Secret Life, Secret Death is also a critically acclaimed independent documentary film. See the trailer and get the DVD at www.secretlifesecretdeath.com

"Visually stunning . . . a remarkable, haunting movie"

-- Rick Kogan, Chicago Tribune & WGN Radio

"Technologically innovative and dazzling"

--Marty Rubin, Gene Siskel Film Center, Chicago

Other books by Genevieve Davis

coming soon from October 7th Studio

Fannie's Kitchen

Humorous, poignant stories and incomparable
Viennese recipes from Davis's Austrian Grandmother,
Fannie Baier

Coming in 2013

The Fantastic Adventures of the 100 Gorditas

A bilingual book in English and Spanish about the
escapades of a time traveling pack of
mischievous nine year old girls

Coming in 2014

The Brides' Tale

An erotic fairy tale of the star-crossed, medieval
romance between a court lady and a monk

Coming in 2014

www.october7studio.com

Secret Life
Secret Death

Genevieve Davis

October 7th Studio

Secret Life, Secret Death

This is a work of non-fiction. Some of the names have been
changed out of consideration for present day descendants

To all the people who helped me get the book and the movie off the ground

Minnie on Drexel Boulevard in Chicago

Contents

ACKNOWLEDGMENTS

There were many people who encouraged me to tell my Grandmother Minnie's story. Let me tell you about some of them.

Thanks to Tim Samuelson for his unabashed, enthusiastic interest in my project and the pieces of information he unearthed and contributed to the project..

Thanks to Prof. Emeritus Art Robson for his trenchant thoughts and intellectual guidance, since that first day at Beloit College, when I saw him walk into the Greek Drama classroom with those wacky green eyes, holding out his paper coffee cup before him, like a libation bearer on a Greek vase.

Thank you to my parents for sharing their stories. And to my brother Rob, who copied the Apache Dance photos for me at the Library of Congress in Washington, D.C.. He did that in the morning of the same day he flew to Israel for a business trip. I guess that morning was his free time and I thank him for that!

Thank you to Arthur Bilek for sharing information with me on Big Jim Colosimo and his world.

Many thanks to Pat Printz for encouraging me to write about

Minnie's story and for serving as an eyewitness on Spread Eagle in the 30's and 40's.

Thanks to Voyageur Publisher Bill Meindl for believing in the importance of telling Minnie's story and inviting me to write about it for their magazine. Chapter One was published in the Winter/Spring 2007 edition.

Thanks to Virg Laszewski for friendship and accommodations. Thanks to Marty Rubin for believing in the project. Thanks to Terese Hiles Olson and Urszula Tempska for their friendship and penetrating insight.

Thank you to Virginia Anderson and May Tchao, early readers who provided invaluable thoughts and reactions. Thanks to David Glaeser, Art Robson, Alisha Benson and Craig Jacobsen, Terese Hiles-Olson, Barbara Meyer-Spidell, Lynn Weborg, and Pat Smith for reading and commenting.

Thank you to Tom Uyehara and Dan Mihm for coming to the rescue with technical support for computers and software.

A big thanks to Chicago Chef, Phillip Speciale, for permission to use his terrific recipes. For more recipes, I thank James D'Archangelis, my Mom, my cousin George, and Manuela Ciri.

Thanks to Robert Golden for telling me about the early history of Spread Eagle. Thanks to people who contributed stories about bootlegging: Mike Monte, Laura H, Dave Euhlberg, Jim Crosby, Linda, Richard, Sharon, and my cousins Becky and George. And thanks to people who contributed pictures, William J. Helmer, Marzena, Edna, Linda, Dave Euhlberg and Mike Monte.

Last but not least, let me thank my editor, Gellis Fleming, and my agent, James Davis, for giving 110% to the project.

Vintage Chicago, the city whose mysteries unravel in the stories

photo courtesy of Tim Samuelson

INTRODUCTION

๛ ๛ ๛ ๛ ๛ ๛ ๛ ๛ ๛ ๛

This book represents ten years of sleuthing out Minnie's story. My Great Aunt Lily's letters were a gold mine of information, once I knew how to understand them. So were my Dad's stories, his VA records, and my Mom's stories.

The tempestuous childhood I had growing up with my brothers, in retrospect, gives veracity to the existence of potent family secrets. We were not told about them. We did not know about them. But as children, we lived with their emotions. I had no idea until I began researching Minnie's story that those emotions were handed down the generations through this strange looking lady whose pictures I looked at occasionally, uncomprehendingly. I was told she was my Dad's mother. She would have been my grandmother, but she died before I was born.

As I followed Minnie's trail, I found so many intriguing stories along the way that fascinated me. Strangely enough, I have come to love not only her stories but also the stories of the people she associated with. I am fond of all the stories, you know, the way you love a red-haired stepchild.

Minnie at the Hollywood in the late 1930's

Chapter One

ఌఌఌఌఌఌఌ

On the Trail of a Black Sheep

On a damp fall day in late September, I was driving north from Milwaukee on country 1roads in my aging Toyota. I had my hand on the skeleton key to the family closet, ready to unlock secrets, intentional mysteries, things that had been deliberately left unsaid in my family. The trip would soon become the first stop on a journey to the dark side of human nature.

On the three hour drive through wet farm land and pine forests, I thought about my dad's mother. She was the reason I was headed up north. My grandmother Minnie died at age 56, in 1948, three years before my birth. Now in 2003, I was on my way to find out the truth about her life in northern Wisconsin. My dad, who passed away right after Christmas in 1991, never said much about his mother, but he did leave me with a few facts. I knew that she and her husband Johnny, a Greek, had owned the Hollywood Hotel in a little town in Wisconsin, where I was headed, two miles across the border from Iron Mountain, Michigan.

And I knew she landed up there after a roller coaster life during the Roaring 20's in Chicago, which my dad had characterized as a "boom and bust" existence. He told me they lived "high off the hog" one day and were "scraping the bottom of the barrel" the next. And he was often left alone all night as a child in Chicago. The man of the house was a guy he once described as a "minor Mafioso." Dad thought this man was his father, until years later he discovered he was the illegitimate son of someone his mother had known back in Philadelphia.

Dad liked to tell the story that when he was five years old, his mother took him to the funeral of Big Jim Colosimo in Chicago, who had been murdered by his infamous successor, Al Capone in 1920. When Dad was seven, that Mafioso he thought was his father left for good without saying even goodbye. When Dad was eleven, his mother sent him to Philadelphia to live with her parents. He would not to see her again until he was an adult.

Well, none of what I knew about my grandmother added up to a picture that made much sense to me. Why would someone leave their kid alone and go out all night? Why would someone send their own child away? And what in the world were the two of them doing at a gangster funeral?

My Mom did not like her mother-in-law, Minnie. She characterized her as "a drunk with a cold personality." One more thing I knew about Minnie: she hennaed her hair a brilliant red - a fact my mother would impart with great revulsion. When I had my own fling with red hair, it really unnerved her.

Mom herself had been to the Hollywood several times, as a young woman in the late 1940's. Her description of the place never quite made sense to me, either. "She ran a kind of trysting place up north, where pretty girls, nicely dressed, would spend the weekend with older men - judges, lawyers and other officials of the own. There were sounds of moaning and toilets flushing in the night. There was a bidet in every room. I had to ask your father what that was for." Mom said that Minnie's husband was usually taking care of matters in the bar, while Minnie could usually be found in the kitchen. "She cooked breakfast for everyone in the morning."

Minnie herself gives a glimpse of life at the Hollywood, in a letter to Dad, on letterhead from the bar:

Hollywood Hotel Bar

"A Fine Place – Just Like Home"

July 29, 1945

Dear Son:

Snapshot of the North Country from Minnie's album

Received your letter today so I thought I'd better answer it at once as I am the worlds worst letter riter. Well today is really one hot schorer [scorcher], and you know how I hate that, never could take the hot weather, otherwise am feeling pretty good again. . . things are kind of quite [quiet] the people seem to go more to resort towns that is where there is swimming boating etc, our business always seems better here when its colder. . . Boy its hot I think when we close up we will take a ride maybe I can get a little air. . . "

Her letter speaks of recent illness, a slump in business, and a nearly unspoken feeling of claustrophobia.

3

To begin to unlock the mystery of her life, I had one name I could research -- "Big Jim Colosimo." If he was a big shot in Chicago in the gangster era, maybe I could find some info on him in the library. He wasn't too hard to find. Yes, he was a gangster. Yes, he was executed – maybe even by Al Capone - in the foyer of his own night club. His lavish mob funeral cortege was gawked at by a crowd of 5,000 people, who milled in front of the Colosimo Café on 22nd and Wabash when it stopped there, on its way to the cemetery. "Expensive floral tributes surrounded a bronze coffin. The fifty three pallbearers included judges and Congressmen. One thousand First Ward Democrats marched in the funeral procession to Oak Woods, accompanied by two brass bands." [www.gambino]

I read that Big Jim Colosimo's was known as the "Whoremaster of Chicago." His main business was in the sale of women and children. Colosimo's brothels were peopled by the wholesale abduction, imprisonment and rape of U.S. citizens. Often these victims would be approached with an appealing job offer, which then led to their kidnapping. Colosimo's extensive political connections, as evidenced in the apparently distinguished mourners at his funeral, allowed him to operate without interference from the Law.

I began to see Minnie's story in a new light. I wondered if my grandmother, about whom I had heard so little, had somehow gotten caught up in this enormous web of human misery. It would explain their "boom and bust" existence, her being out all night and her Mafioso boyfriend. I learned that many women in prostitution were single mothers, like Minnie, because it was impossible to get a job, due to the social stigma.

I now had a bigger picture to work with. What I knew for sure was Minnie was a young mother on her own, she couldn't get a regular job, she probably had to work nights and leave her child alone (as many people did in those days), she had no financial security and she had a live-in Mafia boyfriend. My dad had long since died by the time I came to wonder if she had been trafficked into prostitution. My cousin Doris, in her early 80's, who I spoke to a couple of times on the phone, made some provocative statements. "You know, your grandmother was kind of a black sheep," she once told me on the phone. "She played fast and loose." And then clammed up on the details.

So here I was on my way to find out what I could about this business up in Florence County, the old Hollywood Hotel. I figured I could find a few old timers, like my Mom who was then in her late 70's, people who had been around when Minnie owned the Hollywood. When I arrived in town, I found a sign in front of a metal warehouse-type building, proclaiming the "New Hollywood Supper Club." I wasn't surprised at the recent vintage of the building, because I had already heard that the old Hollywood had burned down, from an Iron Mountain dentist I had met some time ago at an art fair when he stopped at my booth. Also in "town," which was really just a curve on the highway, were two more restaurants and two bars. This little "metropolis" was surrounded by bare trees that had already dropped their leaves, by lonely pines and by lovely lakes. The whole place had an air of desolation. The name of the town? *Spread Eagle*.

I pulled up into a dirt parking lot and went into a bar. It was a basic kind of Wisconsin bar, dark and sort of homey, with a small handful of people drinking and smoking at the bar. I pulled my envelope out, with the snapshots of the old Hollywood, of my grandmother and her husband and showed the pictures around. But everybody in there was too young to have been around back then and no one recognized them. But then an older man came in, a pleasant looking fellow with black glasses and a friendly demeanor. He looked closely at the photos. *"Sure!* I remember the old Hollywood," he intoned with great inflection in his voice, which carried a slight eastern accent. "What kind of a place was it?" I asked. "It was a **whorehouse!**" he replied, without hesitation. Eureka! There it was - my answer! And I had only been in town 15 minutes!

Pat looked at the pictures, but he didn't recognize either my grandmother or her husband. He was in his early 70's so he would have been just a kid back then. But he did say that there had been a number of brothels there in Spread Eagle in the 30's and 40's. "We had no law, he explained. "The sheriff was part time and just collected payoffs."

I was not surprised to hear what Pat had to say, because I had already read the Report and Recommendations of the Wisconsin Legislative Committee to Investigate the White Slave Traffic. The report tells that prostitution and local politics were enmeshed in a quid pro quo relationship in nearly every Wisconsin city and town in 1913-1914, a generation before my grandmother got to Spread Eagle.

I understood how that worked in Chicago. But I didn't entirely understand yet how things worked up in the North Country. Everything was different up there. It was remote, sparsely populated. And they had their own weather up there, too. The next morning, though it was only October 1st, the ground and the tall pines outside my motel room were dusted with snow.

I drove over to the county courthouse in Florence, to research the title on the Hollywood. I found that Minnie purchased the property along with her husband, John Vill, in 1936, from one savvy guy, who happened to be the Register of Deeds. I say this because only minutes before, acting not in his official capacity, but as a private citizen, he had purchased the Hollywood from the county, along with a bunch of other properties that had reverted to the county for tax delinquency. You can just imagine what he paid. Nice cottage industry!

Johnny at the Hollywood

After my morning at the courthouse, I headed to a main street diner for some home cooking. I ordered sirloin tips, the special. While I was waiting seated in a booth, drinking a cup of tea, a man came up to my table, who had heard about me and my project.

"How did you know who I was?" I asked him.

"I got your description from the bartender." Whoa! Really small town! "You should talk to my Dad about the old Hollywood," he suggested. He's over at the senior center right now, having lunch.

A few blocks away at the senior center, a bare bones kind of place, I found lunch being patiently awaited at a couple of tables, by a handful of silent seniors. I sat down and passed around my envelope of snapshots. At first, they didn't show much interest in the pictures. They were there for more important matters - lunch. But then, the father of the man I had spoken to had the snapshots in his hand and began talking about the old Hollywood. He was a silver-haired man, way up in his 80's and tall.

"It was a whorehouse!" he stated matter-of-factly, just like Pat did the night before. He and his wife looked at the pictures together. She had a soft, mild mannered appearance, lady-like with white hair in a cauliflower do.

"That's Johnny Vill," she said.

Yeah, I remember him. Johnny Vill," her husband said.

"Do you know who this is?" I showed them the pic of Minnie on the steps. They were both stumped.

"I was a deputy sheriff," the lady said, with a gleam in her eye. "I used to go on raids to the brothels with the sheriff. We rounded up the girls and took 'em to headquarters where they got fines."

Another lady chimed in, "One time I went to the gynecologist in Iron Mountain and in walked a row of painted ladies there in the waiting room."

The pictures went around the table, to another lady. "Johnny Vill was an ordinary man, friendly and polite, short and stocky, dark hair, chunky." She added, matter of factly, "A number of local officials owned slot machines in partnership with the Hollywood."

I wanted to know more, but just then lunch was put on the table and my dusty old snapshots took a back seat to pork chops, instant mashed potatoes and frozen green beans. "You should talk to Dino Geppetto over in Iron Mountain," someone said, before they all dove into their dinner.

Minnie and Johnny up north in the 1930's

I got in the car and drove back through Spread Eagle on Highway 2, crossed the border between Wisconsin and the Michigan UP, and arrived in Iron Mountain 20 minutes later. There, I pulled up to a ranch house, where I found Dino, a friendly guy in his 70's, with intense black eyes and a head of completely black hair, slicked straight back from his forehead. I wanted to take him out to a coffee shop, someplace where we could talk in private, but he had broken his leg and couldn't leave his house. Thus all the information he volunteered was given within earshot of his wife, a small, wiry woman up in years, also sporting solid black hair, [perhaps they shared the same "Nice and Easy" box] who hovered in the next room in front of her TV, turned way down low.

I handed Dino the pictures of Minnie and Johnny. A diabolical smile spread across his face. "Johnny Vill never worked a day in his life. He always stood out. He always had a nice suit," he said with admiration, "and drove a new car." Yeah, during the Depression lots of people were just scraping by or had fallen through the bottom. However, I think Dino's memory may have improved on reality, because Minnie and Johnny had an older car and were constantly remortgaging their real estate.

"The Hollywood was a place where you could rent a room for an hour or two. Or you could get a girl there in the bar. . . . It was like a blind pig" [meaning, it was a place that looked like a legitimate business, but had a hidden illegal aspect to it]. His black eyes shined. "It was a wild place." He explained, "the girls were from out of town, from Chicago or Milwaukee." Minnie he didn't remember.

I asked Dino, "Who was managing the girls?" "It was a man's job to run the girls." Hmmm, so that meant Johnny was in charge of that? I wondered why it was "a man's job."

"What about the sheriff?" I asked.

"In the old days, the sheriff would get people in and out of trouble with the law, in exchange for money," Dino said, bluntly. This

10

explained a little more about what Pat had told me the night before, that the sheriff had just been there to collect payoffs.

After my conversation with Dino, I called on a lady on the outskirts of Iron Mountain who was related to people who owned a brothel on the curve in the highway, back in the old days.

I found her at home, feeding her small army of adorable yellow finches that flew loose in her house. She described the frontier atmosphere in the town back in the 30's and 40's. "A few crooked local officials had control of the town," she told me. Then she volunteered a startling viewpoint. "Everybody ran a clean business. That's just how everyone made a living back then. There was nothing wrong with it."

She described a guy who had owned another brothel in the curve of the road in Spread Eagle. "He was a big Swede. And *mean*. He bought his wife when she was thirteen from her family in Minnesota." Yes, there were still people selling their own children back then. "He had twenty kids with her and was very mean to her. They had the brothel next door to the Hollywood and bought the land from John Vill." The Register of Deeds records bear this out.

"*He* ran the girls – that was a *man's* occupation. Yes, there were places like Betty's High Hat, some places which were run by a madam, but usually it was a *man's* job." There was that statement again. *It was a man's job.* What did they mean by that?

Some time later, I found this quote in an 1893 *Herald* newspaper article in the Wisconsin State Historical Society archives and wondered if this was the kind of brutality that required a man, a certain kind of man, to do the job.

> While I was at Bill Anderson's dive at Eagle River I heard a girl screaming in the bar-room, and on going in found a small, frail-looking girl, about 15 years old, lying on the floor, with the blood running out of her mouth, while the burly bartender, with his knees upon her breast, was

11

choking her. Several men stood about the room. The cause of this horrible scene was the refusal of the poor young girl to submit to the attentions of a half a score of male brutes, who had been selected by the proprietor. I afterward succeeded in getting the girl liberated.

I drove the side roads on the way back to Florence, in the dying light. The lakes glowed with an iridescent light in the growing gloom. Pine trees were silhouetted against the twilight sky. As I drove, I was trying to imagine what Minnie thought when she came up here. Did she think this was a good deal, a better life than she had in Chicago? Or did she think she had fallen off the face of the earth and landed in the middle of nowhere?

Hanging out at the Hollywood

I tried to catch up with Pat Printz again up north, but only got his answering machine. However, when I gave him a call again when I got back to Milwaukee, I got him and he proved to be a walking encyclopedia. "How did the prostitution work up there?" I asked,

Pat explained, "As soon as a man comes in, the woman comes up to him and they have a couple of drinks together. The Madam works the floor – if a guy likes someone else, she switches them around. The girls had *two* functions" [i.e. selling booze *and* their bodies.] "All the girls were from Chicago." That tallied with what the black haired guy told me in Iron Mountain. "They were well behaved and had to be able to hold their liquor and to act respectably." That tallied with Mom's description of pretty women dressed in nice clothes. "Girls lived the good life – a lot loved it." Or, more likely, I thought, it was only for salesmanship purposes that they appeared so.

The 1914 report of the Wisconsin Legislative Committee on White Slave Traffic describes conditions in the lives of prostitutes:

> Their earnings are taken from them or must be turned over to their 'lovers' or 'pimps' or 'madams,' so they have little or no money. . . The unfortunate women . . . are made to feel absolutely dependent upon the 'madam' and 'pimps' for everything which they need, and are sometimes threatened with more or less severe violence in case of any mutiny. In this way they soon lose all ambition in life, and following the path of least resistance, resort to drink and drugs to palliate their unfortunate position.

Pat ticked off names, "There was Betty's High Hat. That was a lounge and brothel back in the woods. The Green Garage was just a brothel, with no bar. Women worked back and forth between the Hollywood and the Riverside Bar." He characterized the brothel business as "lucrative." I had found in the Register of Deeds records that Minnie and Johnny paid cash for their place in 1936, at the height of the Depression, which seems unusual. But they soon mortgaged it. When the mortgage was paid off, they re-mortgaged it. Minnie and Johnny, themselves, were not rolling in money. Their fortunes went up and down. In a letter to my dad, Minnie envies her competitor, the Riverside, "if they close to-morow I guess they can't kick. They are tying up all the real-estate now they can. Right now they have an all girl band and a woman organ player." Sounded picturesque, like the movie *Some Like It Hot!*

In his candid manner, Pat mentioned another place that would serve children booze. He went there to drink with his pals when they were kids. The report of the Wisconsin commission on vice confirms the nearly universal distribution of liquor to minors at the time.

"We had no law," Pat reiterated. "Local officials pulled the town together and created a mafia atmosphere. Fines [for prostitution] went to the judge and the sheriff." In the 30's and 40's, the sheriff, an elected official, held his position without pay. "The sheriff was just there to collect payoffs. A raid happened when someone was not being paid off properly. Prostitutes were arrested. Fines were paid. Not to the county, but to the sheriff's own pockets. "

Johnny and Minnie on the steps of the Hollywood

Mom's careful observation from her youth, of "judges, lawyers and other local officials spending the weekend with young attractively dressed girls," was another dimension to this quid pro quo relationship. Perks, along with payoffs or fines allowed brothels to thrive under the ogling eye of local representatives of the law.Some of these same local officials owned the slot machines and reaped a huge percentage of these profits, too. I remembered something about slot machines in that letter from Minnie to Dad and looked it up. Here is a fine description of the situation on June 29, 1945.

> As far as slot machines they are positively out, no doubt you read how the governor signed the Anti-gambling Bill. They claim even Bingo is out if that is so I think the Riverside will close up. They put on about three times as many enforcement's agents so that will keep us closed pretty tight as far as the one o'clock closing for awhile. [*Name deleted*], the operator of the slot machines was in tonite and took out all the machines and said the people needn't expect any-thing for at least two years, so I guess that's that.

I looked up the 1945 anti-gambling bill Minnie is referring to on the web, and found that it is the foundation of the current law on gambling in taverns in Wisconsin.

> The legislative response to widespread tavern gambling was Chapter 374, Laws of 1945. Also known as the Thomson Antigambling Law, for its sponsor, Assemblyman Vernon W. Thomson (later attorney general and governor), the law provided for the seizure and destruction of any slot machine or gambling device found in a tavern and the revocation of the establishment's alcohol beverage license. **Any law enforcement official aware of illegal gambling who failed to take appropriate action was subject to removal from office by the governor.** Well-publicized raids resulted in the confiscation of many illegal gambling machines. ["Evolution"]

With three times the state enforcement agents on duty, as Minnie's letter reports, the local law officials were in danger of being prosecuted themselves for knowledge of illegal gambling. And so the tolerance for those slot machines came to an end.

One last surprising gem of information from Pat. Some of the customers were "Milwaukee, Chicago, Detroit money. The Mob came in to enjoy themselves; they [the brothels] were a guy's hangout. They all carried shotguns, pistols, machine guns. Mobsters partied and had fun here. They could run around armed with tommy guns and no one would say anything."

Yeah, gangsters like to get out of town too, and go fishing, hunting, swimming and boating and have a good time on vacation, like other wealthy people from Chicago. [Hollatz]

"The mobsters always brought money into the area," Pat said. "Sure! The mobsters from Chicago were always good to people here. They would bring up tires, which were hard to buy, and give those away. They gave away food and clothing for the kids up here."

Finally, I asked Pat if he thought it was a good deal to come here in the midst of the Great Depression in the 30's to run the Hollywood. "Yes," he said. "Clean, fresh air, nice countryside, steady money, no trouble." But in the same breath he said, "Whoever was the toughest survived in this business."

Well, it probably was a good deal. Minnie toughed it out in a rough business. Yet no one I talked to remembered her in a tiny town where she had lived for 12 years. Her husband, her business, yes. But not her. I sensed a certain wistfulness in the Hollywood's motto printed on their letterhead, "A Fine Place – Just Like Home." A good deal, yes, but was it good enough?

A few months before her death in 1948, my Grandmother came to Milwaukee for the christening of her first grandchild, my older brother, Rob. Mom says Minnie was so drunk that she was afraid to let her hold her baby. Minnie's death certificate reports her death in October at age 54 from "heart failure, due to alcohol over indulgent."

Two decades later, the story of Minnie's life was still fresh in her sister Lily's mind, when she wrote the following in a letter to Dad, marked *"Personal and Confidential."* I had already read the letter quite a few times over the years. But I didn't understand what she was getting at until now.

> She had a lovely – generous nature – very sentimental was a beautiful girl. . . . By nature your mother was not born for that life – one saw what it done to her. It completely changed her expression. . . She was not a mercenary person. Only dreamed of love, home and family.

Minnie outside at the Hollywood. Note the Victory Rolls in her hairdo, placing the picture around the time of World War II

*Minnie and Lily in Fairmount Park in Philadelphia, taken by one of their artist
brothers. "That picture I have of her sitting on the grass with me is excellent –
the dress was pink" – my Great Aunt Lily*

Chapter Two

ॐॐॐॐॐॐॐ

Up Against a Cruel Situation

My Great Aunt Lily was quite a gal. I was eleven years old when she came from Philly for a visit and impressed the hell out of me, with her wily intelligence and unabashed manner. She was different from the women in the early 1960's, somnambulant, suburban world I was stuck in, women whose demure demeanor was just as fake as their red lipstick.

Aunt Lily was a widow in her 70's, with her own perspicacious way of looking at things. She was blunt and to the point. She had her own style, too. She liked to wear tailored pants, when everybody else was wearing dresses or pedal pushers. She had a face like a horse, with a big schnaz, olive skin and a deep voice. She didn't subscribe to the feminine mystique. Aunt Lily stood out from the pack of adult women of my world: the frustrated, reined-in moms and stifling teachers, who were all trying to make me into one of them.

One night after dinner, Aunt Lily read my palm. She grabbed my thumb and wiggled it to see if it would bend backward. It didn't. With a wink to me, she glanced over at my mother. "Stubborn!" she pronounced. My mother rolled her eyes.

Aunt Lily was a long-winded raconteur. She was in majestic command of any conversation and took a leisurely hour to make a point. She spun anecdotes that grew wider and wider of the mark, until I'd lose the thread of her conversation. I'd nod from time to time to be polite, but was convinced she had doddered into the aimless conversation of an old lady. However, at the end

My Great Aunt Lily – note the ballet hands

of an hour's run, she'd abruptly veer back to her original topic of conversation, beaming with a triumphant expression, and recap how she had illustrated her point over and over, with all those tangled digressions I just couldn't follow.

When I left in the morning for school, Aunt Lily would regale my mother with her unwieldy tales all day, following her through the house, while my Mom cooked and cleaned. Lily even followed her into the bathroom, perching on the edge of the tub, because she was in the middle of a story and had to finish it, while Mom answered the call of nature as best she could in company.

Aunt Lily had a droll sense of humor. I remember her standing in the hallway one time, staring down at a pile of pastel colored pills in the palm of her hand and laughing. "Might as well just croak!" she mused.

The only other member of the Frank family, besides Aunt Lily, to come all the way out from Philadelphia to visit us in Milwaukee, was my Dad's cousin Karl. He was the son of Lily's charming but alcoholic younger brother Auggie. Uncle Karl by this time was a stocky middle-aged man, with kind of crazy eyes, bushy eyebrows, and a bristly, salt and pepper crew cut. He seemed different from other adults I knew, because he was a lot of fun. Uncle Karl would tell stories all day long I didn't understand, but he and my Dad guffawed long and hard over them, as they sloshed down whiskeys tinkling with ice, their breath pungent with strong spirits.

One time when I was about five years old, Uncle Karl asked me, "What do you want to be when you grow up?"

"A psychiatrist!" I chirped, but then wondered if that was the right word. I meant I wanted to hold a sassy dummy on my knee, and say what I really thought, without moving my lips. Maybe the word I said was wrong, because after I said "psychiatrist" Uncle Karl's hairy brow furrowed and his glassy eyes drifted over the floor. For once he was speechless. Yes, I'm sure that gave him food for thought in his semi-smashed state: his cousin's little girl wanted to be a top level professional during the 50's, when women were seldom spotted working outside their own kitchens.

When I was in college and had an internship in Washington, D.C., I paid Aunt Lily a visit in Philly. She was living in an attic apartment, above her niece, Olga, the daughter of Lily's sister Olga.

This Olga was a sandy haired, pleasantly plump gal, who was the only person I ever saw try to compete with Aunt Lily in conversation. They were like two trains trying to run on the same track. Like after dinner one night, we were paging through a dusty old photo album, and they found a picture of my Dad in his salad days, dressed in a double-breasted pin stripe suit. They thought that was really choice and exclaimed in their nasal Philadelphiaese:

Lily: *"Aaaaow!* Doesn't she look *just* like *Fraaaancis !"*

Olga: "*Aaaaow!* Doesn't she look *just* like *Fraaaancis !"*

Lily*: "Aaaaow! Doesn't she look just like Fraaaancis !*

Olga: "*Aaaaow!* Doesn't she look *just* like *Fraaaancis !"*

Lily held the picture up to my face. *"Yeah! Just like Fraaaancis!"* Lily really had to get in the last word. It was a matter of principle.

My Dad

Never heard the Philly expression "Aaaaaaaow!" before? Sure you have, when you stepped on a cat's tail by mistake. I was cringing, but not over that exclamation. No, I was chagrined, because how could they possibly compare a young college girl like me, with beautiful, long blonde hair, to an old fart like my Dad?

When Lily and I went upstairs to get ready for bed, I looked at the two double beds side by side in the cozy attic bedroom. Uh oh, I thought. "Um, Aunt Lily, I didn't bring a nightie. I, ah, usually sleep in the nude," I confessed. I liked to do that, because it felt nice on the skin to slide in between the sheets. I also thought it was sophisticated.

"Sure, go ahead!" Lily exclaimed. "Knock yourself out!"

I shyly waited until she was in the bathroom to get undressed and slip into bed. The next morning, Aunt Lily jumped out of bed, whipped off her pajama top and padded around the room, with her bare pancake boobs flapping in the breeze. She was yakking away, while I, sophisticated young thing that I was, remained as long as possible under the covers, too embarrassed to get out of bed naked.

Now, many years later, I realize Aunt Lily was just trying to make me feel at home. But back then, she, like, out-nakedized me!

Speaking of nudes, Aunt Lily was an art lover, who sent my father an enchanting Art Noveau gouache, "Temple of Aphrodite," that a friend of hers had painted and exhibited in Paris. Dad admired it when it hung in his grandparents house in Philly, and Aunt Lily remembered that. I was about twelve when we unwrapped the painting and my parents hung it in our living room. It seemed to me exotic and divinely voluptuous, mystical in an ethereal way, not like the grisly scenes of suffering they showed us in the Catholic Church.

Some years later, Lily gave us another painting, a watercolor her brother Arthur painted of her when she was a girl. Every time I saw that one, it boggled my mind and made me wish I could paint like that. Lily herself had taken art classes in night school as a young woman, while working for the electric company making maps of the city. Lily took up painting again in her 80's in her usual unabashed way, working in a primitive style. When I was in my late 20's, every couple of months, a box with Aunt Lily's scrawl on it arrived at my scruffy apartment. Unpacking it was an adventure in polyester - plaid pants with a matching vest, a camel pants suit with fake leopard cuffs and collar, and a belted, mint green, hip-length coat, that I actually did wear for bicycle riding.

"Temple of Aphrodite" by Inez Livingston Delaney

In a letter to my parents, Lily wrote, "I love to sew, so make clothes. I believe in jeans. I seem to inherit them from my mother who was quite a successful Haute couters [couturiere]. Genevieve is finding herself. She is talented and willing to work. I love her. One has to battle to make it in this world."

My parents, who were still paying off my college tuition bill, had a different view of my art rat lifestyle. I worked at temp jobs painting scenery or typing, while I took painting classes and hung out with the art dregs of the town. No career, marriage or family appeared on the horizon, nothing which they would have viewed as a sign of success. Nice to know Lily understood. Apparently her artist brother Arthur painted scenery, too, in his back yard, so she told me.

Arthur was a painter, who lived the bohemian life, the classic version of it, in Paris in the 1920's, which is enough to make any American painter green with envy. However, that famous expatriate, Ernest Hemingway, wrote some charming sarcasm about his fellow expates in Paris.

> The scum of Greenwich Village, New York, has been skimmed off and deposited in large ladlesful on that section of Paris adjacent to the Café Rotonde. [Monmartre] New scum, of course, has risen to take the place of the old, but the oldest scum, the thickest scum and the scummiest scum has come across the ocean . . . [Hemingway]

What exactly did Hemingway mean by "scum"? Writers like himself, men who slithered away their nights drunk in brothels, their mornings passed out face down in bed like a moth stuck to a windshield, and their afternoons pounding out their angst onto a typewriter. And perhaps painters like Arthur. My Dad confided that his Uncle Arthur left behind a wife and daughter, when he crossed the ocean to live in Paris with a "lady patron." He hung out at the Café Dome, located at the same intersection as Hemmingway's Café Rotonde, with his fellow American art rats. But to customers he passed himself off as a Parisian, the better to sell his paintings.

Mommie and Poppie

"Mommie," the mother of Minnie, Lily, Arthur, and the rest of the kids, started a ladies' tailoring business, in Philadelphia, after giving birth in America, to her first three children. A highly skilled clothing designer and pattern drafter, she had been

Lily painted by her brother Arthur

apprenticed to the trade in Europe. In Philly, she attracted "all the mainline trade," Philly-speak for *upscale clientele*. But when Mommie brought Poppie, into the business and taught him the trade, it was a business decision she would eternally regret.

Poppie had already bombed out unpacking china at Wanamaker's, a grandiose Philly department store, and also delivering milk to homes by horse and cart. To make matters worse, a friend of his at the dairy asked Poppie if he wanted to go into business with him, selling the new hot item, pasteurized milk. Lily wrote, "but you know Poppie's ego if he did not think it up – he stubbornly held out – well his friend became one of the owners of the Willis-Jones [Dairy] and died aboard his yacht – so much for being bull headed."

Poppie

In spite of the fact that he was pretty much a loser and "bull headed" to boot, Poppie was a devilishly good looking man, whose looks lasted well into middle age. He cut quite a figure in this photo, in a three piece suit, with a cigar dangling from his fingers. Just imagine the thrill his sexy appearance wrought on ladies coming to The Frank Dress Shop to have their fashionable dresses made to order.

Mommie intercepted love letters written to Poppie, that revealed a love affair between her husband and the forelady of her shop. That prompted Mommie to quit the shop and their home all together. She took her half grown children, Minnie, Lily, Walter [who later became a fashion illustrator] and August with her. Poppie remained, running the dress shop, or rather *ruining* the dress shop, "spending the money on women." The shop's finances and reputation suffered.

After a while, Poppie was going over to Mommie's every night, Lily wrote, "begging her to come back." After four months she did, but by that time he had run their business into the ground. Thus, they retired while still in their 50's, letting the upkeep for themselves, as well as their four youngest kids, fall to their five grown children. But then Poppie "felt he lost face, so he became sarcastic, trying to blame everything on Mommie." Hmmm. Maybe she cut him off before he had that affair. Lily and Minnie were impressionable preadolescents, when this disaster occurred. Later, they quit school and went to work to earn their keep. In Dad's VA records, he reported his grandparents sent their children out to work at age 14.

Forty-nine years after Dad was born, Lily sent him a letter relating the circumstances of his birth. She mailed it to his office, rather than our house where she usually sent letters, maybe in case Mom didn't know the whole truth. Lily was careful to couch her letter in oblique terms, so that if someone read it at work, they wouldn't know exactly what it meant. But if you knew the middle and the end of the story of Minnie's life, like my Dad did, you could understand her description of the love affair that brought Dad into the world.

Feb 1, 1963

Dear Francis –

I requested your card in order to write this letter direct to you. I want to clarify your mother to you. I feel that I know truly the whole affair as we were one year apart and grew up together.

Well the first thing in Philly the thing to do in our time was to get to the dances. We started having a lot of good clean fun. Finally we were going more and more with just two boys. Most of the time we double dated that was our agreement. I did not fall in love but your mother fell head over heel – then anyone is vulnerable. She had a lovely – generous nature – very sentimental, was a beautiful girl. A girl like that is prey for a weak, selfish person. In all respects to him it is hard for those people to fight their parents – Well she started dating alone which was a big mistake. When I said how about our pact, which was never to date alone – we had arguments and you know her temper – but the big thing she was madly in love. That was natural he was good looking – well built and alot of personality.

It was then a known thing of the middle class with a little money, they were too fired with ambition and plan too much who and when they should marry etc., but their parents sanctioned their going steady with a girl and even encouraged them to get engaged, so they have a less dangerous outlet than promiscuity. . . [Lily then mentions two instances of it happening currently in the Frank family] . . . But that is beside the point, only to help you understand how a girl in love is up against a cruel situation. No wonder they say they achieve their end but lose their soul. [Lily means the men who would do that]

You look like him. He was alright, but I think Mama dominated. When trouble came they made it hard to trace him – however she had some pride so gave up. But the affair ruined a nice person's life. Maybe he suffered too one never knows.

I give John [a brother] credit he wanted her in his house. Arthur too – but their wives

Photo: Library of Congress

– but she felt better at Olgas – after to get away from them she grabbed at the first straw – which was all wrong – that was the greatest tragedy. By nature your mother was not born for that life – one saw what it done to her. It completely changed her expression. She was not a mercenary person only dreamed of love, home and family.

Why did Minnie go to live with their older sister Olga? Poppie turned her out. He knew that she had had a love affair, because she was pregnant with my Dad.

Some girls were lucky and married the father of their baby, like Olga, if you call it lucky to marry a drunk. Some families simply kept their daughter and her baby in their home. Others sent their pregnant daughter away to have her baby, and with some sleight of hand on her return, raised the child as one of their own or gave it to a relative to raise. But not Poppie and Mommie. No. There was no man to marry, because he had disappeared. And there was no sleight of hand on Minnie's behalf. Just the boot.

Dance Halls

Okay. Dance halls. Ooom pa pa music and "good, clean fun", right? No, no, no, no, no!

"Oh dance halls! Carol, my octogenarian friend exclaimed, rolling her eyes. "My father used to go to one in Cazenovia. He and his friends would get so *drunk*, they would throw people out the second story *window."*

"Didn't people get hurt doing that?" I asked.

"Yes, I imagine they did," she replied. Carol's father, the same age as Minnie, later became a lawyer and a judge.

I came across some pretty lurid descriptions of dance halls in vice commission reports across the country, from the 1910's, like "drunken carousals" [Wis Vice] and "wild, riotous, drunken orgy." [Phila Vice]. There was no problem getting served when you were underage, because "saloon-keepers and dance hall owners have only one end in view and that is profit." [JUV, 1921-22]

Why were the vice commissions studying dance halls? Because they were "breeding-places of vice." [Phila Vice, 21] "The girls are attracted to the unregulated dance halls not only by a love of pleasure but by a sense of adventure."[Addams, 1914: 151] But once there, like Minnie, "hundreds of young girls are annually started on the road to ruin. [JUV: 1919]

"With blood aroused by liquor, their animal spirits fanned to flame by the mad music, [teens] simply threw caution and restraint to the winds in a manner they would never do elsewhere. [Bowen: 5] That "mad music" was Ragtime, played by a live

Tango Photos: LOC

band. It was just coming up from the South and the way couples danced to it was new, too. "Couples dance with bodies and faces plastered close together." [Hart of the Civic League, in Teasdale Commission] And, "a great many seeming to try and outdo each other in vulgar dancing." [WVC: 65]

Where were the police during all this craziness? In cooperation with the brewery, saloon and vice interests, their role was to turn a blind eye. A Philadelphia investigator explains

> By 1 a.m. a great number, both men and women, were crazy drunk. . . Beer flowed like water. . . Girls and fellows were in all sorts of positions—jumping over tables, singing and dancing. One fellow threw a chair clear across the room. Another got up on a chair and the chair broke under him, whereupon he threw the pieces all over the place. . . a gang of 6 or 8 fellows got out a piece of stage scenery, took it onto the dance floor during the intermission, and would sail it nearly the length of the floor on its edge, then it would topple over with a crash. . . Up until 12 p.m. (midnight) there were three policemen on duty, but they only stood around the entrance downstairs. . .

The Intimate Tango

And that was just for openers. Here's what things looked like in the wee hours of the night.

> After 1 a.m. it was not uncommon to see couples fall down while dancing. . . There was positively no restriction to the tough dancing and I saw the most lewd and wanton actions by many couples on the floor. The Turkey-Trot, Wiggle, Spot Dancing and every kind of licentious dancing was indulged in.

I saw unmistakable signs of sensual passions during the dancing, and one girl I noticed was so worked up that she had to leave the floor and go into the ladies parlor. There was no question from her actions what the matter was." [Phila Vice: 73-75]

I'm still trying to figure that one out.

Some unscrupulous men also took advantage of the ignorance of girls in sexual matters. The Wisconsin Vice Commission found that "there are a lot of girls that become pregnant that don't know the machinery which brings about pregnancy. . . parents keep these things hidden from the child." [Wis Vice, 114] Not too effective a philosophy, given teenagers' penchant for thrills and exploring the unknown.

I'm trying to picture my Grandmother and Great Aunt Lily at the dance hall, in that free-wheeling atmosphere. The photo at the head of this chapter shows Minnie and Lily elegantly decked out in their summer whites. Fashionably dressed by their mother, the ladies tailor, Lily and Minnie must have attracted a lot of attention at the dance hall. "Most of the time we double dated - that was our agreement," Lily wrote. They looked out for each other.

Still a racy dance, today!

So, what were these "lewd and wanton actions" the vice investigator talked about? Well, there was a dance called the "Grizzly Bear," also known as "Bearcatting." Dancers embraced in a sloppy bear hug and lumbered from side to side across the dance floor. They tried to outlaw it in the big Chicago dance halls, but it was too popular. [CT "Officer 666: 1] The Lame Duck was a dance in which one partner flopped against the other. Not without humor, no, but what was so scandalous about these Animal Dances was full body contact, something never seen before in public. Like the Bunny Hug. Sounds cute, doesn't it? Bunny Hug dancers locked in a full body embrace and undulated like rabbits, humping in time to the music. Add alcohol and you have something that never looked like a waltz.

Then there was the Tango. This sensuous dance arrived from the brothels of Buenos Aires by way of Paris, where even the French nobility were unable to resists its tempestuous charm. A female vice investigator reported, "the tango . . . when danced extremely, is enough to arouse the passions of anyone." [Wis Vice, 65].

It would be hard to imagine dances more racy than Bearcatting, Bunny Hugging and the Tango, but there were plenty more. A Chicago investigator wrote, "Men and women become intoxicated and dance indecently such dances as 'Walkin' the Dog,' 'On the Puppy's Tail,' 'Shaking the Shimmy,' 'The Dip,' 'The Stationary Wiggle.'" [Bowen, 4] These dances, along with the Slow Drag, came up north from the juke joints of the Delta. If you think about those names, you can pretty much picture the action.

Soooooooo romantic!

You may be wondering why Minnie and Lily were out on their own, unsupervised. In a letter written in the same year as Minnie's affair, a chaplain for a place that helped prostituted girls return to normal life, cited that many European born parents:

> do not realize the dangers of American city-life for their young and unsuspecting daughters and allow them the fullest license as regards late hours, amusements and companions. . . [the girls] begin to float down stream . . . they meet the rake who takes them out into the saloon

and then to the questionable dance hall, the country picnic and finally the roadhouse. The conductors of such places pander to the passions of the young, they allow minors to drink intoxicant drinks, they evade police surveillance. [Meyer]

So did all that wild dancing the vice investigators observed at the dance halls lead to sex? An investigator at a dance hall in "City No. 32, reports,

> in the vicinity of the hall and outside of the building, found a number of couples lying on the grass under the trees and in dark corners. [Wis Vice]

Cheap sleeps were hawked.

> Toward the end of a dance, when every one was much intoxicated, a man passed through the hall calling out, 'Good rooms for rent at _____Hotel.' [Bowen, 10]

And for after hours entertainment,

> Policemen report that girls are often found on the back porch of their own homes at 3 or 4 A.M. engaged in immorality with their escorts after returning from a dance. [WLI, Hart]

Single motherhood, was the frequent result of such liaisons, and was cited as a causative factor in prostitution, by vice commission reports around the country.

Yes, from the dance hall, to hotel rooms, to a girl's back porch, there were plenty of places for a couple to couple. There was another place for privacy, that had the allure of novelty and the romance of wind-blown adventure. "Automobiles are always standing at the door of this hall during dances, and joy rides to secluded places are said to be frequent." [WLI, Hart] My grandfather, the man with dancing shoes, was a traveling salesman with his own car. Lily described him as "good looking, well built and a lot of personality." *And* he had a car. He must have cut quite a figure on the dance floor and he must have seemed like a great catch.

Lily in slacks, 1920ish – pretty much unheard of

Lily and Minnie were probably already working to earn their keep by the time they were 17 and 18 years old. Preying on unskilled working girls had to be a piece of cake, because they were not paid a living wage, but were expected to live subsidized in their parent's home. Girls, who lived in rented rooms away from home, soon found they could not live on the $4 to $5 a week they were paid to be department store clerks or factory workers. Seamstresses and domestics made even less. Minnie and Lily already knew from personal experience in the workforce that they couldn't make it on their own in the world. How hard would it be for a middle class man to dazzle a young working gal with his relative wealth and social position?

You have to wonder anyone would get engaged to someone they weren't planning on marrying. In 1914, the "double standard" meant sex was okay for guys, but not okay for women unless they were married.   Or engaged.   Syphilis and gonorrhea were potentially fatal diseases and a major risk in sexual encounters, because treatment was unreliable.   Thus a man could be advised by his doctor he was cured, but later find he wasn't, when he married and disaster struck his new wife and family.   But a sexually inexperienced, disease-free girl could be convinced with an engagement, to provide "a less dangerous outlet than promiscuity."   And of course, she didn't know he was planning to disappear.

The risk of conception in such an affair was a matter of Russian Roulette, because in 1914, the only female method of controlling fertility was abortion.   That was an illegal, nightmarish option, practiced without medical supervision, effected by a visit to a midwife, or by "herb teas, turpentine, steaming, rolling downstairs, inserting slippery elm, knitting needles, shoe-hooks." [Sanger, Margaret]   Birth control pioneer and nurse, Margaret Sanger, observed in her practice that hemorrhage or septicemia often followed any kind of abortion, with fatal results.   [Sanger, Margaret]   Sanger later introduced the vulcanized rubber diaphragm and jelly method in the mid 1930's. Condoms were around in 1914, but weren't in general usage until World War II, when they were issued by the U.S. military.

When Minnie and Lily went to dances together, they both knew there were temptations and dangers.   The dance hall was rife with predators, professional and amateur.   Free flowing booze and wild dancing, made it easy for a girl to lose her judgment.

> Two half-drunk girls were each surrounded by a group of boys who were soliciting them.   These girls permitted the vilest liberties to be taken. [WLI, Hart]

> A vice investigator followed two couples to a hotel into which one of the girls was dragged against her protest."   [WLI, Hart].

The dance hall was a pimp's playground, where he trolled for new recruits.

> He tells 'the down-trodden working girl' that her wages are a mere pittance and that he can procure a better place for her with higher wages if she will trust him. [Addams, 1912: 152]

Madams and prostitutes worked the crowd and drummed up business.

> . . . three-fifths of the women were fast streetwalkers, inmates of several sporting houses and madams. [Phila Vice]

And last, but not least -

> It was then a known thing of the middle class with a little money, they were too fired with ambition and plan too much who and when they should marry etc., but their parents sanctioned their going steady with a girl and even encouraged them to get engaged, so they have a less dangerous outlet than promiscuity. . . [Lily's letter]

That was the minefield Lily and Minnie danced over.

But the two sisters had very different personalities. On the one hand, Aunt Lily was easy going and level-headed. She had a philosophical outlook on things. A look at her pictures as a young woman shows a very straight forward person with obvious intelligence and a certain penetrating discernment, a faculty which enabled her to observe objectively. Minnie, on the other hand, was much more emotional than her younger sister, Lily, who wrote, "She had a lovely – generous nature – very sentimental, was a beautiful girl." And Minnie was more hot headed, too, because Lily also wrote, "we had arguments and you know her temper."

The two sisters navigated the temptations and dangers of the dance hall by sticking together and double dating. But then

Minnie "started dating alone," with Davis, the fellow she was engaged to, a prosperous, good looking young man she had fallen in love with. "Then anyone is vulnerable," Lily wrote. This new arrangement "was a big mistake. . . A girl like that is prey for a weak, selfish person." But Lily couldn't sway her hot headed sister. "When I said how about our pact, which was never to date alone – we had arguments and you know her temper – but the big thing she was madly in love."

A gal with hopes and dreams

Who knows what Lily's beau was like, because she left only this backward glance at him, after Minnie's disastrous affair: "Needless to say I dropped the boy I was going with, who was urging me to marry him. But I was suspicious – so went in for art."

Perspicacious, yes Lily was that, for sure, even at seventeen years of age. But she also had a secret advantage. Dad told me Lily's ovaries never developed. So her judgment, even at age seventeen, wasn't affected by raging hormones.

Legalities

"When trouble came, his family made it hard to trace him," Lily wrote. That's because Davis had a serious double legal liability - for *breach of promise* when he promised to marry Minnie, and for *bastardy*, which we now call paternity. That's why his family advised him to disappear. And disappear he did. I found on his 1917 draft card, he was working as an adjuster for International Harvester in Jacksonville, Florida, claiming exemption from military service because he was now married to someone else.

I later learned two interesting facts about my grandfather. One, the girl he did marry two years later, was the college educated daughter of prosperous plantation owners, back home in rural Virginia, where his grandparents had lived.

The other fact I learned from my Davis cousin Becky, who told me "in the old days, the Davises were very particular about who their children married." Becky was one of a multitude of Virginia cousins I was lucky to meet as a result of this research project. One Davis cousin I met, George, looked so much like my Dad it was uncanny! George made Crab Imperial when I visited him in his country cottage near a harbor town on the Chesapeake. You'll find his recipe at the end of the chapter.

Davis's father Harry had been a successful dry goods business owner in Richmond, a widower who lost his first wife when Davis was young. He waited more than a decade to remarry, picking a gal just a few years older than his own children. She moved in with Harry and Davis, along with her two educated brothers. One brother was a general practice lawyer. The other brother was a bonding clerk, who worked for the sheriff and the courts processing convicted prisoners. This second wife must be who Lily is referring to when she says of Davis, "he was all right but I think Mama dominated." Could it be that the love affair between Davis and Minnie was Harry's second wife's idea in the first place?

Or perhaps, it was his father Harry's idea. Harry was the son of a wealthy, antebellum, slave-owning planter. That's why "the

Davises were very particular about who their children married."
Plus, a marriage to a pregnant, high school drop out, the working
daughter of disgraced, retired, immigrant tailors probably wasn't
what the President of his own company and his young upscale
wife had in mind for Davis. Perhaps Harry's second wife and her
brothers, both in the legal business, advised Davis to get out of the
way for a while, making it "hard to trace him." Lily wrote, "In all
respects to him [Davis] it is hard for those people to fight their
parents." Yeah, and the woman he married was a college
graduate, the daughter of wealthy plantation-owning parents.

Perhaps the loss of Minnie and their baby haunted Davis for the
rest of his life. I learned he never had any other children. It
would be hard to imagine that he never thought of the pretty girl
he had had so much fun dancing with, or wondered how she was
faring, after he turned his back on her and left on her own with his
only child.

A lawsuit for either breach of promise or bastardy could result in
expensive punitive damages. The Wisconsin Vice Commission
reports a legal case, in which a young woman met a man at dances
twice a month, where he bought her drinks and they danced
together. But one evening, they left the dance hall ostensibly to
get something to eat at a restaurant. But instead, he took her to a
rented room, where he promised to marry her, then locked the
door, pocketed the key and forcibly had sex with her. The next
day the same scenario was repeated, with the man who brought a
friend of his, who also raped her. "After that I was brought in the
family way," her testimony reads. "He offered me $300 because
he could not marry me because his father would not have it." She
miscarried. The Wisconsin State Supreme Court awarded her
$3,650 in damages for breach of promise. In 1913 that amount was
several times the annual income of most young men. That's why
Davis disappeared out of state.

However, this kind of conviction was rare in comparison to the
ruin thousands of young women faced, when an engagement
ended in single motherhood. "The affair ruined a nice person's
life," Lily wrote. Yeah. That was bad, leaving her with a baby.
Everybody knew what happened to single mothers. No one

would hire them and they wound up in prostitution. "Men like that achieve their end, but loose their soul." The way Lily saw it, Davis paid the greater price for sending Minnie with her baby down the road to ruin.

Cruel Situation

Minnie started out her adult life engaged to be married and head-over-heels in love with Davis. But when she learned she would soon be a mother, this state of bliss was turned upside down. Minnie was abandoned by her fiancé, put out by her parents, and shunned by society at large. Minnie was indeed "up against a cruel situation," as her sister wrote.

This kind of situation led some girls to take desperate measures, like Maria Sexton, 23, who worked at the Chicago Box Factory in 1907 and had been rejected by her fiancé "Joe." On a rainy day, she shot herself in an alley near her fiancé's apartment. A waterlogged note addressed to him was found on her body. It read,

> You have a comfortable home and relatives and friends to help you pass the dreary hours of your life; a good position and you earn enough money for any man to be satisfied with. You have no worry for the outcome of the future. What have I? The cold shoulder from every one, no home. . . It is not the one that you are harming, but two . . .

When "Joe" was summoned at the inquest into her death, it was revealed that he had read that letter. He displayed a chilly sang froid at the death of his fiancée and their unborn child. But since his behavior was not *criminal*, he was not charged in connection with her death. Had she lived, however, she could have sued him for bastardy *and* breach of promise in civil court. [Lindberg: 158]

What was the difference between a young woman like Maria Sexton and Minnie? Minnie was a rebel with a fiery temper. I can see it in her picture when she is only 12 years old. At first glance, she looks girlishly demure with her pretty eyes, delicate features,

42

and her blonde hair tied up in a big hair bow. But when I looked at her eyes close up, I noted a fierce defiance. The strength of an angry rebel was a good quality to have, if you suddenly found yourself a social outcast.

Poppie and Mommie in Philly

Minnie could have gone to a home for "unwed mothers," and stayed with other pregnant girls, who were going to give their children up for adoption. But she had already lost the love of Davis and the love of her parents. All she had left in the world was this little baby on the way. And what about her family of eight brothers and sisters? Lily wrote, "I give John credit. He wanted her in his house. Arthur too – but their wives." That had to have hurt. Evangelist Gipsy Smith expressed the prevailing caution of the day, when she said, "You are too afraid to risk your white reputations to help the woman t hat has fallen." Minnie never kept any pictures of her older brothers or sisters in her photo album, so you can tell how she felt about the way they treated her. She kept pictures of her two younger brothers, Walter and Auggie – who were both still living at home with Lily and their parents.

Minnie also kept pictures of Olga, the sister who had to get married to the drunk and then had a bunch more kids with him. Olga was warm, spirited and friendly. Minnie moved in with them and had my Dad in the Women's Homeopathic Hospital in Philly. She signed in as "May Davis." The nurses weren't fooled and checked the box marked "illegitimate" on Dad's birth certificate. Minnie named him Francis Carl Davis, Jr., after his father, perhaps wistfully hoping that they would reunite, or maybe hoping she could get her hands on him and sue him.

Life with Olga and "her rotten husband and a lot of children," [another Lily letter] had to have been chaotic. Mom said of Olga's husband, "Anytime he had a little money he would spend it on drink." Mom also said that the older brothers and sisters contributed to Olga's and her children's support. Lily said their parents did, too, back when they were working. She comments, "Olga's life . . . seemed terrible to us." Yeah, having to marry a guy who was a lush. That was bad. Of course, people could do the math when the first child was born. But still, that was the difference between the two sisters' situations. Olga married, maintaining her social respectability. It was a way to save her standing with her family and society. When Davis disappeared, there was nobody for Minnie to marry.

Or was there? Lily wrote, "after, to get away from them, she grabbed at the first straw." She was talking about Tony Coglioni. Who knows what Tony told her to get her to Chicago. But it "was all wrong," Lily wrote. "That was the greatest tragedy. By nature your mother was not born for that life - one saw what it done to her. It completely changed her expression. . . She was not a mercenary person, only dreamed of love, home and family."

I have read and re-read the above paragraph many, many times. It sounds like something dire and horrible had happened to

Minnie, that she had fallen into a living hell. Now I understand what a chilling tale Lily was telling.

Yes, a "girl in love is up against a cruel situation," as this testimony of a witness to the Teasdale Commission, in the Wisconsin Vice Report, confirms.

Statement of witness WXS, City No_____, p. 182

> The class of men that go to those dance halls are only waiting to make some virtuous girl their prey. . . I think it is one of the most harmful amusements there is for young people. The dance itself is all right, --but not those public dance halls. There are so many young girls who go there, and that is where they get their first drink, their first invitation to go with a man, [i.e. for sex] and these men are past masters in the art of winning young girls.

Another witness to the Teasdale commission further explains the "cruel situation" in the statement of witness MXE, City No_____p. 184

> The man will take the girl out and tell her how much he loves her, and pretty soon he has the best of her [i.e. her virginity] through promises of marriage. He says, 'well, now if anything happens, I will marry you.' Pretty soon [the man is out of the picture] . . the first thing the poor girl is gone [i.e. pregnant]. She is thrown out of her home. She is in bad at home. You are not going to employ her, because she has a bad name. Where is the woman going? The last resort for her is a sporting house [a brothel]. She is not going to lie out here in the street, is she? The man has no punishment at all. He can go to your [exclusive]_____Club, or to your churches and can marry the daughter of the richest man in the city; and he really is to blame for this poor girl's going wrong. The ladies will pat him on the back and put him up for the highest office in the city. It has been done [many times].

Who were these witnesses WXS and MXE who understood so clearly the potential dangers in the dance hall? Church ladies? Social reformers? WXS had at one time been a school teacher. But now she was a madam who ran a brothel. Witness MXE was another cathouse madam.

Yeah. It was a "cruel situation" for a girl who had fallen in love, and was now headed for a living hell. All Davis had to do was to lay low, for a little while. Then he could come back home and it was life as usual for him. He got married two years later. A reformer wrote, "The demon that ruined her you will take into your homes, to your dinners, to meet your daughters. You will marry your daughter to a scoundrel if he can dress well and drive in an automobile." [Smith in Lindberg, 2005, 135]

Philosophical as always, Lily pondered, "Maybe he suffered too one never knows."

My Cousin George's Crab Imperial

1 lb. Back fin crab meat

1 T finely chopped green pepper

1 T finely chopped pimento

1 beaten egg

1/2 c. Hellmann's mayonnaise

1 t salt or to taste

1/2 t white pepper

1 T mustard or Old Bay Seasoning

Parboil and peel green pepper strips before chopping. Pick crabmeat for shell and membrane, being careful not to break up lumps.

Mix all ingredients, except crab. Let stand a minimum of an hour. Fold carefully into crabmeat. Spoon into shells. Top with mayo and paprika. Bake at 350 degrees for 15 minutes.

As a Midwesterner, I don't think I'd ever had crab before I met my cousin George for the first time and had his incomparable Crab Imperial. George was about 79 when I drove to his cottage on the Chesapeake a few years ago. He told me I looked like his mother, who had been a Davis. George fixed this dish himself, with with the help of "Debra," his husky-voiced helper whose complexion was so dark, I could barely make her out in the shadowy interior of George's cottage. She wasn't a transvestite, exactly, because she was dressed in sweat pants and a baseball cap. But it seemed certain to me that she either was - or had recently been - a man.

Emboldened by my first adventure in real seafood at George's, I ordered crab when I was out one time with my older brother, Rob. We went to a big outdoor seafood joint on the Jersey shore. I thought I had ordered crab legs at the counter, because I read that the dinner came with a wooden mallet. When they called our number, I went back to the busy counter to pick up our food, which they had thoughtfully covered with brown paper to keep off the flies in the outdoor setting on the harbor.

Back at our table, I pulled the brown paper off my tray, and nearly jumped up out of my seat into the water, because underneath the paper were lurking six whole crabs. I'm not kidding! Plus a mallet to bust them up with. My brother didn't know what to do with them, so I took my tray and marched back to the counter, where they frowned and sent me to the kitchen window, where I grimaced to the food service person at the window, "Hey, I need to have this taken out of the shell."

"You're supposed to do it yourself!" The harried clerk sniffed."I don't know how to do it!" I protested. The clerk looked at me with anxious incredulity. "Look," I fretted, "I'm from Wisconsin.

When we get fish, it's frozen, the heads are cut off and the tails and fins have been removed, there's nothing looking back at you on the plate. It's just a fillet. I don't know how to eat this. What am I supposed to do with it?"

The chef, a thirty-five-ish well-fed guy, dressed in white, overheard me ranting and came over and sent the clerk on her way. He gave me a searching look, with a half smile on his face. "Alright," he said with amusement. "I'll do one, so you know how to do it." I watched aghast, as he whacked the crab with the mallet, and cracked the back open. He swirled his hands around something white. "Dat's da lungs," he grunted, scooping them up and throwing them into the tall wastebasket.

I grabbed a hold of my stomach, panicking at the thought of eviscerating a crab on my own. I watched with horror as he dismantled the entire crab. Then he handed me back the tray and said decisively, "There. Now you know how to do it!"

Ay yiye! I looked dubiously at the tray of crabs and back at the chef. "Uh, thanks!" I gulped. I returned to our table, where my brother Rob was patiently waiting to begin eating his dinner.

"You can order something else," he generously offered.

I contemplated the tray of crabs. I drew in a breath. "Well, if Captain James could do it, I guess I can handle it, too," I reasoned. I was referring to Captain James Davis, an ancestor I had recently learned about, who sailed *The Virginia* to Jamestowne in 1609-10, during the Starving Time. Jamestowne dwellers were being picked off by disease from their drinking water, which they had polluted themselves with refuse, and by Native American snipers bent on retribution for cruelties delivered at the hands of the English. The colonists were so hungry they were digging up corpses and eating them. Captain James, however, had been sent to establish a fort at nearby Point Comfort, by colony leader George Percy. When Percy visited the fort, he complained to Captain James that it was "so well stored that the crab fishes where with they had fed their hogs would have been a great relief unto us and saved many of our lives." [Percy]

I demolished the tray of crabs with as much Jamestowne zeal as I could muster. However, I didn't notice that the whole time I was cracking crabs and sucking out the meat, my brother had sat there uncomplaining and consumed an entire soft-shell crab, sandwiched between two slices of bread, while I conducted my gustatory tour de force!

Minnie about age 10

She may have cute, fluffy hair tied back in a big bow and wear a pretty blouse and necklace, but this little girl is one fiery rebel

Vintage Chicago photo courtesy of Tim Samuelson

Chapter Three

❧❧❧❧❧❧❧❧❧❧

Chicago Ain't No Sissy Town

Chicago. Concrete streets and sidewalks radiate heat. Smog swirls round and round, so thick I want to gag on the acrid smell of it. On the Lakefront, massive cubes of steel fall away, yielding to the poetry of wild, powerful, blue waves. Always cooler by the lake. Brisk. Air smells of water and car exhaust from Lake Shore Drive. Breezy, chilly even on a hot day. Never the same from hour to hour. The lake is always changing, opaque, translucent, pearl, pale green, cerulean blue, steely gray, ultramarine. Clouds scud by. Big barges way out on the water look stationary, but look away and look back, they're in a different place. Sailboats congregate on a pretty day. In winter sometimes steam hovers over the icy, blue waters. When I see that I know for a moment I have glimpsed the divine.

Chicago people are friendly, down to earth, missing that crisp attitude you get in other big cities, like New York and Paris. Even people I know from China, Poland and France seem to absorb the Chicago character, acquiring the direct, relaxed, unadorned demeanor of Midwesterners. What you see is what you get.

The downtown streets are full of people during the day. They move at a moderate pace, not strolling, but not breaking their necks to get anywhere, either. Even the big caterpillar winding its way to the Ogilvie train station in the evening is purposeful, but never in a rush. Everyone streams in an orderly way over the bridges that span the Chicago River, past solitary beggars shaking styrofoam coffee cups, jingling a little change at the bottom of it.

Fierce wind swoops down the tall buildings of the Loop, finding its way through the seams of my heaviest coat and grabbing onto my insides. One late winter I got an ear ache just traipsing around downtown in a wicked wind going from CVS pharmacy to pharmacy, looking for one on a Sunday that had all-day bus passes in stock. On a cool but sunny day in the Loop, my body longs to warm up in the sunlight. I pass through a slice beaming down through the deep canyons of high rise office buildings, but the moment is too brief. Sometimes the Windy City almost knocks you over with a sudden gust as you cross an intersection.

The air is so thick with car exhaust I can almost taste it. *Whoosh, zip, vroom.* Traffic whizzes by. *Grrrrrrrrrrrr,* an L train rumbles, approaching. Stainless steel cars roar and rattle as they rush *clackity-clack* over my head, while I try not put my hands over my ears, walking on the street below. Just looking up from down below makes my stomach sink, when I look at the criss-cross structure of the elevated track running down the middle of the street, with rivets bleeding rust onto the steel trusses. Climbing up three or four flights of exterior stairs, and waiting up there on the exposed platform for a train to thunder into the station is an exercise in vertigo. I get on the car and it tilts at impossible angles like a roller coaster, as it bends around the corners of buildings in the Loop. Cornices, decorative heads, and business signs in third story windows go by in a moosh of images.

Most people in Milwaukee don't relish the trip down to Chicago, with its steely, hard, harsh, uncompromising sophistication. It's only two hours away, yet the way people talk about it, it's like it's a banana republic. "It's dirty, it's dangerous and what ever you do, don't mess with a Chicago cop." When I drive down there, I always take the wrong turn in my car. If I take public transportation, I get goofed up on that. Either way, I wind up getting lost in the Big, Ugly City. To me Chicago was always a major inconvenience. That is, until I started making regular trips to trace the footsteps of the Grandmother I never knew, through the underworld of bootleggers, pimps, crooks, and mobsters. That's when I became intrigued with the City.

I was surprised to learn what a young city Chicago was. A mere 120 years before I was born, the city was just an outpost in the wilderness, a handful of flimsy shacks, perched on the marshy shore of Lake Michigan. If you will meander with me down to the swamp where the great City of Chicago sprang up almost overnight, I'll show you how the sale of women, that my Grandmother was headed for on a train to Chicago with Tony Coglioni, was part and parcel of the development of the City itself.

Along the way, we'll look at such fascinating questions as, why is Chicago there in the first place? What did European fashion have to do with it? How did the Father of Chicago come to be thrown in prison twice? When did prostitution arrive in town? How did the Civil War and the Great Fire affect the sale of women? What did First Ward Alderman Hinky Dink Kenna mean when he said, "Chicago ain't no sissy town"? In my search for the answers to these questions, I found the Bad and the Ugly sides of human nature and, perhaps, a little of the Good.

Beginnings

The Father of Chicago, Jean Baptiste Point du Sable, was the child of a French pirate ship's mate on the Black Sea Gull. His father sailed the Caribbean to plunder English merchant ships that brought goods for colonists, rob returning slaving ships loaded down with money, and pillage poorly guarded Spanish colonies. Point du Sable's mother was a woman with African roots, who was enslaved on the French colony of Saint-Domingue - now called Haiti. The conditions of slavery under which Point de Sable's mother lived were brutal in the extreme. Africans were literally worked to death in the sugar cane fields. The Saint-Domingue slave market was insatiable, claiming a third of all

Africans kidnapped to the New World. Even uncontrollable slaves in the U.S. were sold to traders there. [Ball]

Around 1774, when the Father of Chicago was in his 20's, he arrived on the shores of Lake Michigan by canoe and the skin of his teeth. He had already been shipwrecked off the coast of New Orleans, caught without his papers identifying him as a free man, and been arrested by authorities in New Orleans - as a runaway slave. A French priest intervened on his behalf, obtained his release and helped him get him out of the city and up the river.

Thus, Point Du Sable headed 1,400 miles up the Mississippi, for the portage at "Shikaakwa." [McCafferty] Into his canoes he stashed trade goods - guns, ammunition, alcohol, knives, iron tomahawk heads, brass cooking pots, copper ingots, blankets, cloth, needles, thread and beads. Upon arrival Point du Sable set up a trading post. There he did business with Potowatomi villagers, camped on the shore of Lake Michigan, who traded pelts of beaver, martin, mink, otter, and fox for his European trade goods. They had named the place "Shikaakwa," after the wild onion that released its pungent odor, as it waved its fronds in the breezy swamp along the shores of Lake Michigan. Today, 20,000 Native Americans live in Chicago, representing a variety of nations, including the Potowatomi.

When du Sable got there, Europeans were already in the Shikaakwa area, French *voyageurs*, who traveled the wilderness, trading with Native people for beaver and other pelts. French *voyageurs* paddled the rivers and Great Lakes in large birch bark canoes, which might be as long as 36 feet. Many Native American women found the *voyageurs* exotic and attractive. They offered the adventure of traveling in the wilderness, and not the least of their charms were that they controlled desirable trade goods. In turn, the *voyageurs* were attracted to Native American women for their experience at wilderness living, processing and packing furs, and preparing food in the wild. In addition, the knowledge Native women had of the terrain, social customs, and languages of Native people were invaluable to the *voyageur*. Native women and *voyageurs* formed liaisons, ranging from traditional marriages in the Native or European way, to simple verbal agreements to cohabit which were made and broken at will. The children of these unions came to be known as the *Metis,* whose culture was a mélange of French and Native customs. By the 1820's an estimated 15,000 Metis lived in the Great Lakes region. [www.uwgb]

Personally, I have witnessed plenty of canoe landings, like the one Point du Sable made at "Shikaakwa." Part of the inaugural events of any buck skinner rendezvous worth its salt, is a reenactment of fur traders landing in a canoe and greeted by Native Americans. The authentic part of the event having been completed, the entire camp then indulges in four days of beer swilling, belching, and loafing, while lamely impersonating fur traders. They hoodwink the public with tall tales and dicey merchandise, which includes the pelts of poor trapped animals hanging in front of their tents. Men wear buckskins they sewed themselves, from deer they shot themselves, with a musket or bow and

Photo: *Helen Davis*

arrow. Many of them do their own cooking, making the most delicious meals over an open fire, because not every woman wants to forgo bathing for four days, crap in a blue box in her nightie, sleep on a leaky air mattress, or wake up to the sound of a drunk puking outside her tent in the middle of the night, or to the theme to Star Wars played on bagpipes at the crack of dawn, by a teenage boy strolling through camp in a great kilt.

Serious re-enactors come to these events, too. French *voyageurs* in stocking caps, leggings and long shirts camp under their canoes. Great Lakes pirates in breeches, waistcoat, and three cornered hat sail on the waters. Scottish military gents swagger through camp in great kilts. Revolutionary War soldiers shoot at British military in red coats. Blue-eyed 1/8 Native Americans entertain in fringed buckskins, in front of their hand-painted tipis.

Flitting from camp to camp, I have been feted on venison flame-broiled steaks, goose roasted on a spit, and exotic stews cooked by mountain men from stuff they killed themselves, like beaver, bear and elk. As it begins to grow dark the camp closes to the public. Lanterns are lit. Guitars, harps and bodruns are played around the campfire. And the entire group sails away into a fantasy world of their own making, lit only by fires and lamplight. In the middle of winter, you can open your closet, inhale the scent of your lovely smoked costumes, and remember just how good it really was - like the day I turned around and saw a strawberry blonde, green-eyed Icelander, in a full suit of armor and great kilt, looking at me and laughing.

The trading post Point du Sable established in America had, as its primary purpose, the collection of beaver pelts. This trade had been going on since the 1600's, when competition for beaver territory, between the Eastern Iroquois and the Great Lakes nations led to the Beaver Wars, from 1630-1700. The French, Dutch, British and Swedish all fueled the conflict, with their supply of arms to both sides, and of course, their demand for beaver pelts.

What was all the fuss about beaver for? Fashion. Back in Europe, the baby-soft fur of the underbelly was felted and made into wide-brimmed, high fashion hats - which were waterproof. I made a Cavalier hat like this for my 1630's impression of the artist daughter of a Scotsman employed in Paris in the French royal guard. But I used black velvet, stiffened with buckram instead of beaver, because I like beaver and I know that beaver, given a choice, prefer to stay inside their own skins. Cavalier hats are nothing if not flamboyant. I was once told "Ya look grand," by a Scottish military captain, in a great kilt worn in a military bustle, whose job it was to shout orders at pike-wielding recruits, marching in formation through camp.

I found out the hard way why women and men in the 1600's like those waterproof beaver hats, when I went to The Trail of History reenactment in northern Illinois, to demonstrate a 17th century artist's studio. As soon as it grew dark, a killer thunderstorm rolled in and everyone was flooded out. They wouldn't allow us to bring in our cars in that night, but two police officers were kind enough to drive me through the sheets of rain, to a dry location to sleep. I rode in the back seat of their squad car that had been stripped of door handles, which made me a little nervous, even though this was just a courtesy ride, not a trip to the hoosegow. As the wipers whirled the cascading rain off the windshield, the two cops made wisecracks about Cheeseheads. Ha ha ha. I rose to the occasion, riposting with jokes about F.I.B.s and F.I.S.H., and, I'm not kidding, I found myself having to explain to those cops what that meant, because for some reason, they had never heard those terms before. Oy vey. "Um, F.I.B. means *something* Illinois *something*," I said. I could tell by the way they exchanged glances, they didn't think that was very funny. Not like they thought *Cheeseheads* was.

By the time I returned to my canvas tent in the morning, thank goodness in a different squad car, my hat was a soggy mess. I had left it on a table where it lay all night touching the wet, sloping wall of the tent, soaking up moisture like a sponge. We were told the entire Trail of History event

The Cavalier Hat - photo: Jeanne Eberlein

was called due to excessive rain. They hauled us out on a flat buckboard, like refugees, with all our possessions stacked beside us, so our cars wouldn't damage the muddy ground. My wet hat, *not* made of beaver fur, dried into a mashed up wad, never regaining its former glory. But at least somewhere in a stream, there were a few beaver snuggled up in a dam together under the water, with their nice fur coats and soft underbellies intact.

Besides making hats out of the luxuriously soft pelt of beaver, the fur was also made into waterproof winter coats in the 1600's and 1700's in Europe. The musk of the beaver served as an exotic ingredient in perfumes. Beaver are good to eat, too, if you like tough, gamey-tasting meat. I was game to try it when it was offered by some nice, buckskinner friends some years ago at the

Prairie Villa Rendezvous in Prairie du Chien. After all, the beaver was already dead and I figured I might as well eat it. The same friends offered me the use of their bathing basin in the privacy of their tent, filled with fresh water heated over their fire. Deluxe!

Point du Sable married Kittahawa, [*Fleet Footed*] and was adopted into her tribe, the Potowatomis. Then in 1779 during the American Revolution, Point du Sable fell under suspicion, again for his heritage. The British suspected him of being a French spy, detained him briefly, and let him go. The French supported the American Revolution and this support was recruited in Paris by Ben Franklin, who was famous around town for his wild man hats made of American fur. Dubbing him "The Natural Man" the Parisians, especially *les femmes*, delighted in his charms. Franklin wrote of his celebrity to his daughter, back in America.

My picture is everywhere, on the lids of snuff boxes, on rings, busts. The numbers sold are incredible. . . Your father's face is now as well known as the man in the moon.

Shikaakwa was wide open for development after the Blackhawk War in 1832. Several years later, the Potowatomis were forcibly removed from their camp by the military, who burned their village and crops, and marched them at gun point on "The Trail of Death" to a reservation in Kansas. Potowatomi trails remained, but were given the names Clark Street, Ogden Avenue and Archer Avenue.

Last summer, I was heading to the original site of Point du Sable's log cabin at Pioneer Court, in front of the Chicago Tribune building. I walked along with the crowds of tourists and office workers on Michigan Avenue at rush hour. Just as I was crossing Wacker on my way to the bridge over the Chicago River, I noticed crossing towards me, a beautiful slim, young woman with ginger hair, in leggings and a tunic. I had the sudden feeling, "what's wrong with this picture?" She crooked her finger with a sweet smile on her face, beckoning to a guy in a sporty white car who was waiting at the stop light. I heard her say, enthusiastically, "Come on! You want to have some fun?" There was no response from the white car and she walked dejectedly past me.

I stood there dumbfounded in the crosswalk, thinking about what I had just seen, and was still standing there with my mouth open, when the light changed, and cars honked at me. I leapt back onto the street corner, where she was now standing crestfallen, milling around the crowd of people, searching for another mark. I could see the pressure she was under and sense that her pimp - and there always *is* a pimp - was nearby watching her too. The light changed again, I recrossed the street and walked to the other side

Old Chicago - photo: Library of Congress

of the river, to Pioneer Court in front of the Trib Tower. There I located the plaque marking the original site of Point du Sable's cabin. I sat down to ponder the grim reality of the young woman I had seen in the crosswalk. Then I tried to imagine what it had been like here on the riverfront, before all the people and concrete, when it was just fur traders and Native Americans.

My reverie was interrupted by a call from my director friend May, who was heading over so we could walked to the Gene Siskel Film Center, where my movie was making it's Chicago premiere that night. It was an eerie pleasure to play my film in the same city where my Dad, my Grandmother, Tony Colgioni and Big Jim Colosimo had once treaded the same sidewalks.

Boom Town

In 1832, the stinking marsh "Shikaakwa" began its transformation into the boom town, "Chicago." In 1833, the town impressed an early visitor as a "chaos of mud, rubbish and confusion." [Latrobe] Newcomers stayed in houses and hotels, made of hastily milled clapboards with cracks gaping so wide, the wind whistled through them. One traveler wrote of his first night in town that the wind "blew so hard that I fancied the roof of the boarding house in which we were would have fallen about my ears." [David, 53-66] When the temperature dropped to 29 degrees below zero that winter, people roasted themselves in front of a roaring fire, with heavy coats over their backs to stay warm. [Cleaver] It was so cold that one chronicler had to give up writing until it warmed up, because he found his ink froze before it could leave his pen. [Hoffman]

Despite the cold people enjoyed themselves that first winter grouse and duck hunting, ice skating, joy riding in horse drawn sleighs, improvised from saplings and buffalo robes, and even theoccasional music concert. [Cleaver, 1833]. Yet the new town was so wild, people woke up in the middle of the night to the sound of wolves, howling as they ran through the streets. [Hoffmann]

In the spring, Chicago – at swamp level with Lake Michigan - was a muddy mess. It wasn't unusual to see horses slopping their way through knee deep mud. Signs cautioned travelers: *Fastest Route to China, Slough of Despond* and *No Bottom Here*. Road conditions prompted this local joke: A man comes across a gentleman mired up to his chest in mud and asks, "Do you require assistance?"

"No, no. Thank you, though." the gentleman replied. "You see, I've a good horse underneath me!" [Maggio]

In spite of the boom town conditions, a couple of years later the town was bulging at the seams.

Strangers, to the amount of some hundreds more, fill our public houses and streets, our wharves are covered with men, women and children, just landed from the vessels, and even some storehouses have been thrown open to receive the unsheltered emigrants, who had else remained under the open sky upon the wharves. [The Chicago American]

Chicago 1833 – just a few houses on a marsh

Carpenters, masons, and laborers arrived to get the town built. Along with them came land speculators, lawyers, merchants, livestock dealers, peddlers, doctors, inn keepers, newspaper editors and school teachers, to maintain the new town. [Hoffman] Also drawn to the prairie town by the scent of new money were parasites: gamblers, pickpockets, thieves, card sharps, con men, gun men, counterfeiters, hoodlums and rowdies. [Asbury: 37] By year's end in 1835, the boom town had a population of only 3,279 people, and yet the town board was already coping with the sale of women, when it passed an ordinance imposing fines on -

> Whoever keeps or maintains a house of ill-fame . . . patronizes the same or lets any house, room or

other premises for any such purpose . . . All prostitutes, solicitors to prostitution, and all persons of evil fame or report, plying their vocation on the streets, alleys or public houses

One night a few years ago, when I was walking to a milonga in Little Italy, I noticed that many of the houses I passed had a long front stairway leading up to a high first floor, with a garden level below that was half underground. This architectural quirk, I later learned, was due to the raising of the streets of the entire City.

With the constant problems of cholera, dysentery and malaria, there had been no doubt in anyone's mine that the City's swampy location was a health hazard. But the question was, what's to be done about it? The City tried ditching the roads and building wood plank roads and sidewalks, with unsatisfactory results. Then in 1855 the City hired Boston engineer, Ellis S. Chesbrough, to tackle the problem. He came up with a radical solution: they

would raise the level of the entire city, so that roads could drain into a sewer system, which the city would construct under the raised streets. It was a crazy idea that no one had tried anywhere else, but Chicago embraced it. Over the next twenty years, the whole city was raised from between four to fourteen feet. Houses were jacked up, while new, higher foundations were built underneath them.

Those architectural quirks I noticed were the result of economizing by homeowners, who didn't want to pay to raise their house to meet the

Peculiar architecture

higher street level. They simply punched a new front door on the second floor and built a staircase leading up to it. They had to or they would have had to climb in and out a window, once the land around the house was buried until the original first floor was half underground.

Prostitution

By the time the streets were being raised in Chicago, prostitution and the misery that accompanies it were a firmly entrenched reality, as seen in tragedies reported in the newspapers. An article reported a "terribly diseased," seventeen year old prostituted teenager was raped by "ten men who went up there of a Sunday and violated her, one after another." [CT "Horrible"] In the same year, a 23 year old inmate of a Chicago brothel took a legal dose of opium, in a state of despair over her life in prostitution. The reporter described her life in the brothel as "misery that earth cannot elsewhere parallel." [CT, 7/21/1859]

Collateral Damage   photo Library of Congress

Also in 1859, the death of a 17 year old child prostitute was reported, from "inflammation of the bowels." [Ibid] When gonorrhea infected the uterus, the infection easily spread to the bowel and then to the blood. The result: lethal septicemia. As prostituted individuals fatally succumbed to venereal disease, as well as alcoholism, drug addiction, and violent death by murder, suicide, or as the result of assault and battery, they were replaced through the criminal recruitment of new individuals. Abduction and rape of teenage children were a constant problem in the City. In 1857, twelve-year old Christina Davis was abducted in the train station, on her arrival to Chicago. Described as "an unusually bright and intelligent child," Davis had come to Chicago to search for her father and to find work as a house servant. [CT "Outrageous"] Three people who had conspired inher abduction, including a hackman and a brothel madam, were convicted. [CT "Recorders Court"]

In 1860, the attempted abduction of Lizzie Engels produced a conspiracy conviction of two procurers and a brothel madam. During the trial, Ellen Frances Herbert, testifying on behalf of Lizzie Engels, reported that she herself had been abducted when she sought work through an employment agency, which sent her to what turned out to be a brothel. There she was drugged and raped. When she made a complaint to police officer M.M. Gillespe, according to the newspaper he "made base proposals to her and on her persistent refusal" put her in jail overnight, where he raped her. The next day she was convicted and sent to prison on his testimony, that she was an inmate of a house of prostitution. [CT "Lizzie"]

The rate of attrition in human trafficking was high in the mid 1800's. An 1859 study by William M. Sanger, M.D., revealed mortality statistics. "The average duration of the prostitute's life, after beginning her career, does not exceed four years. One-fourth . . . die yearly." [Sanger, Wm.] Prostitution deaths from suicide, syphilis, gonorrhea, alcoholism, drug addiction, and murder were recurring tragedies in the vicious cycle of attrition and replenishment in prostitution. Maggie McLeran, a "handsome girl" who had come to Chicago at age seventeen to learn millinery, had been left with child when her lover abandoned her. She spent the next two years in brothels. As a result, McLeran developed a "furious temper, in the exhibition of which she would draw a weapon and use it on the slightest provocation." When she left prostitution to live with a hackman, he also deserted her. After running into him outside a confection and oyster bar on Clark and Quincy and being rebuffed, she bought adose of morphine for fifty cents at a drug store and died in the arms of a female friend. [CT "The City"]

The Cost   photo Library of Congress

"It bears absolutely no resemblance to sex." That's what Arthur Bilek, told me when we had lunch in an Evanston restaurant in 2008. He is the author of the *The First Vice Lord* and also the retired Chief of Police for the Cook County Sheriff. A tall man of 80 years, with a full head of white hair, Bilek shook his head disparagingly as he gave voice to years of experience in law enforcement, "Prostitution is the most negative of negative experiences." [Bilek, Personal Interview, 2008].

That is why Hattie Wilson and Katie Thompson, two sixteen year old prostituted teenagers, killed themselves by taking laudanum [an opiate] and strychnine [rat poison] in the basement of a brothel, in what was their second, double suicide attempt. Their suicide note reported in the Trib, read,

I hope we have made a sure thing of it this time, as we are tired of living. Goodbye, everybody. [CT "Double"]

The brothel trade grew by leaps and bounds during the Civil War, which took place between 1861 and 1865. Chicago was the wartime hub of rail transportation in the Midwest, where soldiers stopped on their way to the eastern fronts. The City experienced a dramatic increase in prostitution, in an estimated 200 brothels with 2,000 inmates. [Asbury: 95, 96]. By 1862 it was estimated that the Union capital in Washington D.C. had over twice that number of houses, with 7,500 prostitutes. Richmond, the capital of the Confederacy, had similar numbers of prostituted women. Reportedly, venereal disease "among soldiers was prevalent and largely uncontrolled." Estimates of infection in troops ran as high as 45%. [Lowry]

Personally, I have done a lot of Civil War reenactments, as a refugee. And let me tell you, you never see anyone doing an impression of a prostitute in and amongst all those Confederate and Union men. One August at Gettysburg I camped with a small group of Confederates who turned me from a refugee into a rebel soldier. They liked my own battered, gray tweed, wool suit jacket and lent me a kepi and a pair of wool trousers. The sergeant showed me how to load and shoot a musket. "Push the ramrod down with your pinky. That way if the gun goes off, you won't lose your trigger finger," he advised. Hmmmm. Maybe I shouldn't be doing this, if I'm an artist. The next morning, we got up early and marched over the still damp grasses of the Pickett's Charge field, where 10,000 men had died on the afternoon of July 3, 1863. When we got up to the top of the gently rising field, we ran into a group of Union soldiers, who - unbeknownst to us - had been watching our ascent. We all shook hands in a friendly way.

There can be prejudice against women on the battlefield at reenactments. Actually, during the real Civil War, quite a few women were out on the battlefields. Some passed as men in uniform. Some were daughters of the regiment, dressed in trousers and knee length wool skirts, and marched alongside their fathers or husbands. When I tried my hand at cavalry reenacting at an event in Illinois, the sergeant told me, "If I can't tell you're not a man, then you can be in the battle." Fortunately, I had already had some experience under my belt, at another reenactment as cavalry soldier during battle. I also brought a little Colonel Sanders mustache and goatee, which I had made from the combings of my hairbrush.

The next morning at muster, I stood at attention next to the guy who had loaned me the Union cavalry uniform and the horse. He told me later, he was trying to figure out who this strange guy was standing next to him.

The sergeant shouted out "Davis."

Cavalry Reenactment, the author on the left

I answered "Here" in my gruffest voice. Before he could call the next name on his list, I barked, "How 'bout a kiss, Sir?"

Without missing a beat or breaking character, the sergeant looked up from his roster and croaked, "I don't want a kiss from *anyone* in this company." *Ha, ha, ha.* Shortly afterward, I was trampled under my horse. Fortunately I lived to tell the tale, but that put the kibosh on my career in the cavalry.

During the real Civil War, the pressure was on for new recruits – to prostitution. In 1864, a mother complained to the Chicago courts that a pimp named Antonio Delight "has for some time attempted to get [her underage daughter] under his control." [CT "Conspiracy] Mr. Delight was described in another newspaper article as a man of "low, vicious and vulgar habits." [CT, 1/14, 1869] Not the kind of man you'd want hanging around your kid.

In 1864, a hearse pulled up to a Mr. Fox's house. The driver delivered a coffin, with the mysterious explanation, "That's your daughter. . . " Inside the coffin the Foxes found:

> the lifeless body of a fine looking girl of seventeen or eighteen, whom the agonized parents instantly recognized as their daughter "Kitty," who had disappeared from her home nearly two months ago.

Apparently, their daughter's "good looks and youthful manner attracted the attention of a Mrs. Herrick, the keeper of one of the State Street sepulchers," so read the newspaper account. The cause of death was determined to be "inflammation of the bowels," that symptom of unchecked gonorrhea, for which there was no cure until the mid 20th century. [CT "Sad Death"]

The tragedy of Kitty Fox's death was followed by the suicide of her friend, eighteen year old Ann Wallace. Wallace a sensitive, beautiful girl, arrived in Chicago from a town in southeastern Illinois a month earlier. Back home, her parents believed she was working as a seamstress in the City. But in 1864, seamstresses were paid starvation wages. A young woman, such as Wallace, living on her own in the City as a seamstress, would spend twelve hour days working in a dress shop or doing piece work at home. In spite of the long working hours, she would find out almost immediately, after paying her weekly rent for a room in a lodging house, that she could not make enough money to feed or clothe herself.

That's why Annie Bell, the madam of the Clark Street brothel where Anne Wallace had been an inmate, testified at the Coroner's inquest, that she had:

> known the deceased about three weeks. She came to my house about that time ago in company with Kitty Fox. . . after Kitty's death, she became very melancholy and told me she did not wish to live. She cried very much and talked almost constantly of Kitty and her sudden death and her spirits were much affected. . . On Friday I went out and when I returned found the deceased in violent spasms. I was alarmed and asked her what was the matter, when she told me she had taken poison.

Satan's Mile vintage photo: Library of Congress

Ann Wallace had given her parents no inkling that she had been the inmate of a house of prostitution, when she visited them back home, a couple of times during the month she had lived in Chicago. At the inquest, they "wrung their hands and sobbed in an agony of grief that drew tears from nearly all present." [CT "Suicides: Prostitution"]

The reporter commented on the "frequency of suicides" of women in prostitution, which

> will excite with wonder and startle with horror. But when we consider how weak the ties which bind them to earth--how few and feeble the friendships they have formed, and how little the

future gives them of hope, we shall cease to marvel and only wonder that life is tolerable to them. . . " [Ibid]

Jane Addams Studies Conditions of Prostitution

Premature death from venereal disease, assault and battery, psychological damage, social ostracism, alcoholism, drug addiction, arrest, imprisonment, and acts of sexual violence – all these were the hazards of prostitution, identified by Jane Addams in 1912. [Addams, 1912] The same damage is present in today's prostitution. In 2006, Janice Raymond found that survivors had experienced more severe trauma than returning combat soldiers, with symptoms of extreme depression, anxiety, and nearly 100% alcohol and drug addiction. In addition survivors are at risk for self-mutilation, suicide attempts [which runs nearly 50%], and murder. Raymond found that 84% of survivors had been victims of aggravated assault, 78% were victims of sexual violence by pimps and johns who committed these crimes on the individual an average of 49 times in a year, 53% were victims of sexual torture, and 27% had been mutilated. [Raymond]

Brothels boomed in Chicago during the Civil War. A special law was enacted in the City in the beginning of 1864, to accommodate prostitution business. The new law required that before police could make any arrests, a complaint against a brothel had to be filed by "two respectable householders." Further, raids were to be conducted only during daylight, apparently so as not to interrupt trade during peak hours. The new law also provided a gaping loophole for politicians, frequently netted in raids with their pants down around their ankles - no one found inside a brothel should be arrested who was "merely a casual visitor." Thus at the time of Fox and Wallace's deaths, brothels enjoyed what a reporter described as "the abundant protection of the law." Money might be raked in by the bushel, while "men in high office and social position may gratify their lusts without fear of detection or disgrace." [CT "Houses"] Under the new law, the lives of Kitty Fox and Ann Wallace became collateral damage.

Slaughterhouse Town

Chicago was a slaughterhouse town, whose Union Stock Yards ran for acres and acres on the south side. Here farm animals were transported by train to be butchered by thousands of workers. Fresh water came was pumped in from the Chicago River, while waste drained into "Bubbly Creek," also a favorite location for dumping human bodies. The entire area had an unhealthy air of rotting flesh. Poorer neighborhoods clustered around the undesirable location. "Back o'the yards" was Connelly's Patch, a hard scrabble Irish neighborhood. The "Black Belt," which housed the City's growing population of black workers up from the south for industrial jobs, ran along the rail corridor that serviced the stockyards, where the smell of soot and cinders from the trains added to the heavy air. [www.chicagohs]

The Great Fire

In 1871, the Great Fire blew through Chicago. The gigantic firestorm demolished everything in its path, including brothels. Pandemonium ruled as people poured out of their homes in the downtown and on the North Side. Firebrands of debris flew overhead. What would you do if you were in the path of a such a monstrous conflagration? I'd run like hell for water. That's just what Chicagoans did in 1871. They fled to the river and the beaches and also headed out to the prairies outside of town.

> The streets were crowded with men looking for their wives and children, children looking for mothers, husbands for wives, and wives for husbands. . . Horses and cows were running loose up and down the streets. . . Men, women and children loaded with everything you can conceive were blocking up the sidewalks . . they went, hurrying, pushing, scrambling, crowding, jostling, shouting, and laughing even. . . [Gallagher]

The giant fire, spurred by its own updraft, blew gusts of fire so hot they melted mortar and iron, toppling brick, steel and stone buildings in the downtown. Brothels had been sprinkled throughout the central city, in places called Shinbone Alley, Under the Willow, Mother Conley's Patch, and the rookeries of Wells Street [i.e. the upper stories]. The hungry fire consumed their flimsy, wood-frame structures like matches.

The Great Chicago Fire

Some inmates rushed into the caverns of the Washington Street tunnel under the Chicago River. There in the smoky darkness, waiting out the fire, huddled

> bankers and thieves, merchants and gamblers, artisans and loafers, clergymen and burglars, matrons and rag-pickers, maidens and prostitutes—representatives of virtue and vice, industry and improvidence, in every grade, . . . There were bruises and groans, blows and piercing shrieks, prayers, imprecations, pocket-picking, and indignities unmentionable. [Luzerne: 78]

Between 200-300 people lost their lives in the fire. Thousands were without homes. The Loop and the North side were burned to the ground. Entire sections of the City had been transformed into an eerie ghost town. "One is unable to form any idea of where he is -- lost among the streets that contain not a house for miles," observed a railway worker. In the aftermath of the fire, "Roughs and thieves from all parts of the country flocked here for plunder. In most cases the party caught in the act has been shot on the spot." [Wicker]

In the midst of such devastation, the brothels reappeared immediately in the South Loop neighborhood, opening for business in real estate that had escaped the fire, on Customs House Place.

In the 50 year building boom that followed the Great Fire, architects came from all over the country to create a new metropolis of brick and stone. Mark Twain observed the evolving cityscape: "It is hopeless for the occasional visitor to try to keep up with Chicago. She outgrows his prophecies faster than he can make them. She is always a novelty; for she is never the Chicago you saw when you passed through the last time." [Twain: 1883.]

The rich enjoyed the splendor of the newly rebuilt downtown, where they stashed their money in banks and the stock exchange, shopped for luxuries in department stores, and attended the opera, symphony and plays. And just a few blocks away, along the near South Side river wharves, the streets of the Levee teemed with vice. Not only had brothels congregated in the seedy district, but also appearing alongside them were saloons, gambling joints, cheap hotels, squalid tenements, flop houses, peep shows, burlesque theaters, dance halls and opium dens. Perhaps that is what prompted Rudyard Kipling to complain, in 1891, that Chicago "is inhabited by savages." [Kipling]

Like moths to a flame, highbrow Chicago slummers and tourists flocked to the seedy life on the Levee, a cesspool of vice and crime. And an army of ne'er do wells were ready to fleece them for all they were worth - gamblers, thugs, muggers, pickpockets, violent thieves, con artists, murderers, opium addicts, cocaine addicts, pimp and madams. Thus, Mark Twain's character Satan makes this wry comment to a Newcomer, in Hell. "The trouble with you Chicago people is, that you think you are the best people down here; whereas you are merely the most numerous. [Twain: 1897]

Chicago's Levee was notorious all over the country as place of pleasure. But in reality it was a black hole of thinly disguised human misery, waiting to devour the lives of those who came there. The Levee was a desperate realm where predator and prey locked together in a death grip, unrestrained by law and order. The political climate in Chicago provided the ideal backdrop for such a place to exist. "Chicago is unique. It is the only completely corrupt city in America," quipped Charles Merriam, unsuccessful candidate for mayor in 1911.

Boodle

In 1893, the Chicago Herald wrote that "the average representative in the City Council is . . . a disreputable that can be bought and sold as hogs are bought and sold at the stockyards." [Stead, 1894, footnote: 183] So what were they talking about? That Chicago specialty: boodle. That seducer of aldermen. Boodle had to be paid by anyone wanting to install anything in the city streets - for example, the L train, power lines, phone lines, electricity, gas, water, pneumatic tubes, railways, street cars, or even such simple things as a balcony hanging out into the street, or merchandize on the sidewalk.

With 2000 miles of City streets to be milked in 1894, boodle was a gold mine, that paid out an estimated $5million/year, directly into the aldermen's pockets. [Stead, 1894: 173-4] Members of the City Council were paid $3 for each weekly meeting, netting them $156 a year. [Stead, 1894: 176] Yet many aldermen owned luxurious mansions in town, and equally splendid country estates, which they claimed they could afford through good investments. Alderman Nathan T. Brenner confided, "There are only three aldermen in the entire 68 who are not able and willing to steal a red hot stove." Brenner would know, because in addition to being the 7th Ward Alderman in 1896-8, ["Report"] he, himself, owned an elegant mansion at 5839 N. Sheridan Rd. ["Preliminary"] In addition, his presence in the City Council was arguably a conflict of interest, as he was also the President of the American Insulated Wire and Cable Co.

Honest City Council members were cattle prodded into voting along with the boodle pack, with threats like, "You won't get a can of garbage moved out of your ward till hell freezes over." [Wendt and Kogan: 40]

View of the South Loop in the early 1900's - Photo: Library of Congress

British Journalist, William T. Stead, observed the under-the-table deals of the City Council.

> A safe man, who can keep quiet and not take more than his share, [acts as] a go-between between corporations and aldermen. . . [he] contacts the boodle boss, 'to ascertain whether the boys are

hungry. . .' He strikes a deal with the boodle boss, or head of the ring, for $500 - 1,500 per alderman. The go-between deposits money in a safe deposit box in his own name. Some time after the vote, the money is discreetly placed in his [the alderman's] overcoat pocket. [Stead, 1894: 177-8]

In a good year an alderman would rake in 15-20 K a year. [Asbury, 1940, footnote:157, quoting the Record, February 19, 1894] In the late 1800's that was a fortune. Stead observed that Mayor Carter Harrison, Sr. could also be bought, with an envelope stuffed with cash, stashed under the pillow of a couch in his office. [Stead, 1894: 184]

Boodle is how bills were passed in spite of public condemnation. [Stead, 1894: 176]. And the City was left high and dry. Not only did the City *not* receive a nickel of the boodle, but the City also did not receive the return it should have on taxes, from the corporations that got the City contracts. That's because the crooked alderman made sure tax assessments for the companies dishing out boodle were set low. [Wendt and Kogan: 34, 35] Wealthy industrialists who doled out boodle were laughing all the way to the bank.

First Ward Aldermen

Two Levee rats, "Bathhouse" John Coughlin and "Hinky Dink" Kenna, began serving in the City Council as aldermen in the 1890's, and could not be routed out of office for more than a generation. They represented the First Ward, which included not only the Levee, but also the downtown Loop. Kenna and Coughlin won their elections through chicanery, paying drunks and illegal immigrants to vote for them multiple times on election day, at different polling places. They also rigged elections through the machinations of crooked poll workers, who falsified election returns on their behalf.

John "Bathhouse" Coughlin, grew up Irish-American in Connolly's Patch, and left school to go to work at age 11, in a bathhouse. A barely educated saloon and bathhouse owner,

Kenna and Coughlin, Fat Cat Adlermen

Coughlin was elected in 1893 and remained in power for 45 years until his death in 1938. The alderman was a peacock, known for his collection of loud suits, "which included at any one time, some combination of silk hat, pink gloves, yellow shoes, green coat, lavender pants, cream-colored vest, diamond studs, and floral embroidery." [Kendall] His ridiculous poems, like "Ode to a Bowl of Soup," were served up Chicago newspapers as local political folly. In spite of his buffoonery and flamboyant personality, there was nothing to laugh at about a man who tampered with his own elections, paid out huge sums in graft and - to use his own words - made "a mockery and a sham" out of Chicago politics. [Ibid] Coughlin was a force to be reckoned with.

Along with fellow First Ward Aldermen Kenna, the two aldermen ran a highly lucrative protection racket, extorting money from the crooked businesses on the Levee. Graft paid out of this fund was used to paralyze law and order, and allow the prostitution of women and girls as young as 13. Michael "Hinky Dink" Kenna, Coughlin's partner in derailing the criminal justice system on the Levee, was a 5'1" saloon owner. Kenna came to power in 1897 and remained in office for the next 26 years, until 1923. Kenna himself owned several Levee bars, including the Clark Street, "Workingman's Exchange." Like many saloons, Kenna offered 5-cent beers and free lunch every day of the week to the unemployed.

Upstairs from the Workingman's Exchange, Kenna ran the Alaska Hotel, a flophouse, which accommodated up to 300 men, who could be primed with 50 cents and a glass of beer, each time they hit the polls on election day. Kenna's bar was located in the 800 block of S. Clark St., [Kendall] in a block lined with pawn shops, brothels, rag picker nests, saloons and gambling houses, called "Little Cheyenne."

Today, the block still has a men's hotel, cheap restaurants, a liquor store and pawnbrokers. In fact, I met a nice pawnbroker there, who gave me free parking in his lot, while I was shooting the upper stories through snow flurries. The upper stories looked pretty much the same as they did in the old days. I used the footage for the brothel sequence and also the fire escape, which was where a crazed voodoo queen tosses a brothel inmate out of a third story window.

Little Cheyenne was described by a police detective active in the 1890's as being :

Green screen movie scene throwing Laura Johnson off a Clark Street fire escape

about as tough and vicious a place as there was on the face of the earth. Around the doors of these places could be seen gaudily-bedecked females, half-clad in flashy finery, dresses which never came below their knees, with many colored stockings and fancy shoes. Many of them wore bodices cut so low that they did not amount to much more than a belt. [Wooldredge: 410]

Aldermen Kenna and Coughlin maintained a stranglehold on the First Ward, through their extra-legal protection racket, extorting money from crooked Levee businesses. With graft paid out of this fund, the two aldermen paralyzed the criminal justice system and disenfranchised the rights of thousands of underage girls and women, who were denied protection under the law as U.S. citizens. Kenna and Coughlin had their own police captain in place, who could be counted on to *not* enforce the law. They also had court "fixers," who – for a substantial fee – would obtain a dismissal or a "not guilty" verdict for clients. The aldermen even had a system of obtaining pardons for convicted criminals with certain governors - the ones who could be bought.

"Justice shops," the police courts in the City of Chicago, were places where "justice was literally for sale." [Willrich: 3] Justices of the Peace were appointed by the governor. Police magistrates were appointed by the mayor. There were no educational standards whatsoever for appointees, who were characterized as "burly, vulgar minded political henchmen." [Ross: 106 and 133-4]. They made decisions on cases of vice, assault and petty theft. [Willrich: 13] In 1892, a grand jury investigating the justice system complained that justices and magistrates, lacked "proper comprehension of the rules of law, justice and honesty." [Willrich: 17]

All kinds of wheeling and dealing went on in the courts. The First Ward Aldermen received kickbacks from side deals with the judge, as well as kickbacks from the bail bondsmen and the aldermen's fixer. The convicted who couldn't afford to pay, were sentenced to the Bridewell House of Corrections.

The Progressive Era

In the face of overwhelming corruption in City government, the burden of controlling problems generated by rampant prostitution in Chicago was taken up by Progressives. Some were mayors of the city, like William Dever and a few were City aldermen. Some were Chicago District Attorneys, who worked hard for justice for the women and children caught up in the prostitution industry. There were also downtown businessmen and civic groups, like the Committee of Fifteen and the Civic Federation, which is still active today, as a government watchdog agency.

The attempts by Progressives to put criminals, who dealt in the trade in women, out of business were continually thwarted by First Ward police captains on-the-take, who would order raids only on brothels that were not paying for "protection." Sometimes raids were conducted by an honest police officer but those arrests never came to fruition in the courts, because police officials shuffled the paperwork, or the courts dismissed the cases, under the influence of graft. And that honest policeman would likely find [Addams, 1912:Chapter 2] himself transferred out of the First Ward, to some remote location. However in 1915, the Kate Adams Law, recommended by the Committee of Fifteen, was approved by the City Council. Under this law, landlords became liable for renting out their property to brothels. The law required convicted property owners to cancel leases with brothels and keep the property vacant for a year. Progressives filed suit against 80 Levee real estate owners, with an impressive 71 convictions obtained. [CT, 10/4/1915]

Vintage Chicago - Photo: Library of Congress

Squeamish Victorian mores were an impediment to the Progressives' efforts. Prominent Civic Federation member, Adolph Nathan, complained of the "mawkish sentiment of sensitiveness which taboos an open discussion of the subject." [CT, 2/7/1897] The word "prostitution" itself was considered obscene. Social activist, Jane Addams elaborated - "In every large city throughout the world thousands of women are so set aside as outcasts from decent society, that it is considered an impropriety to speak the very work which designates them." And indeed, Addams herself does not write the word in her book on prostitution, called, *A New Conscience and an Ancient Evil.*" [Addams, 1912: 3]

Victorian euphemisms, such as "ruined," "immoral," "loose" and "fallen," were used to designate the women and children of prostitution. Such language provokes misunderstanding today of the Progressive efforts to put an end to the suffering caused by prostitution. Pioneering investigative journalist, William Stead clarified in 1885, that he objected to the "atrocities, brutalities, and unnatural crimes" of prostitution. He was fighting against "sexual criminality, as opposed to sexual immorality." [Stead, 1885]

Chicago Vice Commission Studies Prostitution

In 1910, an investigation into prostitution in Chicago was ordered by Mayor Fred Busse, who appointed thirty individuals to the Chicago Vice Commission. Their detailed report, published the following year, *The Social Evil in Chicago* was banned from the U.S. Mail, for violating obscenity laws.

The Commission discovered that the general lack of sex education among young women and girls made them easy pickings for procurers, who exploited their ignorance. Sex education was immediately implemented in the schools in 1912, under the name "Social Hygiene," with the backing of School Superintendent Ella Flagg Young. One school trustee fumed that the information, "has poisonous tendencies and will put impure thoughts into the minds of the children." But this Victorian notion was refuted by another trustee, who countered, "There is no safety in ignorance." [CT "Educational"]

Jane Addams reported in 1914 that over half "of all the young women in the nation between the ages of sixteen and twenty, are engaged in some gainful occupation." However, starvation wages paid to unskilled female workers prevented them from making enough to live on. [Addams, 1912: 56]

The Chicago Vice Commission identified starvation wages as an important cause of prostitution. The study found that working women and children were likely to find they could not make ends meet, in jobs as sales clerks at department stores, domestics, waitresses, laundry workers, factory workers, and dressmakers, that all paid $5.00 per week or less. This simple entry in the report speaks volumes: "Rosie. Works in millinery store, learning the trade. Salary $4 and can't hardly exist." [CVC, 189] The Commission's investigations revealed that women's wages were insufficient to live on. Many workers turned to theft and prostitution to survive.

Present day Clark St. detail from the past

Addams reported how a factory girl was unable to make ends meet on her wages of six dollars a week. "She habitually spent two dollars a week for her room, three dollars for her board, and sixty cents a week for carfare." The young woman was unable to clothe herself with the forty cents a week remaining of her wages. She had her old shoes resoled twice in the seven months she worked her factory job, until she could no longer wear them and having "but ninety cents towards a new pair, she gave up her struggle; to use her own contemptuous phrase, she 'sold out for a pair of shoes.'" [Addams, 1912: 76]

Many young women were the sole breadwinners for their families, Addams found when she interviewed thirty-four young women at a rescue home. One was a young widow of seventeen years, who entered prostitution to pay for her own support and the care of her baby in her sister's household. Another young woman supported her mother through prostitution.

Another girl Addams interviewed had left her small town in Indiana at age fifteen, to go to Chicago to support her family. Her mother was ill, her father too old to work, and her brother had been stricken with rheumatism. The girl obtained a job as a department store clerk, but was unable to make ends meet even for herself on the five dollars a week she was paid. "She was constantly filled with a corroding worry for 'the folks at home.'" A coworker at the department store told her about how to make "appointments for money in the noon hour at downtown hotels." Then, after doing this for several months, "the young girl made an arrangement with an older woman to be on call in the evenings whenever she was summoned by telephone." Finally she entered prostitution full time in order to pay for her family's support and send her brother for a one year treatment in a sanitarium in Hot Springs, Arkansas. [Addams, 1912: 62]

Chicago department store owner, Marshall Fields, paid starvation wages to women. Ironically his son and heir was shot to death, while slumming one night in a brothel on the Levee, the Everleigh Club. Plush furnishings, inmates in evening gowns and high prices did not change the fact, that what the Everleigh sisters were selling were the bodies of women, who could not make a living wage on the outside, including in an establishment like Field's department store.

"Girls of tenderest age were mercilessly ground into dollars; their young life's blood dyed deep the fabrics which brought Field riches," wrote Samuel Paynter Wilson in 1910 [Wilson, 57-61]. One young woman had come to Chicago to find work because her family back home had just lost their father. She was offered a job working at a department store counter at $5 a week. Paynter did the math: "The YWCA charges $5.25 for a room and board, two persons in a room." When the young woman protested to the store manager, that she could not support herself on such a sum, the "brazen rascal had the effrontery to ask her if she did not have 'some friend' on the outside who would help her." Apparently that's how it was done by shop girls in Paris. [Stead, 1984: 245] If that it sounds far fetched consider this: a recent documentary film, reports that today the world's largest retailer regularly counsels its employees on how to supplement *their* starvation wages – with state and federal welfare programs. [Greenwald]

An even more treacherous problem the Commission identified was the high death rate from venereal disease in prostitution. "Fresh young girls must be continually supplied to take the place of those who die." [CVC: 40] Edward Sims, U.S. District Attorney declared "Prostitution literally consumes thousands of girls each year."

L Station back in the day – photo Library of Congress

The Commission also found that it was almost impossible for a young woman, in the course of daily life, to avoid coming into contact with the "direct, persistent, often concerted efforts of procurers." We would now call them "traffickers." The ranks of traffickers "include both men and women, bartenders, waiters in saloons and restaurants, managers and employees in theaters, nickel shows, penny picture arcades, employers, floor walkers and inspectors in stores and shops." There were also "hackmen, expressmen and runners at railway stations and boat landings," on the lookout for naive country girls, who needed lodging. They would deliver their charges to brothels, where they were imprisoned, raped and beaten into submission. Other traffickers included certain midwives and doctors, along with "fortune tellers, cadets, keepers and attendants in dance halls, private recreation parks, hotels and flats." Even the post office wasn't safe. The general delivery window, where new arrivals in town picked up their mail, was "watched as a secret and safe way of spotting, inveigling and trapping young girls." [CVC: 230-1]

Other traps for young women were placed in the want ads, luring girls and young women to Chicago for jobs at good wages. Another method of entrapment practiced by procurers was to travel to nearby cities in Indiana and Wisconsin, to "entice young

girls to the big cities under various glittering but false promises."
[Clabaugh] Traffickers also practiced their deception at "rest
rooms in department stores [where there were comfortable
lounges], and even at the counters in certain departments; at
theaters, especially on amateur nights; at employment agencies
including those connected with mercantile and industrial
establishments." [CVC: 230-1] In short, traffickers were at work,
everywhere a young woman in Chicago might go in public.

The criminal activity of obtaining and selling these women and
children to brothels was known at the time as *white slavery*. Art
Bilek, the Ex-Police Chief of the Cook County Sheriff defined
"white slavery" thus:

> Girls . . . were induced through flattery, money,
> promises of good jobs, or other equally bogus
> offerings to go to another city far from their homes
> where they ended up against their will in brothels.
> In many cases, these women, whose ages ranged
> from fifteen to twenty-five, were initially held
> captive in the resorts by physical force or
> intimidation. . . raped and made to undergo
> repeated acts of sexual violence until they
> submitted. [Bilek, 2008: 95].

Why was there no one there to stop it?

> "The Commission does not condemn the personnel
> of the *police* as a whole, but it does condemn the
> *System* . . . which makes it easier for the police to
> accept graft from the tremendous profits reaped
> from the sale in women's bodies than to honestly
> do their duty." [CVC: 29]

The rights of U.S. citizens who became crime victims were
nullified by graft.

Following the publication of the Chicago Vice Commission report,
The City received so much pressure from its citizens and civic
groups, that State's Attorney Wayman ordered vigorous raids

against the red light district in 1912. In retaliation, brothel owners who had been shut, down sent flocks of garishly dressed, prostituted women out into residential neighborhoods, where they attracted crowds of followers as they fanned out, ringing doorbells in search of apartments. It was a staged event, and the uproar it caused stayed convictions of the brothel owners. However, Mayor Harrison, who espoused an "open city" policy for the Levee, had to bow to public pressure, and eliminate First Ward Police Chief McSweeny from office, for failing to close those dives that the State's Attorney took action against. In addition, two police inspectors and a police lieutenant were convicted of graft and removed from office.

Present day doorways in Printer's Row

Corruption at the Time of Minnie's Arrival

The Juvenile Protection Society reported that after being dispersed from the Levee, brothels were "honeycombing the south, north and west sides," and had also moved to roadhouses in outlying suburbs. Brothels, they complained, were still "protected first and last by the police." They judged the City to be the worst in the country, for its massive prostitution of women and children. [CT "Chicago's Vice"]

Corruption in Chicago reached new depths under the leadership of Mayor "Big Bill" Thompson, elected in 1915. During his two term administration, which lasted until 1923, violent crime doubled in the City. [Behr: 183-4] Following his master plan for a "wide open" city, Thompson appointed corrupt police administrators, including new Chief of Police Detectives, Nicholas Hunt. Three years earlier during that clean-up, Hunt had resigned from the police force, in a corruption scandal which exposed his protection of the brothels. Thompson's star appointee in 1915, however, was Police Chief Charles Healey, who went on trial the following year. He was charged with malfeasance in office and conspiring to nullify anti-gambling laws. Healey's "little green book" was presented as evidence in the trial, containing his handwritten notes. In it, he had recorded weekly fees for police protection paid by saloon and brothel owners. He had also entered a list of joints that could be raided because they were not paying for protection. In spite of such damning evidence, Healey was acquitted. He was defended by the famous lawyer, Clarence Darrow. [Darrow]

Big Bill Thompson also replaced capable City officials with his own corrupt appointees. These men collected payoffs in all areas of City service, from public transportation to the construction of roads, schools and hospitals. State of Illinois Governor Len Small, elected in 1921, granted pardons to Thompson's convicted appointees and gangsters. This pack included convicted bootlegger boss, Edward "Spike" O'Donnell and notorious white slavers, Harry and Anna Guzik. [Behr, 183-4] The Guziks, after receiving their gubernatorial pardon, went right back to doing business on the Levee. There they operated a "disorderly hotel at 516 S. Wabash . . . [where] male 'ropers' on the street ballyhoo the place, like a barker at a street carnival." Despite vigorous complaints to the police by other businesses in the area, the

Guziks' hotel was left alone. With a crooked Mayor and Police Chief in town and the Governor's pardon, how could anyone stop them? [ICS: 18]

Under wide spread corruption, thousands of young women lost their lives, as collateral damage in the prostitution business. There is no doubt that a quid pro quo relationship existed between the giant prostitution industry and fat-cat City Aldermen, police captains, lieutenants, detectives and cops on the beat. Judges, police magistrates and court fixers raked in their share of graft. During quite a few administrations, even the Chief of Police and the Mayor jumped on the bandwagon and led the City on an unbridled course of violence and corruption.

This is the Chicago my Grandmother and my Dad found when they got off the train from Philadelphia, in 1916: a city that would make a banana republic green with envy.

Library of Congress Panoramic of Old Chicago

Chapter Four

❧ ❧ ❧ ❧ ❧ ❧ ❧ ❧ ❧ ❧

Big Jim Colosimo

It was a story that Dad liked to tell. When he was five years old, his mother took him to Big Jim Colosimo's funeral. I was sitting out at my lake house in the wilderness, where I had a lot of time to think, and I started wondering: who was this Big Jim Colosimo and what was my five -year old Dad doing at his funeral? Maybe Big Jim Colosimo was just a figment of my Dad's imagination. Was the story, you know, something Dad had dreamed up to make up for his rotten childhood? Or was Big Jim Colosimo for real?

I went to the library and got a book on Chicago Gangsters, because I started this project before the internet got going. There he was, Chapter One - Big Jim Colosimo. Wow. The first big crime boss in Chicago. And he specialized in the brothel trade - in the sale of women and children. That is, until he was shot in the foyer of his own nightclub in 1920. Dad said Al Capone did it.

Colosimo Profile

So who was Big Jim Colosimo? He was a corpulent, Southern Italian man, with oiled black hair and a large, soup strainer moustache, shrouding his upper lip. He had dark brown eyes that were warm and friendly, but when the gloves were off and he meant business, his gaze became a cold, penetrating stare. This picture of Colosimo was taken the only time he was ever arrested. He confronts the camera with the glare of a dangerous animal in a cage. It was a cage he knew he would break out of in a matter of hours, grabbing his freedom through sheer power. As he looks out at you, Colosimo drips with brute charm and the hulking menace of a great beast. You can hear him growl through his bared teeth. This picture of him, with his great fat hand dangling over his crotch like a giant crab, always gives me the creeps. What on earth were Dad and his Mom doing at the funeral of a guy like that?

Colosimo was a spiffy dresser, his bulk draped in an expensive suit, white for summers, tweed for fall. His other nickname was "Diamond Jim." It's just a shame that guys can't dress to the nines, like women do. Still, Colosimo managed to indulge his love of diamonds by wearing them studded on his garters, suspender clasps and belt buckle. He had diamonds set on his tie pins, cuff links and the rings on his fingers. He even carried a bag of diamonds in his pocket, so he could take them out and sift them back and forth between his hands. [Asbury, 312]

He was born Vincenzo Colosimo in the little town of Colosimi, near Cosenza in Calabria, [Bilek, Email] and emigrated to America in May of 1891, when he was thirteen. [Bilek, 2008: 28] He lived with his father on Polk Street, a run down tenement neighborhood, in the heart of the red light district, where kids climbed over piles of uncollected garbage and animal manure. Kids also witnessed scenes of prostitution through brothel windows, solicitation conducted openly on the streets, brawling drunks stumbling out of saloons, and pickpockets, thieves and the scum of the earth lurking in every doorway on the Levee. As a kid, Colosimo worked the streets, selling shoelaces, gum, and newspapers, shining shoes and picking pockets. These tasks were usually doled out by a child labor padrone, who was just as mean as Fagin in Charles Dicken's novel, *Oliver Twist*. Colosimo was also a messenger boy on the Levee. [Bilek, 2008: 34] Prostitutes sent their errand boys to the druggist to pick up their fix of morphine or cocaine. Sampling those drugs were the perks of the messenger business. And being a messenger boy on the Levee was a school unto itself, because that's the way kids learned how illegal trades, like prostitution, worked from the inside.

A few years later, Colosimo lived with the family of labor padrone, Emilio de Stefano. One of Emilio's sons, Rocco, later grew up to be Colosimo's crooked lawyer. Called now by his American nickname, "Big Jim," Colosimo grew to be

Natty Dresser

handsome, with broad shoulders, he was a loud-spoken extrovert with a winning manner and was talented in the art of making friends. He was also cunning, strong willed, unscrupulous and very capable with his fists. All this made him an imposing figure who commanded respect wherever he went." [Bilek, 2008: 77]

As was the case with many boys growing up in the crime infested Levee, Big Jim graduated to prostituting girls, when he was just eighteen years old. Here was an opportunity to put his cunning, his controlling nature, and his brutishness to the test. But after a brush with the law, he turned to working for the City of Chicago, as a street sweeper - a grunt job doled out to Italian immigrants by Italian labor bosses. The street cleaners, or "White Wings" as they were called, wore a white uniform, as they pushed a cart and shoveled up manure that fell to the pavement, behind horse drawn vehicles. [Bilek, 2008: 38] [Bilek, Email]

With his affable personality, his ability to command respect, and a penchant for control, Big Jim soon organized his fellow street cleaners into a union, an athletic group, and also a voting block, for First Ward Aldermen and notorious dive keepers, Hinky Dink Kenna and Bathhouse John Coughlin. In gratitude, Kenna made him a Democratic precinct captain. Thus on election day, when saloons were closed, Colosimo rounded up winos, took them to the polling place to vote Democratic, and then provided a few "thank you" drinks, courtesy of the Aldermen. Colosimo also bought votes for fifty cents a head, carting voters from one polling place another, so they could, in the immortal words of Al Capone, vote early and vote often." In exchange, Alderman Kenna granted Colosimo immunity from arrest. That was like a "Get Out of Jail Free" card that he could play as often as he liked.

Vittoria Moresco

Soon Colosimo was running girls again, this time out of a chop suey joint on Clark Street. Then in 1902, he married brothel madam Vittoria Moresco, who came complete with her own pair of Levee brothels. From these beginnings, with his immunity from prosecution, Colosimo expanded his brothel operations over the years, into a syndicate that soon controlled 200 brothels on the Levee.

By this time, the Levee had become a "disgrace to the city . . . [lurking] in the shadow of the big loop office buildings." [CT "Officer 666," p. 1] In 1903, downtown businessmen, who had been trying for some time to shut down the Levee, finally applied enough pressure to Mayor Harrison's office, to get him to order the Levee closed by the police. Harrison was a corrupt official, who had advocated a "wide open city" for prostitution and gambling, contributing in no small part to the existence of a huge prostitution industry.

Working on insider information, Colosimo's operation bought up prime property and leases in the South 22nd Street area, in anticipation of the raids which would soon be conducted on the brothels of Customs House Place. Then, when the Customs House prostitution managers were turned out of their digs, Colosimo's organization sublet brothel real estate to them on the South Levee, at sky high rates. Secondly, Colosimo hit them up for protection money, threatening that if they didn't pay they would be shut down - by the police. "The police did not simply make arrests. They tore in with fire axes and cut the hangings, chopped the pianos, split up the woodwork, wrecked the joint." [CT, "Officer 666," p. 2] Several years later, an investigation of property owners on the South Levee revealed the presence of the cleverly organized vice syndicate, headed by Colosimo and run by his cronies. [CVC: 847] In 1912, State's Attorney Wayman discovered that while various "dummy" property owners were listed on 50 real estate deeds for Levee houses of prostitution, the electric bills for all the properties were paid for by one man - Colosimo. [CT, "Officer 666," p. 2] When a Progressive City administration went after the South Levee, Colosimo opened up operations in suburbs, whose governments he could control with payoffs.

In addition to prostitution, Colosimo's organization ran gambling emporiums and labor rackets, siphoning off cash from unions, such as the one Big Jim had started for the White Wings. Last, and certainly not least, Colosoimo was the First Ward Aldermen's "bagman," collecting protection money from the brothels and other crooked businesses on the Levee, like gambling joints and saloons that stayed open after closing hours.

Protection money was divvied up between the police force, public officials, the two First Ward Aldermen and Colosimo. The Law then extended "protection" to the criminals – brothel owners, madams, pimps, and traffickers – instead of protecting the rights of U.S. Citizens when they became victims of those criminals. Police officers, detectives and captains were paid regular bribes to forgo their duty to protect young women and underage girls.

Thus they turned a blind eye, while young women were abducted, raped and battered, and kept under equally brutal conditions as inmates in brothels. Social activist, Jane Addams remarked, "The fortunes of the police are so tied up to those who profit by this trade [of vice] that the most well-meaning man upon the force is constantly handicapped." [Addams. 1912: 43]

In 1910, The Chicago Vice Commission a committee was appointed by the City to investigate prostitution. Their 1911 report stated, "The Commission does not condemn the personnel of the *police* as a whole, but it does condemn the *System* . . . which makes it easier for the police to accept graft from the tremendous profits reaped from the sale in women's bodies than to honestly do their duty." [CVC, 29] Thus the ugly business of luring girls and women to Chicago with false promises, committing the crimes of kidnap, rape and battery on them until their will was broken, and then selling their bodies in brothels, might continue without the law stepping in to protect its citizens.

In 1914, Jane Addams complained, "the politician higher up receives his share of the toll which this business pays that it may remain undisturbed." [Addams. 1912: 36]. Colosimo satisfied the insatiable greed of many Chicago politicians and at times, even mayors, DA's, governors and other officials of the state of Illinois. It was also within Colosimo's power to provide officials with perks, like wining and dining them in his restaurant and providing access to women for sale in his brothels.

Colosimo's power was more than *quid pro quo* immunity. A "maker and breaker of political aspirations," Colosimo twisted law and order to his own ends. [CT, "Obituary"] Through his machinations, he brought about the paralysis of the police, local politicians and many judges, DA's and mayors, all of whom were elected public servants, whose salaries were paid for by tax dollars, and whose job it was to protect the citizens of Chicago from crime.

It was weird to think that my Dad and my Grandmother had been to the funeral of an arch criminal like that, that they had been in the same room with such a ruthless guy, even it was only to view his lifeless body. But that was no ordinary funeral. In the first place, Colosimo had been murdered, execution style, with a bullet in the back of his head, in the foyer of his own nightclub. Nobody was ever convicted of his murder. Dad said Al Capone did it. Some say it was Frankie Yale, from New York. But some witnesses interviewed by the police, had observed a man hurrying away from scene of the crime, with a big scar on his face. [Chicago Herald,"Big Jim"] Capone's moon face had a couple of big slices across his jaw. He got that in a fracas over an off-color comment he had made to a woman about her hips, within earshot of her brother, at Frankie Yale's Harvard Inn in New York, where he worked as a bouncer. The slashes on his face were only part one of a plan of revenge, that led to a death contract being put out on Capone. Capone took that as his cue to exit New York and start over in Colosimo's operation in Chicago. Those reports of witnesses who had seen that gunman with a scar on his face were recanted the next day. So was that insider information a five-year old kid had heard, that Capone pulled the trigger? Or did Dad just get his facts mixed up?

Colosimo Cafe

While he stoked his nefarious, empire, Colosimo maintained the fiction that he operated just one business, the Colosimo Cafe, a hot place around town for night life on the Levee, located under the L track, at 2128 S. Wabash. It was the same place where he was executed on May 11, 1920. He had his place decorated in Grand Italian Opera style, with gilded archways draped with red velvet curtains, painted of scenes of Italy on the walls, and gold plated crystal chandeliers hanging down from above. [www.myalcapone] Behind the scenes, were "a hundred bottles of rare wines" and "towering stacks of cheese he had collected." [CDN, "Murder"] Colosimo roved from table to table, greeting guests, suggesting a specialty, like Caruso's favorites – chicken liver spaghetti and pork ravioli. [Find recipes at the end of the chapter] For a dollar and a quarter, you could order frog legs or the spring chicken dinner, featuring half a milk-fed bird, fried in butter.

The floor show featured pretty, lyric opera singer, Dale Winter, as well as Grand Opera singers, like Tenor, Isadoro Prati, who sang arias during the dinner hour. This entertainment alternated with "refined cabaret." [www.myalcapone] By "refined" was meant performers who did stuff with their clothes on, you know, like a jazz band or a ragtime pianist. But that didn't preclude a character singer crooning suggestive songs, or a fan dance artist

Colosimo Funeral Cortege at the Colosimo Cafe

wearing nothing behind her waving, peek-a-boo ostrich plumes, or a chanteuse, appearing bare-breasted, in pasties and a drape wrapped around her waist. [Ibid]

Colosimo's Cafe catered to "After-Theater Parties," for slummers - like millionaires, celebrities, novelists and even school teachers. They came for the thrill of rubbing shoulders with bad company - "painted women and maudlin women, and drunken men, . . . thieves and gamblers and crooked coppers and lords and dukes of the badlands." Even the chief of police could be seen after hours, "taking his high ball in the north room at 2 a.m." [CT May 21, 1920]. The Colosimo Cafe had a casino upstairs, where patrons went after dinner to blow their money on poker, craps, faro and chuck-a-luck. [Bilek, 2008: 199]

Funeral

Colosimo's funeral took place in his home, at 3156 Vernon Avenue, [CHE, "Hold 4"] on a spring day in May. It was the first lavish gangster funeral in Chicago, a spectacular event that hit the papers running. Outside his South Side residence, a "throng of automobiles" had collected. [CHE, "Big Jim"] A large crowd milled around in front of his house, comprised of public officials, cabaret singers, actors, gamblers, waiters and curious people from the neighborhood. [CT "Courts"]. Meanwhile, the tableau inside the house was priceless:

> A quartet stood by in the parlor and sang amid the silver mounted candles, the flower pieces and the bared heads of rough faced men weeping. It was a funeral that sent a thrill through the ward and brought hundreds of residents and habitués crowding and shoving for a peep at the famous bronze casket. Outside the home the underworld stood massed in solid formation." [CHE, "Big Jim"]

I remember Dad saying that it was crowded inside, and they had to wait in line a long time to view the body. That meant they were inside the house. So were they there because they were residents of the neighborhood and wanted a "peep at the famous bronze casket?" Or was it because they were part of the underworld "massed in solid formation?" Or was there another reason? Dad had told me that his step father, Tony Coglioni was a "minor Mafioso." Was there a connection there?

After the wake, the swarm of people fell in line into a long procession behind the hearse, which wove through Chicago's South Side streets. "A cavalcade such as moved behind the funeral car of Caesar," is how a Trib reporter described it. [CT, "Obit"] The list of names of the small army of actual and honorary pallbearers [CT "Courts"] [CHE, "Hold 4"] was a who's who of Chicago characters, who had grown fat off the sale of women and children.

Heading the list were elected officials: nine alderman, including the First Ward's diminutive "Hinky Dink" Kenna and the portly "Bathhouse" John Coughlin, three judges, a Congressman, a State Representative, the Assistant State's Attorney, a former U.S. Assistant District Attorney and a number of Chicago Democrat party leaders. No sense of shame hindered them from appearing in public at the funeral of the man who

My five-year old Dad

for more than a decade has been recognized as the overlord of Chicago's underworld. Such tribute from men set up to make and enforce our laws to a man, who in much of his life was a law unto himself, is more than the tribute of friendship. It is the tribute to power." [CT, "Obit"]

The list of honorary pallbearers went on and on. There were opera singers, saloon and dive keepers, who kept gambling joints called "French Lick Springs," "Friars Cafe" and "Midnight Frolic." And there were names of people who had been part of Colosimo's dark empire: the lawyers who defended pimps, traffickers, madams and prostitutes in court, and the bail bondsman who sprang them out of jail so, they could get back to making money for the empire. There were the physicians, knowledgeable in the medicine of prostitution, who provided medical care to Colosimo's inmates, so the empire could wring as much cash out of them as possible, before their commercial value was used up. These characters formed the funeral cortege, along with Colosimo's employees and associates: dance hall owners, dive owners, saloon keepers, bookies, gamblers, pimps, panders, prostitutes, waiters and cabaret singers.

And that is the gangster funeral my five year old Dad attended with his mother.

Colosimo's right hand man, Johnny Torrio presided over the entire affair, surrounded by his "goon squad" of flunkies. Torrio wept, "Big Jim and I were like brothers." Torrio had, in fact, been a relative of Colosimo's by marriage. Colosimo's wife Vittoria, the brothel madam, was Torrio's aunt. And it was Torrio who footed the bill for the expensive funeral. Yes, it was a fine public display of grief, a terrific drama, engineered by Torrio, himself - in more ways than one. Because it was general knowledge that Torrio had ordered the execution of Colosimo - his uncle, by marriage. That is, until Colosimo divorced his first wife, the fleshy, middle aged Vittoria Moresco, just a month before his death, and immediately married young, classy, svelte, lyric opera singer, Dale Winter.

Dale Winter

Yes, the 49 year old vice lord Colosimo died a newlywed. Toward the end of the wake, Dale Winter his bride of 3 weeks, made an appearance. She was the young chanteuse, who wowed the crowd nightly at the Colosimo Café, dressed in elegant, sinewy gowns, her golden brown hair coiffed in fluffy waves under a sequined headband. She had a pristine, an off-limits air, as she warbled arias from light opera. But at the wake, Winter made a pathos-filled entrance, just at the moment crooked First Ward Alderman Coughlin intoned a prayer for his partner in graft, the deceased, with the multitude inside the house murmuring the responses. To the sound of this chanting, Winter, wearing a simple black dress, leaned heavily on the arm of Rocco de Stefano, as the two descended the staircase with all eyes upon them. Rocco was Colosimo's step brother – he and Big Jim had been raised together. [CHE, "Colosimo Cortege"]

Dale Winter was a rare character. She had been the star of Big Jim's nightclub for six years, where she "glided skillfully away from leering, tipsy patrons," no small feat in a joint like the Colosimo Café. [CDN, "Big Jim"] In the beginning, Winter had been engaged to violinist, Arthur Fabbri, who had introduced her to Colosimo. However, Fabbri was sorry he had done that, when his engagement to Winter died a slow death during the first year she sang at the club. Fabbri was not supplanted in Winter's affections by the barrage of attractive marriage proposals she received from well heeled, upscale customers. No, those offers she sonambulantly brushed away. Fabbri made his exit, because Colosimo finally laid down the law for Fabbri to keep away from Winter. And that was weird, because Fabbri had the impression that Winter was afraid of Big Jim. [CDN, "Find Dale's Ex"]

The lovely Dale Winter

And while this rivalry was going on, Winter was also receiving great job offers to star in New York musicals and the Siegfried follies, at much higher pay. She turned down those offers, too. You have to wonder, why a glamorous, talented singer would prefer headlining in an underworld nightclub, in the middle of the red light district, to becoming a Broadway star? Well, on the sly,

Winter had entered into a sinister, sub rosa liaison with Colosimo, a married man, known around town as the "Whoremaster of Chicago." Not that there weren't perks that went along with the affair. Colosimo gave her luxurious clothes, diamond jewelry, a pleasure horse, cash, expensive digs at the Lexington Hotel [Bilek, 2008: 206] and singing lessons with the famous Chicago Opera star Tito Ruffo. Of course, Dale could have paid for these things herself, if she had accepted any of the plumb jobs she was continually offered. Yes there was something strange, indeed, about that secret relationship with Colosimo.

The peculiar eulogy Winter made after Colosimo's murder, in an interview with a Trib reporter, gives a clue to what was at the heart of their relationship: "I respected him and admired him . . . he had a heart of pure gold." [CT, "Divorced"] A peculiar description of a vice lord, who made his living off of cruelty to women. Peculiar indeed. She made another statement to a Daily News reporter, which belies the perverse adulation of a victim of abuse:

> 'He was my god,' she half hysterically declared. 'Really and truly, he was my god. All of us around him were little things - nothings. I am nothing without him.' [CDN, "Big Jim"]

How did he do it? How did an overfed, married, middle aged criminal hold a beautiful, talented singer like Winter in thrall? How did he keep her away from her own fiancé, and a host of wealthy admirers, and the great job offers she received during their six year affair? It wasn't the luxury goods he lavished on her. No, that was just stuff. And she could have had that without him. Would stuff make you say "Really and truly, he was my god?" Uh uh.

No, Colosimo kept Winter in thrall, with the brutality of the pimp he had been in his youth, and always would be. Far from having "a heart of pure gold," he was rotten to the core. But he knew from years of practice, just how to undermine a woman's sense of self, how to make even a talented singer like Winter feel like "nothing without him." He had the expertise of a pimp, and knew just how to apply the right mixture of coercion and tenderness, brutality and generosity, to make a woman do his bidding - no matter how ugly it might be. Colosimo was a master of bullying and intimidation. Extorting what he wanted out of women was second nature to him. And what he wanted in this case, was to possess Dale Winter exclusively, body and soul.

The predatory magnetism of the pimp is aptly described by Dr. Ben Reitman, who was acquainted with men who were pimps, throughout his personal as well as his professional life.

> The pimp has dark eyes. . . that emanate something. When he looks at a woman he does something to her. Call it hypnosis if you will. It may be black magic, it may be the power of the devil, but it is something that women sense or fear and cannot get away from. I have seen a pimp come into a crowded roomful of fifty people and look around and have seen the girls of loose morals shiver and flush and get nervous, begin to fix their hair, feel their breasts, cross their legs and look at the pimp as a bird does at a snake. . . . the pimp has a charm, something in his body that arouses passion in the souls of women. They feel his vibration. They sense his power." [Reitman: 186-7]

A pimp is a sadist. And Colosimo was one of them. Love, hate, love, hate. A woman's psyche became putty in his fat hands. He had the predator instinct to crush whatever got in his way. Like when he pummeled tough brothel madam Georgie Spenser senseless with brass knuckles, and helped himself to three $100 bills from her wallet, for protection money for the First Ward Aldermen. [Bilek, 2008: 80]. He stopped at nothing, not even murder to get his own way. He bent Dale Winter to his will, just like he did everyone else in town, from policemen, judges, and elected officials, including the Mayor, to prostituted women and underage girls. Colosimo had pimp written all over him.

The widowed Dale Winter appeared diffident and shadowy at the funeral, leaning heavily on Rocco de Stefano's arm,

> walking as if she were about to faint, a handkerchief showing ghostly beneath the veiling over her face, Dale Winter squeezed into the space against the funeral roses beside the casket . . . The dignitaries paid Dale homage. Their hats came off [CHE, "Big Jim"]

Photo Courtesy of William J. Helmer

Winter, barely able to walk, was half led, half dragged to the head automobile of the funeral cortege, again by Rocco de Stefano, Colosimo's step brother. Rocco was also the executor of Big Jim's will, and mastermind of the legal management of Colosimo's estate. At the cemetery, Winter was described as "a shrouded figure in black, about which there is nothing human but a nervous noise of dry sobbing." She was "literally carried into the first car," by Rocco. [CHE, "Colosimo Cortege"]

Was this a widow-bride, prostrated by grief? Or had Winter been drugged into submission by the family, to prevent her from blabbing to all the press hanging around the funeral? Winter had already spilled the beans to a Herald Examiner reporter the day *before*, about how Big Jim's first wife Vittoria had threatened them both. A medical man like those prostitution doctors on the honorary pall bearer list, could be counted on to drug an angry, uncooperative young widow like Winter, to prevent her from leaking more information about Colosimo's execution to the press. Here's what Winter told that reporter, "She said she would do it . . She walked into the restaurant one night and told us if we didn't stay away from each other she would kill us - Jim and me." [CHE, "Bride Says"]

Winter appeared in public in the same woozy condition some days later, when Rocco again led a wobbly Dale Winter to the probate hearing on Colosimo's estate. Once again he propped her up, while she read a statement to the court, explaining that she did not want any of her husband's assets, because she didn't want people to think she had married him for his money. It was estimated that Colosimo brought in a half a million a year in prostitution and other illegal enterprises. But his astronomical assets had mysteriously disappeared after his death. A few thousand in chump change was all that was left. Plus the noose-like, diamond lavaliere necklace Winter was awarded by the court from his estate, a courtship gift from Colosimo.

The Family

Vittoria Moresco had been Big Jim's wife for 18 years. She was a savvy, dark-haired woman with an operatic figure, who had grown up hard scrabble, in a single room on the Levee, with her Italian parents and seventeen brothers and sisters. Vittoria had given her husband a leg up in the brothel trade. She owned two houses of prostitution when she married Big Jim in 1902, when he was just a two-bit pimp.

Now after Colosimo's death, there was speculation in the news that Vittoria Moresco was on a *vendetta*, after he had disenfranchised her in a quickie divorce. [CDN, "Rehearse"] "I slaved for years in helping Jim make the money he had and I won't let anyone shove me aside," she told the Daily News. "There may be many reasons why Jim was shot down . . . but my belief is that . . . it will be found that his marriage with Dale

Colosimo in a pool of his own blood, before they turned him over

Photo courtesy of William J. Helmer

Winter was at the bottom of it all." [CDN, "Nab New"] On the day of the murder, according to newspaper accounts, Vittoria breezed into town just 2 hours before his death, [CDN, "Rehearse"] and then disappeared. Also disappearing at the same time were the jewels and bonds believed to be in Colosimo's safety deposit boxes in the bank. And then several days after the murder, Vittoria provided a splashy cover-up, when a telegram to her attorney was published in the Chicago Herald and Examiner, in which she requested the contents of the boxes. [CHE, "Hold 4"]

JAMES COLOSIMO.

PROPRIETARIO DEL

COLOSIMO BUFFET E HOTEL.

2001-3-5 ARCHER AVE., CHICAGO.

Telefono: Calumet 1549.

I locali del signor James Colosimo sono stati rimessi completamente a nuovo tanto da essere considerati tra i più eleganti del South Side.

Gli italiani che desiderano gustare vini prelibati, liquori finissimi, si rechno a visitare i locali del signor James Colosmo.

Johnny Torrio was Vittoria's nephew. He was a killer, who had grown up tough on the streets of New York and had been a member of the notorious Five Points gang. That's why Vittoria and Big Jim had called him to Chicago in 1909. They needed help. Some Black Hand extortionists were sending Colosimo letters demanding a large cash payment, *or else*. Torrio came to Chicago and met the extortionists in classic gangster style. The Trib wrote: "That night as three Italians were walking under the Archer Avenue subway below the Rock Island tracks between Clark and La Salle streets a sawed off shotgun spoke." [CT, "Divorced," p. 3] Triple murder was Torrio's first job for his Chicago family.

The Colosimos put him in charge of a brothel and Torrio soon became Big Jim's second in command.

When Colosimo divorced Torrio's Aunt Vittoria, he signed his own death warrant. Because when he divorced Vittoria, he also severed his family connection to Johnny Torrio. Now there was nothing standing in Torrio's way to becoming Number One, because he and Colosimo were no longer family. When Torrio ordered Colosimo's execution, he was merely carrying out the family design: a *vendetta*. Get rid of Big Jim. Keep the business in the family.

So, what were Minnie and my five year old Dad doing at Colosimo's funeral? Had they somehow been drawn into Colosimo's world? Were they part of the family? They key to those questions turned out to be Tony Coglioni. But first, I had to figure out *who* he was. And *that* turned out to be quite an adventure.

Ad Translation from L'Italia August 1909

James Colosimo.

Proprietor of the Colosimo Buffet and Hotel

2001-3-5 Archer Ave. Chicago [Note extra address]

The premises of Mr Colosimo have been completely redecorated, so as to be considered one of the most elegant on the South Side. Italians who want to enjoy fine wines, fine spirits, should go visit the premises of Mr. James Colosimo

Translation by the author.

Recipes

These wonderful recipes come from Chicago Chef Phillip J. Speciale [Speciale] www.great-chicago-italian-recipes.com

Tenor Spaghetti

Spaghetti alla Caruso, a Colosimo Cafe specialty, was named after the famed Italian tenor Enrico Caruso who reigned over the Metropolitan Opera house for eighteen years. Caruso, loved to cook and he loved chicken livers.

INGREDIENTS

  1 pound of chicken livers separated into individual lobes and all visible fat removed
  1 cup of flour for dredging
  2 Tbls of extra virgin olive oil
  2 Tbls of butter
   cloves of garlic, chopped
  1 yellow onion, chopped
  4 oz. of Crimini mushrooms, sliced
  4 oz. of white button mushrooms, sliced
  4 oz. of shitake mushrooms, sliced
  1 cup of dry red wine
  1 28 oz can of San Marzano tomatoes, peeled
  1/4 cup of parsley, chopped
  1/2 tsp of fresh ground black pepper
  1/2 tsp of salt

  1 pound of spaghetti

PREPARATION

  Season the flour with a little salt and pepper.
  Dredge the chicken livers in the flour.
  In a large skillet, saute the chicken livers in the olive oil until brown and firm.
  Remove the livers from the pan and set aside.
  Add the butter to the pan and saute the garlic, onions and mushrooms for 5 minutes

Add the wine and reduce to about half.
Puree the tomatoes and add then to the pan.
Slice the chicken livers in half and add them to the pan.
Season with salt and pepper and cook on low heat for around thirty minutes.
In 6 quarts of boiling salted water cook the spaghetti until al dente.
Drain and plate the pasta.
Cover with the sauce and garnish with parsley.

Serve with Parmesan cheese. Serves 4 people.

Pork Ravioli

Pork is very big in Calabria, and is widely used in cooking.

For the dough, use the well method with 8 eggs, 1/3 cup of water, several cups of flour

FOR THE FILLING

2 lbs. ground pork
1 lb. Ricotta cheese
1 lb fresh or frozen spinach, thawed & dry
½ cup parsley
4 eggs
½ cup bread crumbs
Fresh rosemary and hot red peppers to taste

1 cup grated pecorino or romano cheese

Mix all ingredients. Cut your pasta dough into long wide strips. Place 1 Tablespoon of filling on the pasta several inches from the edge. Fold over and crimp with a fork on all sides. When all ravioli's are done, boil in water until the pasta is al dente.

Drain and sprinkle with extra-virgin olive oil and stir gently until coated. Place in a serving dish and sprinkle with pecorino or romano cheese. Alternatively, you can serve with Pasta Arrabiata sauce.

Pasta

COOK BY FEEL RECIPE which comes from watching my Italian friend, Manuela [from Umbria] make pasta.

You take about two cups of flour, some salt in with that, like about half a teaspoon and make a mound of flour on a bread board. Then you make a well in the center, into which you crack 2 eggs. Hand beat the eggs in the well. Then begin taking forkfuls of flour from the sides of the well and mixing them into the beaten eggs. Continue until the egg mixture gets dry. Then add water a half ounce at a time to the well, continuing to mix in the flour. I cannot do this, without the eggs running out of the well onto the floor, so if it doesn't work for you, either try using a bowl.

Finally you will have a ball of pasta, into which you will roll the unused flour, using up as much as possible. Add flour to the board and knead for a minute. Rub the rolling pin with dry flour and roll out the pasta until it is about 1/8 inch thick. Dust the top of the rolled out dough with flour. Roll up loosely. Slice in ¼ thick rolls.

Spread a clean sheet over your bed. Take the newly cut pasta into bedroom and unroll the pasta loops and lay them on the sheet. I'm not kidding - that's how they do it in Italy. After about an hour, gather up the pasta and drop into boiling water, until al dente, maybe ten minutes. Drain and serve.

R I P, if that's possible

Dad's brownstone on 40th and Michigan Ave.

Chapter Five

❧❧❧❧❧❧❧❧❧❧

Will the Real Tony Coglioni Please Stand Up?

It was like searching for a needle in a haystack. How could I sift through the 2 million people who lived in Chicago in 1916, to find some record of my Grandmother. How was I ever going to solve the mystery of what happened to Minnie and my Dad there? I had only a handful of clues from Dad about his childhood. They lead a boom and bust existence. Dad was often left alone all night. Tony Coglioni was a "minor Mafioso," a bootlegger. And the granddaddy of all clues - Minnie took my five-year old Dad to Big Jim Colosimo's funeral. And then after my trip up north to investigate the old Hollywood in Spread Eagle, I was pretty sure I was looking for a prostitution connection.

City Directories

They were sitting on dusty shelves in the dark in an unused corridor of the library. You had to turn a light switch on just to see your way around. Dreaming there in the darkness, with their two million names, they were just waiting for me to figure out they were there. They slept on the back shelves of a stately Greek Revival building, with gigantic fluted columns reaching up to the third floor. A grove of cherry trees stood in front, their branches holding up pink blossoms to the spring sunlight. And they had been waiting all the time I had been working on my B.S and M.F.A in Art right next door, those old city directories from Chicago. A few years after graduating, I discovered they were there and went back to campus to look in their musty, brown-edged pages for Minnie. But there weren't any women named Minnie Coglioni or May Coglioni and I couldn't tell if any of the listings for Minnie Davis or Minnie Frank or May Davis or May Frank were for her.

There were plenty of Tony Coglionis in the directories, too. Why were there so many guys with such a weird name? One Tony was a listed as laborer, one was a painter, and another one a railroad worker. And there was a Tony who was a clerk living next door to a Coglioni owned grocery, around 12th and State, where some more Coglionis worked. It all looked pretty innocuous. Hard to imagine a laborer, painter, or railroad worker involved in the underworld, or to imagine a grocer and his sons involved in shady business.

But they were there, sleeping in those massive directories, if I could just figure out which listing was the right one.

Genealogist No. 1

Well, when you are stabbing in the dark, you have to start somewhere. So I called the secretary of a genealogy society in Chicago. "I have a Gangland story in my family," I explained. "Is there somebody in your group who might be good?"

I could hear the buttons pop off his shirt drop and hit the floor. "I like to think that I am just the person you need. Gangland activity in Chicago has been a research interest of mine for a long time," he boasted.

"Well, my Dad was taken by his mother to Big Jim Colosimo's funeral. And, um, I think she might have been in prostitution."

"A lot of people went to that funeral," he snapped. "They were just sightseers. You really can't read anything like that into it."

He was referring to the thousands of people milling around the funeral car when it stopped in front of the Colosimo Café. I had seen the pictures in old newspapers.

But that's not the way Dad talked about it. He always remembered it like this: "We had to wait in line a long time to see the body." That meant that they were inside at the wake, because they saw the open casket. That's the kind of thing a kid would remember, because it would be creepy. He wasn't talking about later, in front of the Colosimo Café, because the coffin was closed and piled with flowers, before it was loaded into the glass hearse.

Then it was drawn by horses down to 22nd and Wabash, where everybody gawked at it parked in front of the restaurant.

"Yeah, but . . . "

"It doesn't mean your grandmother . . .was in . . . prosti-tution. " he chided.

"But my Dad . . ."

He hung up. Clearly he was disgusted with my suspicions. That wasn't the only time someone got weird on me over

"Just a party dress"

the course of this project. But I wasn't going to let that stop me. The more I investigated, the more I wanted to know what really happened to her in Chicago.

Costume Lady

I was lucky to have Minnie's photo album. Some of the pictures were unusual, to say the least. Maybe something about the way people were dressed in the snapshots would be telling. I didn't know much about 20th century fashions or vintage wear, even though I had designed plenty of costumes before. But those had been for dance companies - stuff like abstract splatters on body suits. So I took a stack of pictures to a costume expert I had seen give a lecture on vintage costumes. The costume expert met me on a plain wooden bench, down in the stark basement of that beautiful Greek Revival building. The fashion archives were down the hall, hidden behind a heavy fire door marked "Restricted Access," with a secret code pad beside it. I guess that's where they hid the top secret, off limits clothing.

Girls at a barn door up north

She was dating fashions friends But she hunch on Minnie had pulled out into the to have her "No, no," defen- just a dress."

very helpful in photos by the Minnie and her were wearing. resisted my this pic: that just been of a dark resort bright sunlight picture taken. she insisted sively. "This is regular party

These two gals peering out of a barn didn't look to me like dairymaids taking a break from milking cows. You don't milk cows dressed in fancy shoes, silk stockings and satin dresses. But the expert's opinion was a cautious, "They're just wearing house dresses."

With this pic however, she ventured the most I was going to get out of her. "She's dressed to the nines, in a cloche hat, fox fur, shapely shoes and polka dot dress. You can see it's cut on the bias and comes to mid calf. That's a style that came into fashion at the end of the 20's. Okay, well that told me a little something - Minnie wore clothes in the height of fashion in the late 20's and could afford them.

This snapshot reminds me of a description I read of people at crime lord Dion O'Banion's 1924 funeral: "beautifully dressed women of gangland, wrapped in costly furs and supported slowly down the aisles by excellently tailored gentlemen with steel-blue jaws and a furtive glance." [Allsop, 86].

Minnie & friend on Drexel Bd.

O'Banion had been gunned down in his flower shop by Torrio's men, you know, the same guy who ordered Colosimo's execution.

Genealogist No. 2

I emailed the above picture to another Chicago genealogist, to see if she could identify what city park they were taken in. "Oh, this isn't a park. It's Drexel Boulevard," she asserted knowledgeably over the phone. She was looking at the pics on her computer screen. "You can see the big mansions in the background. It's not a park, but a boulevard in the middle of the street. Drexel Boulevard was a fashionable location on the South Side."

"You really know your Chicago!" I remarked, suitably impressed.

"Well, it's a very well known place," she replied modestly. "You know if you think Tony Coglioni was a bootlegger, there might be some trial records for him in the Federal Archives, down here. Volstead Act violations were prosecuted by the U.S. Treasury Department."

Wow! Here was a sympathetic genealogist who wasn't going to lecture me on morality. You could really get somewhere with the right genealogist!

"It's way on the South Side. I could go down there and look," she offered.

"What would that cost?" I asked.

"Oh, I charge fifteen dollars an hour. It'd probably take me half a day."

Federal Archives Trip No. 1

On crisp, cold, wintry day I got on the L for a bone rattling ride, that was the first leg of my trip down to the Federal Archives on the South Side. I was going to check out if U.S. Treasury agents had nabbed Tony Coglioni during Prohibition. I did learn a few things on that trip, but not what I was expecting.

I got off the L and waited at a bus stop in the stiff wind, on a busy street corner in an iffy South Side neighborhood. I was warm and toasty in my winter coat, lined with fake fur, which I had bought with Christmas money from my Mom. I loved it because it was soft and fuzzy and reminded me of the fur lined garments people wore in the Renaissance.

But I immediately realized my mistake in wearing that coat, because I felt like a sitting duck in it at the bus stop. Everyone else was keeping warm in a nylon parka that probably cost more than my coat did. You wouldn't think, I reasoned to myself, that someone would be standing on the street corner in a *real*, full length, fur coat in that neighborhood, but then you wouldn't think a crazy *gringa* with long blonde hair would be running around by herself, waiting for a bus in that neighborhood either.

I turned to a nice, portly, middle aged man, who was also waiting for a bus. "Que tal?" I asked, striking up a conversation in Spanish, hoping our conversation would protect me like a shield. Twenty minutes later we were still talking when the bus arrived, with a screech of hydraulics. We climbed on board, warmed up and yakked for another hour, while the bus floundered, like a sailing ship in a storm, over huge potholes in the road. The bumpy ride was courtesy of the Mob who hold the street resurfacing contracts, so I'm told by a Chicago friend who used to work at the Better Government Association. Lesson #1 - next time, wear a nylon parka.

Finally I arrived at the Federal Archives, tucked away like a fortress, behind a tall iron fence that also contained a military installation. I wrote out my order for the Volstead violations docket and handed it to the taciturn, bored silly archive clerk, who evinced zero interest in my topic of research.

"Lock up all your personal effects," he said in a monotone, pointing to the bank of lockers behind me. Then he issued me a No. 2 pencil and several sheets of blank paper on which I was permitted to take notes. The files arrived half an hour later. I poured over them for the couple of hours, but didn't turn up anything on the Coglioni's. Actually the fact that there were no Coglioni's in the record, in and of itself, told me something. Since

I knew for sure that Tony was a bootlegger, he must have kept up with his underworld connections, and made his payoffs, because he had not run afoul of the Volstead Act. That was Lesson #2.

Lesson #3: A professional genealogist, however congenial and knowledgeable on Chicago she might be, was not necessarily the right person to help find crooks.

City Archive Room

Next time I went down to Chicago, I decided to snoop in the City of Chicago archives. Maybe poking around down there would turn up some clues to my family's mystery. A big, Picasso reared its horse-like head in front of a tall glass building, where up on the 11th Floor I found the Archive Room. It stood at the end of a corridor of courtrooms, where nervous defendants paced in the hallway. The archive room was crammed with old file drawers and metal cabinets, and a conference table in the middle, where several unhappy souls sat, filling out forms to get a copy of their marriage license, so they go down the hall and get a divorce. A couple of genealogists were going blind, hunched over the screens of ancient microfilm machines. And behind the counter at the far end of the room, a single, gloomy civil servant, looking like someone who had crawled out from under a rock, reluctantly fielded requests for information.

"Where are the arrest records?" I asked.

"Just a minute, I'm helping this person." Five minutes go by, while I watch. Then another five. Finally he looked at me and grunted, "over there," pointing with his chin at a metal file drawer full of rolls of microfilm. Jesus. Like he couldn't have jerked his chin when I asked him 10 minutes ago?

A half day of picking through microfilm, ordering records, and waiting while they were fetched from the basement, was enough for me to figure out that Tony Coglioni had no arrest record with the City either. Whatever he had been involved in, as a "minor Mafioso," he kept his nose clean. That, in and of itself, told me how well connected he was in the underworld.

At one point in my research I discovered there was a Morals Court in Chicago where prostitutes were tried. It was a Progressive innovation instituted in 1913 to control the spread of contagious venereal diseases, by testing and treating convicted prostitutes. [CT "Morals Court"]

Maybe I would find some info there that would help solve the family mystery. So I returned to the City Archives next time I went to Chicago. I spent a couple of days hunting for Minnie on a microfiche reader, my brain warped into vertigo by the green swirl of names raking by on the dim screen. It was discouraging, because after two days of researching, I hadn't even dented the surface of the records for the ten years Minnie was in Chicago. Plus I still didn't know what name she used when she was there. And back then, you could fake your name, too, because I saw in the records that a lot of women made up names when they were arrested, like "Pearl Smith." So I gave up. Maybe later, I would know what name she used in Chicago and could look again.

Looking like a two bit chump

One cool thing I did discover. Hidden away in the archive room, inside a dull beige metal cabinet - you know the kind that opens with a twang of rattling doors - tucked between books on the history of the Chicago, I found a little book of recipes by city employees. [See recipe at end of chapter]

One Thing

Finally I came across one tiny concrete fact about Tony Coglioni. It was on an Italian genealogy site. Nearly all the émigrés to America, Argentina or Australia named Coglioni, came from the same, little, hillside town in Calabria, a province in the boot of Italy. A couple mayors of that tiny town had been named Tony Coglioni - that's why there were so many Tony Coglionis in America. They were named after that big man in the little town in Italy.

Snapshots

You can tell a lot from snapshots. Minnie had slapped mucilage on the back of some little pictures of Tony Coglioni and pasted them into her photo album. Here, he really looks like a two-bit chump, a real "minor Mafioso." No flashy tailored suit like in the movies. Just a big attitude clashing with his badly tailored, rumpled suit coat and teensy bow tie. I wondered who he had been standing next to, that prompted Minnie to snip the picture.

Here's a snapshot taken on the South Side, around the time of Colosimo's funeral. Tony looks annoyed, he's still young but paunchy, and stands with his stepson, my cranky 5 year old Dad. What do they look so put out for? There's a story here, but we're just looking at the punch line.

In another snapshot, Minnie and my two year old Dad are with Coglioni. Here, Tony is the only one with a big grin on his kisser. The rest of them looked like a hard, cheerless bunch, maybe because they were at a funeral that day. Or maybe it's because they are a hard, cheerless bunch. Another pic shows them waiting around a mausoleum, dressed in exactly the same WWI era coats and hats. I've learned a lot more about 20th century fashion since I visited the costume lady, because I designed costumes for the film. Based on the clothing styles and Dad's age, I put the picture at about 1917. It's early spring because the leaves are off the trees. Why Tony was grinning is a good question. Maybe it wasn't his family's funeral. And I did say he looked like a two-bit chump didn't I?

My Dad, about six years old with Tony

I took a blow-up of that funeral photo with me when I went to Festa Italiana one summer in Milwaukee, where I pinned it up in my art booth. That was the year I had been invited to join the Festa Italiana Heritage Artisans Tent - by mistake. The invitation went like this. "What part of Italy is your family from?" the woman in charge asked me on the phone. She had gotten my name from a place where I had recently given a lecture on Italian Art.

Hmmmm. I thought to myself a moment. A few years before that, I had forked out a small fortune to show my art work in a different tent at Festa Italiana – the Marketplace. The truth is I don't have a drop of Italian blood in my veins, but I had the feeling that if I made the Coglionis my "family," I was going to get a much better deal.

"They're from Calabria," I chirped.

"Great, you can be our featured artist!" she cheered. "Calabria is the featured province this year!"

"Terrific!" I replied, laughing.

Funeral family portrait - but whose family?`

When I got there, I took my Sharpie and carefully wrote across the bottom of the blow-up of funeral portrait, "Do you know the Coglionis?" Even though the Coglionis were Chicago people, maybe I would get lucky and someone up here in Milwaukee would recognize them.

Lots of people who came by my booth put their reading glasses on and peered at the faces in the photo with curiosity. "Geeze!" they pondered. "Looks like the Sopranos!" Yeah, they *were* a tough looking bunch. But it was the name, Coglioni, that gave me a bite on my line.

Andrea

One guy who stopped by my booth at Festa had a friend in Chicago, with the same last name of Coglioni and gave me his phone number. I called up his friend, Andrea, a nice friendly guy in his late 70's, born just up the mountain from that town where all the Coglionis hailed from in Italy. He spoke with a touch of an Italian accent.

> They were poor farmers, the people back there. Mostly they had olive groves and vineyards on the hillsides. It was so steep, nothing else would grow there. The lucky ones came over and made a fortune or a good position in life for themselves.
>
> My father came here in 1921. He worked for a tailor named Meshbitz in Chicago and also for two more tailors – one was in Milwaukee and he went there once a week on the train. He and a couple of other guys boarded with a family from their hometown in Italy. My father worked hard and saved his money for ten years and then went back and married an Italian girl and had me. Then we all got on the boat and came here and settled in Oak Park.

Enter Al Capone. That's right. Andrea's father moonlighted as a flute player at weddings, banquets, and the Chicago Symphony Orchestra. And for Big Al down in Cicero.

> One Saturday night my dad was standing in the dark, under the L on Racine Avenue in Little Italy with my Uncle Emil, who played the clarinet. They were waiting for Capone's limo to pick them up and take them to Cicero. It was a good job. Capone paid good, and there was always a lot of food, so they could count on a good meal. But while they were waiting there under the L track, my father was held up. They got his wallet and his watch. They even got his gold wedding band.

When Capone's limo drove up shortly after that, Andrea's dad mentioned to the driver he'd just been robbed.

> Next night, they went to play at Capone's again, and waited in the same place under the L. The limo came and when they got in the driver turned around and handed my dad his wedding ring, and his watch and his wallet, with all the money in it!

I laughed. What a great story! "Did any of the people from your home town in Italy work for the Mob?" I asked.

"No, no. We were not big Mafiosi," Andrea contended. "It took a lot of guts to be mafioso, but - it wasn't very smart. Making a living and supporting your family – now that's smart!"

"Yeah, but what about bootleggers?" I wondered.

"Some Italians who came over dabbled in crime. But they just took advantage of Prohibition for a little extra money!" Andrea assured me.

"What about Mafia back home in Italy?"

In his best theatrical voice, Andrea protested, "No, no! We were no Mafioso, never *ever*! We were *only* lovers!"

[Andrea Interview on 3/8/8]

Visit to the City Cultural Historian

Boy, I was really stabbing in the dark, the day I went to see Tim Samuelson, City of Chicago's Cultural Historian. I had uncovered only circuitous, oblique information so far. Nothing concrete yet that could help me solve the mystery of what happened to Minnie and my Dad in Chicago. Tim's name had been given to me by an archivist, one of a collection of lank-haired women with intelligent eyes who staffed the room of a certain library in Chicago, all of whom just really did not want to hear a single thing about my project. Their attitude was as curious as it was disappointing. I never found much of interest in that archive room, merely pawing clumsily through manila folders, wearing their regulation issue white dress gloves, that looked like something my mother had worn to church in the 50's.

Tim Samuelson's idea of history, however, was a horse of a different color. His office in the Loop stood at the end of a long, windowless corridor lined with scroll work capitals and art nouveau terra cotta fragments, saved from Louis Sullivan buildings that had been demolished. I later learned this was Tim's own collection of stuff he had salvaged, beginning at age twelve. I wound my way back to his small office, and there I found a large, cheerful guy with a round face, blue eyes and a big grin, who stood up to greet me with a meaty handshake. "Have a seat!" he intoned pleasantly, gesturing to an orange plastic chair in front of his metal desk. His office was so tiny there was only room for that desk, a bookcase, and a beige metal cabinet with a little paper model of Sullivan's Transportation building perched on top of it.

I took a seat, while Tim sandwiched his bulk on the other side of the desk into a big, black, vinyl desk chair. "Tell me about your research," he proclaimed invitingly, folding his hands across his stomach, interlacing his fingers, and sitting back with a creaking of chair springs. I gave him the rundown so far and then fished out a blurry snapshot from my bag and held it up. "I found this in my Dad's photo album," I ventured. "My Dad wrote next to it, 'The Old Home, Michigan Ave, 1923.' "

I knew it was crazy to show Tim the photo, because I had already poured over every single feature of the tiny snapshot under a magnifying glass looking for a street number, and the only thing I could make out was a small sign affixed to the front of the building that read "Michigan Ave." But where on Michigan had it been? That was a street that went on for miles. I handed Tim the little black and white snapshot and soon realized I was face to face with a guy with a mind like a steel trap.

Tim took the little picture, pulled his glasses down from his forehead and studied it with interest. Then he raised his gaze and muttered, "Let me see," and stood up. He took two strides over to the bookcase next to me and extracted an old, yellowed 1922 Chicago phone book, one that I had not seen in any archive room I had visited. Tim's keen sense for sleuthing out the buried truth led him to perform a minor miracle right in front of me.

Page from Dad's scrapbook

"There we go," Tim said matter-of-factly. "Here's a Tony Coglioni at 4016 S. Michigan Avenue, with a *telephone*." He turned the phone book around and handed it to me. There it was, in black and white.

"Wow!" I sputtered, looking at the listing in disbelief. "That's amazing!"

Tim mused, "It would have been unusual for your average tenement dweller to have a phone back then, but in the prostitution business, it would have been a handy item."

The miracle wasn't over yet. Tim turned to his computer and asked me, "What was that address, again?" I read it out to him from the phone book, wondering what he was up to. Suddenly there on his computer screen loomed a picture of the old, brooding brownstone.

"Holy shit! " I shrieked. "You found it!" Tim was on the City Assessor's website. Now not only did I know exactly where Dad had lived, but the building was still in existence! And that was just the beginning.

After we chewed over that nugget of information, Tim's *Tim at his Frank Lloyd Wright exhibit* blue eyes twinkled and he looked at me hopefully, "How'd ya like to take a drive to the South Side and take a look at it?"

"Absolutely!" I yelped, practically jumping off my chair at the chance to go see the old brownstone. What a great idea! The thought hadn't even occurred to me that I could just drive down to the South Side and see Dad's building that very day!

By the time we walked out of Tim's building in the Loop and over to my minivan parked by the lake, cars were beginning the zoom, zoom, zoom of rush hour. I was going to take South Lake Shore Drive, because it usually didn't turn into a parking lot like the other freeways in town at this time of day. But Tim thought we should take a drive along State Street – forty blocks worth. It seemed outrageous to take the streets during rush hour, but since Tim himself lives on the South Side, I figured he knew what he was doing. Traffic was surprisingly fluid along the route. Tim pointed out historic points of interest along the way, like when we drove through Printer's Row just south of the Loop, he commented, "This used to be called 'Satan's Mile.' That's where all the brothels were." That became a pivotal piece of information, a year later.

We drove through the South Levee, past Big Jim Colosimo's and through Bronzeville, and arrived at 40th and Michigan. There we found my Dad's three story brownstone apartment building, sandwiched in-between two dilapidated factories. We got out of the van and stood behind the iron fence in front and peered up at it.

It was marvelous to see the building for real. It had a lot of personality. The windows were the kind of curved bay windows you see in an Edward Hopper painting, except these were broken and we could see the inside walls had been stripped down to the lathe. A light rain fell, slanting in through the window. Pigeons, darted in and out, narrowly missing the shards of glass still stuck to the panes. Tim remarked, "Looks like somebody started to renovate and then ran out of money. It's too bad."

Looking at the doorway at 4016 S. Michigan

In its decayed, crumbling condition, the old, dark red husk of Dad's apartment building looked mournful. It possessed an eerie presence, which seemed only fitting, considering the misadventures and misery it once contained. We walked around to the back of the building and saw it was crisscrossed with wooden fire escapes. At the end of the street, we could see an L track for the Orange Line, up high atop a cement wall. A long vacant zone stretched out for blocks underneath the L. It was easy to imagine my five year old Dad playing ball there or rough housing in the dirt with other kids, under the "Post No Bills" sign still stenciled onto the wall.

Some months later on the phone, Tim told me he had walked by the building again several times after our visit. "It looked so *lonely*," he murmured with emotion.

"Because it's stripped down and vacant?"

"No. Something else."

"Maybe my Dad left behind some perceptible anguish," I proposed. "He used to wait on the steps all night for his mom to come home."

"Hmmm," Tim mulled thoughtfully. "Maybe that's it."

Couple of Guys at Dad's Brownstone

I went back another time to visit Dad's brownstone. I wanted to see it again and thought I'd take some pictures. Fortieth and Michigan is an "iffy" neighborhood, but I figured if I drove in my minivan and went for a brief visit during the day I'd be okay. When I got there early in the afternoon, I started taking pictures in front of the wrought iron fence, when a couple of guys came strolling by and stopped to watch me work.

"S'up?" one of them inquired.

"Hey there!" I crooned, and we introduced ourselves.

"Cool building," Greg remarked, nonchalantly. "Yeah, this old place look like they had some craps and cards goin' on the first floor, you know and they be doin' the policy numbers, and there be some "criiiiiiiibs" upstairs with the girls. Yeah, and behind that basement door, they be making hooch down there."

I laughed. "My Dad used to live here when he was a kid and his step dad was a bootlegger."

"Dang!" Greg drawled, as his eyes grew wide. "Hey, this was Capone territory, right?"

"Yeah, that's right." I affirmed.

"See?" he crowed knowingly to his companion, Sal. Apparently there had been some prior discussion on the point. There was a heavy smell of booze in the air,

Neighborhood dudes

"How do you know about that old stuff?" I asked Greg.

Sal answered for him, "Oh, he reads a lot."

I smiled. "Can I take your picture?"

"Sure!" Greg chirped and they posed together in front of the old brownstone. I wanted to ask another passerby to take a picture with all three of us in it, but I was afraid my camera would walk away down the street. Sal continued, "You know, my Uncle Wallace, he used to drive for Capone. After that, he drove a cab His funeral was right here at the end of the street," he confided, pointing to the neon "funeral" sign, down at the end of the block.

Small world. I told them about Andrea's Dad, how his stolen wallet and wedding ring were returned by Capone's driver.

"Wow," marveled Greg.

"Maybe that was your step dad Wallace!" I suggested to Sal.

"Yeah. That could be," muttered Sal, looking a little worried. He turned and started to vamoose down the street.

Hmmmmm. What d'I say?

Greg trailed after him, and hollered back at me, "Nice talkin' to ya!" And the two guys continued on their mission, whatever that was, and that was the last I saw of them.

Black and Tan District

Greg was right on the money with that fantasy of illegal activities at dad's brownstone. It had once been on the southern edge of the "Black and Tan" entertainment

Alberta Hunter, the "Sweetheart of Dreamland" [a Chicago Black and Tan] started out singing in a Levee brothel called "Dago Franks"

district in the 1910's and 20's, where nightclubs, brothels and gambling joints were located.   The area is now known as Bronzeville. Black and Tan cabarets featured live New Orleans Jazz by top flight musicians, like Alberta Hunter, Bessie Smith, Ma Rainey, King Oliver and Louis Armstrong and the Hot Five. The cabarets had names like Dreamland, Chocolate Bar, Plantation Cafe, The Deluxe, and The Elite.   In 1922, The Chicago Commission on Race Relations wrote, "The intimate association of Negroes and whites in the cabarets of the South Side has occasioned frequent and heated protests." [CCRR, 323] But, as a police captain pointed out, "There is no law to prevent a white woman from dancing with a sable hued admirer." [CT "Black Belt"]

Patrons of the black and tan cabarets ran the gamut from black stockyard workers and railroad workers to an integrated vice crowd to white slummers out on the town. Here's a newspaper description of the clientele at the Pekin Cafe, at 2700 S. State St.

> In came a mighty black man with two white girls. A scarred white man with three girls. Two well dressed youths hopped up the stairs with two timid girls. Seven young men - they looked like Back o' the Yards, [i.e. the slaughterhouse slums] came with two women, one heavy footed, the other laughing hysterically [i.e. under the influence]. Two fur coated 'high yaller' girls romped up with a slender white man. [Ibid]

You can tell that prostitution was afoot, because the numbers don't match up, except for those kids out on a double date.

In 1921, the same year that Dad and Minnie were living on 40th and Michigan, Trib police reporter John Kelly contributed his take on the Black and Tan neighborhood, which stretched south of 23rd to 39th or by some accounts, even as far south as 55th. "Without a doubt, this district is the foulest spot in Chicago," Kelly seethed. "Black and tan cabarets, buffet flats, soft drink saloons and every sort of vice are flourishing." [Ibid] Another veteran with his fingers on the pulse of the district, was Police Captain John B. Enright, who remarked, "We make raids every week. If we didn't keep right after them, conditions would become unbearable." [Ibid]

Harlem poet Langston Hughes visited the Black and Tans. And back in 1913, Hughes wrote this description of South State Street, known as "The Stroll" -

> a teeming negro street with crowded theatres, restaurants and cabarets. And excitement from noon to noon. Midnight was like day. The street was full of workers and gamblers, prostitutes and pimps, church folks and sinners." [Hughes]

During Prohibition, a young, white Chicagoan, named Irle Waller, worked a job all week and unwound by spending his weekends sleepless, soaking up the excitement of Black and Tan clubs. One of his favorite joints was the Entertainer's Cafe, a hot club on 35th and Michigan that featured the best in New Orleans Jazz, five blocks away from Dad's brownstone. Waller reminisced, "It was impossible to keep your feet from tapping and your hands and fingers from beating on the table along with the rhythms." Waller was an enthusiastic fan of New Orleans Jazz, which was an entirely new kind of music.

> The band would start out slow and sweet and very gradually draw the dancers on to the floor, continuing to intoxicate not only themselves but everyone, including the waiters and all the other help, to a pitch where everything went. The lights were gradually dimmed, lower and lower, until it was almost impossible to see. If you concentrated sharply through the darkness, many of the dancers could be seen fornicating while standing up, swaying slowly to the music, the girls' dresses pulled up. [Waller, 75]

Many owners of the black and tan cabarets had prostitution and gambling taking place right on their premises, in upstairs rooms or down in the cellars. [Waller, 41] And the Entertainer's Cafe that Waller visited was often raided for Prohibition violations, in spite of the owner's touted connections at City Hall. Patrons were frequently arrested and hauled off to the police station, until finally the cabaret was padlocked for good.

How about those "buffet flats" that the police reporter mentioned? Now there was some "excitement," as Langston Hughes had penned. You had to know the right person to get admitted to a buffet flat, which was a private apartment where different flavors of erotic shows took place in various rooms of the apartment. And for a fee, a person could join in the show of their choice. Ruby Smith's story of the night she went with Bessie Smith to a buffet flat in Chicago, is something you can listen to on-line. [http://stomp-off.blogspot.com/2011/06/visit-to-buffet-flat.html]

My Dad

The Black and Tan district was also the home of policy kings, black vice lords who ran numbers rackets. [Lombardo, 34] Policy tickets were for sale everywhere in the district, in beauty salons, barber shops, coal and wood suppliers, dry cleaners, shoeshine parlors, saloons [when drinking was legal], grocery stores, laundries and even candy shops. One of those black vice lords was King Cole, a policy banker and an investor in the Metropolitan Funeral chain. Maybe he owned that funeral home Sal mentioned, where his step dad who drove for Capone had his funeral. [Lombardo, 51] Or it might have been owned by Policy king Daniel McKee Jackson, who ran a family funeral business, along with gambling joints in the district, including a gambling parlor hidden *inside* the funeral home. [Lombardo, 35]

The Evolution of the Neighborhood

According to Tim Samuelson, originally Dad's block and the area south had been built up as an exclusive residential neighborhood, comprised of swank mansions after the Great Fire. Then in the early 1890's the area began to change, in anticipation of the Columbian Exposition, when vacant lots were quickly developed into apartment buildings, hotels, and rooming houses to accommodate the 20 million visitors who came to Chicago to see the Expo.

Property values began to depreciate after the Expo, when ritzy residents of Grand Boulevard, Michigan Avenue, and Drexel Boulevard [where that pic of Minnie was taken] sold off their mansions and moved to the newly fashionable Gold Coast on the North Side and suburbs. [CCRR, 207 - 208] The final blow came at the end of the 1890's, when industry moved into the last of the vacant lots. Dad's brownstone was flanked by factories and there was even a large automobile factory in the next block,

Dad and Minnie at Lake Michigan

on 39th and Michigan. By 1922 and 1923, when Dad, Minnie and Tony lived there, it was a transitional neighborhood, which had slid from chic to cheap.

Another factor contributing to depreciation on the South Side, was the closing of the 22nd Street vice district in 1912 by the police. An estimated 2,000 prostitutes scattered to "clandestine brothels" in houses and flats, which were quickly established in the area immediately to the south, in the Black and Tan district. [CCRR, 209] By 1916, only one brothel had reached as far south as 40th Street. But two years later, in 1918, eight brothels had moved in, less than a block and a half away from the brownstone at 4016 S. Michigan. [CRR 342, maps] When Dad and Minnie were there three years later, there may have been even more.

Once the rents in Dad's neighborhood became affordable on the wages of black workers in the stockyards, railroads, and war industries, the "Black Belt" expanded East from its location bordering the stockyards, into the 40th and Michigan neighborhood and beyond. The black population in Chicago had recently more than doubled, when people came up from the Deep South for war work at wages "offered at more than could be made in the south." [CCRR 2] Censusrecords bear this out, showing the neighborhood was 80% to 95% white in 1910, but by 1920, it was 60-80% black. [CCRR maps] [

Chicago riots in 1919

Dad was probably the most racially prejudiced person I ever met. Fortunately, he was all talk and no action. But there may actually have been some bad childhood experiences lurking behind Dad's attitude, that made him carp about "jigaboos" for as long as anyone was willing listen to him. In Chicago, Dad was playing out in front of the building they lived in, when his mother happened to look out the window and saw Dad being carried down the street in the arms of a black person. She ran after my Dad and managed to get him back. Then a few years later, in 1919 when Dad was almost 4 years old, race riots devastated Chicago, providing a citywide role model of racial hatred for a little boy.

In July 1919, during four days of stifling 95 degree weather, violence erupted all over the South Side. [CCRR, 8] Thirty eight people were killed, 537 were injured in beatings and stabbings, and a thousand were left destitute when their homes were burned or bombed. [CCRR, 1] Black workers going to their jobs in the stockyards were met by organized raids of "gangs and so-called athletic clubs from the South

Police arriving during riot

Side and beaten and thrown into the Drainage Canal," [Waller, 61] Many of those gang kids as well as their victims came from the stockyards area, a hardscrabble district, filled with the stink of rotting flesh and the "cinders, smoke and noise" of railroads. [CCRR8]

State's Attorney Hoyne also blamed "bank robbers, payroll bandits, automobile bandits, highwaymen, and strong-arm crooks," for escalating violence. Who knows what Tony did, or what he and Minnie said, or what Dad saw at the impressionable age of four during the riots. Police and militia descended upon the City to restore order, sometimes one hundred to a block. But State's Attorney Hoyne related that "a great many police officers were grossly unfair in making arrests. They shut their eyes to offenses committed by white men, while they were very vigorous in getting all the colored men they could get." [CCRR, 8] Thirty eight people were killed, but in the end, only four convictions were obtained for murder. [CCRR, 1] The Chicago Commission on Race Relations wrote, "The riot furnished the gang and hoodlum element a chance to indulge in lawlessness." [CCRR, 47] Now there's a model for racial prejudice.

Will the real Tony Coglioni please stand up?

Okay. I knew that Tony Coglioni was a crook, a bootlegger for sure because that was in Dad's VA records, and perhaps Tony had other illegal activities, as well. He had been named for a big man around town in Italy, but he himself was just a chump. I could see that from his pictures. I knew Dad had been told that Tony was his father. And I had been to the brownstone apartment building where Tony once lived with Minnie and my Dad. But there were too many Tony Coglionis to choose from in the city directories. Yes, there was that one listing in the phone book on Michigan Avenue in 1922, but that was the only listing for Tony there. If I could figure out who was the right Tony Colgioni, maybe it would help me solve the mystery of what happened to my Grandmother, because I couldn't find her in any records.

I had a fat file of loose notes, on pages torn out of notebooks and yellow legal pads, with facts scribbled on them on various men with the last name Coglioni. I had a bunch of Tony Coglionis. And there was also a Colgioni grocer at 12th and State and several Coglioni tailors, including one who got into a duel with his wife. She was found dead on the couch, shot in the chest and stabbed in the heart with a stiletto. The husband was found writhing on the floor in a pool of blood from two gunshot wounds. It was thought her would die, but he lived to be acquitted of his wife's murder.

I kept hoping for a clue that would pop out and tell me which one of the Tony Coglionis was the crook. I looked at my monster file crammed with pages of handwritten info on the Coglionis and thought, "Damn it! I must have the information in my hands! I'm just going to sift through all this and figure it out!" I typed up every bit of information I had collected on any Coglionis, from census records, city directories and phone books, court records and draft cards. When I was done, I had a Master Roster of Coglionis in Chicago.

I had four draft cards for Tony Coglionis from World War I. Draft cards are nice sources of information, because they list the man's address, occupation and physical description. If I could just figure out who was who, and what family of Coglionis they belonged to, maybe I could figure out who the Tony was that brought Minnie and my Dad to Chicago.

All right. Tony Coglioni #1 was an immigrant, a laborer. He had a disabled right hand from the description of him on his draft card and also in the ship manifest records, when he came over from Calabria. I never heard anything about Tony having a disabled right hand. That's the kind of thing people would comment on. In the pictures I had of him he looked as though he had two working hands. So Tony #1 was out.

Then I looked at Tony Coglioni #2. On his draft card, he was listed as a railroad laborer, and his physical description reported he was short. On his ship manifest records, when he sailed from Italy, he was listed as 5'3" in height. I called up my mother and asked her how tall Minnie was. Mom said Minnie was a little taller than she was, and Mom, in her salad days, was 5'3." In the photo of Tony and Minnie and my Dad at that funeral, Tony looks a few inches taller than Minnie, so there's no way he could have been 5'3." That meant Tony #2 was out, too.

Then there was Tony Coglioni #3. He was listed in the census as a railroad clerk, who lived in his family home with his father, who owned a grocery store at 12th and State. On his draft card, he claimed exemption from the draft, because he was the sole support of his "sister and her child." Sounded pretty innocuous.

Tony Coglioni #4 was a painter. I corresponded with a descendent of his that I had met on-line. Her Tony Coglioni sounded like a nice guy, a family man. I emailed her pictures of the Tony Coglioni I was looking for, and she emailed back that he wasn't their grandpa.

That left me with Tony Coglioni #3. Maybe he and his father weren't exactly what they said they were in the census. He was the one with the father who had a grocery on 12th and State, the same Tony Coglioni I'd been seeing from the beginning in those dusty, old city directories. Wait a minute, wasn't State Street called *Satan's Mile* in the Levee? Isn't that what Tim Samuelson said, when we drove down to see the old brownstone? Oh, boy! His father may have been a grocer, but this Tony Colgioni grew up in the vice district, surrounded by saloons, drunks, brothels, panders, prostituted women, opium dens, peep shows, gamblers, con men, thieves and every kind of human parasite imaginable.

Scene in an alley on the Levee

Finally, I had the right Tony Coglioni. That's not his real name, of course. What does Coglioni mean? In Spanish it's *cojones*. You figure it out.

Pasta Arrabiata

Here's a nice dish I found in that city employees cookbook, from Jim D'Archangelo, who works in the Human Resources Bureau of the City of Chicago. It's a spicy spaghetti-type dish, something I later learned that Tony Coglioni might have eaten at home, because they like hot food in Calabria, where his family came from in Italy.

6T XV olive oil

5 cloves garlic, sliced thinly

1 tsp. crushed dried red pepper (or more if you like it hot)

1 1/2 lb finely chopped fresh ripe tomatoes (or drained canned, stewed tomatoes)

1 lb. pasta (any type)

1 T coarsely chopped parsley

Salt and coarsely ground black pepper

Heat oil in skillet over low heat until warm. Stir in garlic and cook until garlic is golden brown. Stir in tomatoes and red pepper. Cook 5-6 minutes or until liquid is reduced. Stir frequently and be careful not to burn. Cook pasta and drain. Toss pasta with sauce and serve. Serves 4-5.

Factory and L track next to Dad's brownstone

Minnie at Clarendon Beach in Chicago

Chapter Six

༄་༄་༄་༄་༄་༄་༄་༄་༄་

Chicago Beach Brouhaha

When I got Minnie's photo album, I had to take apart the album, soak the pages in water, and peel the photos apart, because they had dried stuck together, after a couple of floods at Mom's. When I laid them all out and dried them flat, I wondered why there were so many snapshots of Minnie and a girlfriend in funny-looking, old bathing suits at Lake Michigan.

But then in the course of researching other, grimmer parts of Minnie's story, I came across articles about a bathing costume brouhaha in Chicago, that took place between 1919 and 1923. That's when I realized that all those beach pics were a commentary on the battle between the traditional, women's bathing costume, and the new, scandalous, athletic fashion.

Chicago's first public beach had opened twenty years earlier, in 1895. Christening the new beach were more than 300 boys, street urchins from the North Side, swimming in the buff. This au naturel scene prompted the City's Park Commissioners to draw up a list of rules and regulations about what to wear to the beach. Those rules would be challenged by flappers a generation later. [Encyclopedia of Chicago, 4]

By 1919, many women had rejected the traditional women's bathing costume, which required more fabric than anyone would dream of wearing on a hot day today. And that fabric was wool. Ick! Wool was the only fabric around at the time that didn't absorb a lot of water, and more importantly, didn't chill the body when it was wet. Thus, the entire figure was draped in woolen from head to toe, including stockings, hat and beach shoes. Imagine being cloaked from head to toe in soggy wool on a hot day!

The change in what women were opting to wear to the beach was part of a larger revolution, not only in fashion but in women's roles. In response to escalated agitation for Women's Suffrage, along with the monumental contribution of women during the Great War, fashion began to mirror these achievements by

radically transforming what to wear. In 1913, the controversial Women's Suffrage Movement, [which had already been going on since before the Civil War], instigated an intensive campaign of civil disobedience. This included such highly effective tactics as hunger strikes, street marches, and pickets at the Chicago Republican National Convention and the White House.

Then, during the Great War, women proved they could deliver

In the trenches of WW I

the goods, by stepping up to the plate to perform war industry jobs normally done by men, as well serving in the military as nurses and non-combatants. At last, during a special session convened by both houses of Congress in the summer of 1919, the 19th Amendment was passed. The following summer it was ratified, bringing to fruition 72 years of agitating for women to have the vote.

The New Silhouette

Women's fashions evolved in accordance with the new era of women's rights. Corsets were cast aside and hemlines rose from the ankle to as high as the knee. Claustrophobic, heavy clothing evolved into free-flowing, weightless garments, that provided unrestricted freedom of movement. The sheer poundage of fabric used in the dresses of former days was now reduced to something a girl could even play tennis in. The fashionable silhouette of the flapper was achieved by binding the bosom, to resemble the flat chest of a man. The waist dropped to the hip. Thus, the natural curves of a woman's body were replaced, according to *Vogue*, with the sinewy grace of a "boa constrictor."

Women's swim suits were now designed for comfort. Like men's suits. "Women are entitled to the same rights as men," Police Chief Edward Maroney of Highland Park asserted, in 1919, "both on land and in the water. I want them to enjoy swimming here. They can't if they have to wear a lot of camouflage contraptions that restrict freedom of movement." [CT "Beach Peaches"]

But the Commissioner of Public Welfare for the City, Mrs. Louise Osborne Rowe, wanted women's bathing suits to reach just below the kneecap, with stockings gartered above the knee, sleeves that covered the armpit, and hair tucked neatly under a cap. These measures "should rebuke the male stare," she told a Trib reporter, when she visited Clarendon Beach in the same summer of 1919. [CT "Here's Sad"] Further, Rowe was scandalized when she observed young women at the L station, getting on and off the train in their bathing suits. Just imagine *your* surprise if you saw a guy get on the bus today, wearing nothing but a teensy nylon speedo, and you get the picture.

The new fashion exposed a for women that heretofore number of areas hidden from had been armpit, the knee, view: the lower thigh and the calf, the the shoulders. the back below Bosker, 43] The [Lencek and came in new suits also getting luscious attention- of sober navy or colors, instead was still the black. Wool fabric of choice

Miss America 1921

for swim suits. However, lightweight wool, when wet, made the suits cling to the body, revealing features of the anatomy that had previously remained a mystery. The controversy over what women should wear to the beach got so heated in Chicago, that Mayor Big Bill Thompson appointed a committee to investigate women's swimwear and report back to him. In the meantime, the City actually provided a matron on the beach, armed with needle and thread and scraps of fabric, to enforce modesty in beach dress. If she thought what you were wearing was improper, she would hand sew those scraps of fabric to your suit, until you appeared modest in her eyes. You can bet the women's suits she attacked with her needle and thread didn't look fashionable when she was done with them.

News photo – confrontation in Chicago with swimmers

If we compare the two bathers in Minnie's snapshots, we can clearly see the difference in coverage. Minnie wears a dark-colored, traditional, loosely draped swim dress and sash, with a dagged hem, that reaches all the way to her knees. She wears long trunks underneath her swim dress, and covers her lower legs with stockings, and beach shoes. Her outfit is almost identical to what the first Miss America wore in the swimsuit competition in 1921, which was pretty much the whole competition back then, anyway. Minnie's gal pal wears a tight, form fitting, two-piece suit, consisting of a tunic length top and short trunks in a sporty color. Her shoulders, armpits, calves

Minnie and a buddy at Clarendon beach

plus portions of her thighs and back are exposed, and she is comfortably bare of shoes and stockings.

Minnie, her buddy and Dad are cooling off at Chicago's Clarendon Beach, as evidenced by the beach building in the background of another picture.   That look-alike, Miss American outfit would make the year 1921, right at the height of the swimwear brouhaha. The pictures seem to be a wry commentary on what to wear to the beach and the big beach brouhaha. These pictures may even have been inspired by newspaper articles written about their beach, that I found in the Chicago Tribune.

A couple of Chicago cops, Mrs. Theresa Johnson and Mrs. Agnes Walsh, had the job of leading the "less discreet of the mermaids" into the "hoosegow." They were interviewed on their beat, which was the same Clarendon Beach. They told the reporter they favored comfortable suits, but only for the female athlete who came to the beach for exercise. Mrs. Walsh explained, "The type which causes us trouble is the beach nut," the ones who "loll about on the beach." [CT "Lady Cops"] Their police chief added, that he was also "heartily in favor" of the new suit, BUT wanted

News Photo - Girls led off the beach

to do "something to prevent immodest young women from parading on the beach and attracting men bathers by their brazen actions." [Ibid] Let me point out that these "men bathers" the police chief referred to were identically attired, in the same "brazen" suits the women were wearing. It seems a lot of people were having trouble wrapping their brains around the idea of females wearing something comfortable, while seeking relief from the heat.Also on the beat at Clarendon Beach, was male Police Officer Reilly, who weighed in on the subject. "Honest, some of the suits out here'd make a man blush. I'm for skirts and stockings." [Ibid]

Another reporter observed a man he described as a "smart Alec" get his jaw dislocated at the beach. Apparently a bathing beauty stretched out - in the reporter's words - like "Cleopatra" decked him, after the guy invited himself to sit next to her and made "some remark." The masher was hauled off by the beach policeman, while his buddies on the beach were scratching their heads over that one. Of course, the masher's buddies were sporting suits identical to "Cleopatra's." They complained, "Why land on the fellow? Why not arrest the real cause of the trouble?"

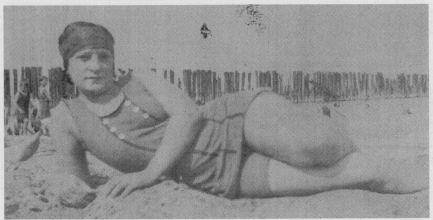

Minnie's buddy a la cleopatra

[CT "As Grandma Says"] The "real cause of the trouble" was addressed by theater journalist, Harry F. Rose, of the Clarendon Beach Hotel, who reasoned, "I don't consider the suits immodest. In the big athletic meets, the athletes run around with very flimsy trunks on and nothing is said about it. It is simply the state of mind in which one looks at these things." [CT "Inquiring"]

News Photo - Girls hauled into paddy wagon

A final voice of reason was found in the Commissioner of Public Works for the City, Charles R. Francis, the man in charge of the City's beaches. "People don't go to the beach to wear a lot of clothes; they go there to bathe." [CT "Council Orders"]

I had pictures of Minnie and Dad on the beach in Chicago. I knew that they had lived in that brownstone with Tony. And I knew that Tony had grown up in the midst of crime on the Levee. But I wanted to know more about their lives. I wanted to know what they did in Chicago, who this guy Tony was and what Dad and Minnie were doing at Big Jim Colosimo's funeral. When Dad was eleven years old, his mother sent him back to Philly, because it was "no life for a child." What were they involved in? If I took a closer look at Tony, the guy who had been raised in Satan's Mile, maybe that would tell me what happened to Dad and Minnie when they got to Chicago.

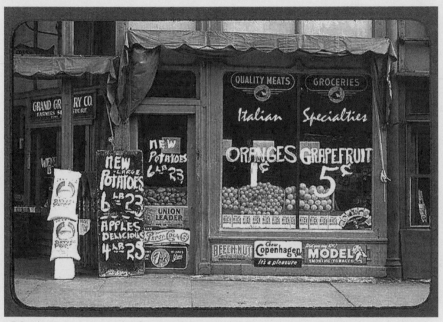

Movie green screen background, imagining Luigi's grocery store on the Levee

Photo: Library of Congress

Chapter Seven

❧❧❧❧❧❧❧❧❧❧

Italian Specialties

Now I knew that Tony Colglioni was spawned on the crime-infested Levee. But if there were no arrest records or bootlegging convictions for Tony, how was I going to find out just what it was that he did? His name and that brownstone apartment building were the only clues I had to follow my Grandmother's trail in Chicago. About the time I reached this point in my research, I found out that the Chicago Tribune Archives were searchable on-line. Of course, it was a long shot that any of the Coglionis would be in the paper, but it was worth a try.

I typed in Coglioni. Nothing. Hmmm. Then I typed in an alternate spelling. Holy shit! I wasn't in the archives for more than five minutes, when a sinister portrait of the man who raised Tony Coglioni tumbled off the screen. I leapt out of my chair in front of the computer and shouted "Eureka!" I never dreamed I would find proof of it in black and white. There it was: *"Luigi Coglioni . . . conducts a saloon and general business."* Yeah, Luigi reported his occupation as "grocer" in the census and city directories. But he was no ordinary grocer.

According to a reporter who visited Luigi's in person, he kept a large "general business" taking up two buildings, on 12th and State Street, the roughest section of the Levee. Luigi's "business" included a general store, grocery, bank and *saloon.* So Luigi was running a saloon in the worst part of the Levee. And the saloons in that neighborhood were generally inhabited by women for sale who, according to Jane Addams, "receive the protection of the saloon keepers." [Addams, 1912: 119] That's what kind of guy Tony Coglioni was raised by – a saloon owner on the Levee.

Chicago newspaper drawing of a padrone

It wasn't hard to run a saloon in Chicago. Eight out of ten Chicago saloons were financed by the breweries, that provided fixtures, rent, liquor license, and beer, in exchange for selling their beer exclusively. Their costs were recovered with a surcharge on each barrel of beer. Thus, Chicago stewed itself in 7,300 saloons in 1907, three times the national average, per capita. [Turner, 575-92]

Luigi was supplied by the Conrad Seipp Brewing Co., one of the largest breweries in America – which may have later secretly supplied beer for Torrio and Capone, during Prohibition. [www.encyclopedia, 2841]

The occasion for the Tribune article is just as interesting as the fact that Luigi ran a saloon. On a hot day in August of 1893, a crowd of four thousand out-of-work immigrant men were gathered at the lakefront around the statue of Christopher Columbus, to protest labor conditions and a general lack of work in the City. All of a sudden a shout of "Coglioni!" went up. One thousand Italians departed from the peaceful throng, ran over to 12th and State, and stormed Colgioni's store. What were they after? Depends on which newspaper account you read. Either it was the one hundred guns stored on the premises of Luigi's store that belonged to the Italian Sharpshooters Society, or it was the flags that the Sharpshooters Society carried in parades. When the mob made their demands known to Colgioni, he called in back-up, because the Trib reporter wrote that suddenly,

> the gong of a patrol wagon was heard and a moment later thirty big blue-coated policemen . . . were in the midst of the mob. As the policemen leaped to the ground and fell into line the mob began to waver and fall back. [Trib #1]

The crowd then swarmed back to the nearby Lakefront, where the mood of the throng changed.

> It was an unruly mob and in an ugly frame of mind. The police watched it narrowly." Many of the immigrants carried heavy railroad coupling bolts, bricks wrapped in newspapers, barrel staves or shovels as weapons. The throwing of missiles at the police . . . [was] the signal for the rush of the police [who] fell among them and scattered them, sending the crowd running pell-mell in every direction. The officers used canes, batons or boots as the case demanded and spared no part of the anatomies that were in reach. [CT, "Italians"]

It had been a tradition to hold peaceful socialist meetings on Sundays at Lakefront Park, throughout much of the 1870's and 1880's. However, the riot was part of a wave of labor unrest in the City in the early 1890's. The Panic of 1893 had brought about the collapse of 500 banks. In the financial crunch that followed, many people's savings evaporated, 15,000 companies went out of business, and unemployment reached a crushing 18%. Many workers suffered severe cuts in pay or lost their jobs entirely. Many people could no longer afford the basics.

There were 30,000 unemployed men in Chicago. Many slept in flop houses, foul smelling, vermin-ridden rooms. There men slept on bunk beds stacked four high, which were made of a piece of canvas tacked to the ball on on end and a pole on the other. Other men slept on the floor. The air was stale with tobacco smoke and a coal burning stove. These Levee flop houses became a kind of school for crime, where unemployed laborers mixed with pickpockets, thieves and con men. [Stead p. 163] But hoards of unemployed men didn't even have the 10 cents to spring for a night in a Levee flophouse, and slept on the Lakefront in the

Alderman Kenna's Saloon

summer and in the basement of police stations and City Hall in chilly weather. Religious and charitable institutions also provided relief, such as Jane Addam's Hull House and St. Vincent de Paul.

Men gathered in the 7,300 saloons of Chicago, either because they were roomers and had no parlors at home, or because they didn't have a home. That's why saloon owners like Alderman Kenna provided a free lunch for the unemployed. Fellow saloon owner Hank North daily served up 36 gallons soup and 72 loaves of bread at his bar. [Stead, 1894:163] On extremely cold nights, some saloons gave shelter in their basements [STEAD, 1894:127]

Labor Unrest

The riot that began at Luigi's store echoed much bloodier events that took place a few months earlier in Chicago, during the Haymarket Riot. On May 1st of the same year, there had been a huge demonstration in favor of the eight-hour work day, when a parade of 80,000 workers strode down Michigan Avenue. The event was part of a general strike all across the country, which had been called by the American Federation of Labor Unions. Over the next two days skirmishes broke out between workers and the police, at two Chicago factories. One policeman was killed and the First Infantry Regiment was put on alert. [CT, May 4, 1893]

On May 4 events reached a tragic climax at Haymarket Square, an open market near Desplaines Ave. and Randolph St., where a crowd of 1,500 workers were listening to speakers denounce the recent run-ins between workers and the police. At the same time, a phalanx of two hundred policemen marched in silence, shoulder to shoulder, heading up Desplaines Street to the Square.

> The glittering stars were no sooner seen than a large bomb was thrown into the midst of the police. The explosions shook the buildings in the vicinity and played terrible havoc among the police. It demoralized them and the Anarchists and rioters poured in a shower of bullets before the first action of the police was taken. Then the air overhead the fighting mass was a blaze of flashing fire.. . . bystanders on the sidewalk fled for their lives, and numbers were trampled upon in the mad haste of the crowd to get away. The groans of those hit could be heard above the rattle of the revolvers. [The crowd was then fired upon] by a thoroughly enraged police. [CT, May 4, 1893]

The nearby Desplaines police station served as a makeshift hospital, where ten doctors, five nurses and several priests attended to the wounded and dying. "Blood flowed in streams from wounds, pooled on the floor until it was red and slippery." Three more doctors tended the injured at nearby drug stores. The death toll stood at seven police officers and "an unknown number of civilians." [Ibid]

Mayor Thompson was on the scene at the police station at midnight, "wearing a pallor not unlike marble." He told reporters,

"Free speech is a right but accompanied with murder and dynamite is a crime to be suppressed at all hazards." [Ibid] Thus, just a few months later, the police were eager to disperse the large, armed throng of demonstrators at Luigi's store and down on the Lakefront.

Finally fifty years later, the eight-hour work day went into effect, when the Fair Labor Standards Acts was passed under the New Deal in 1938. So if you're feeling droopy on the job towards the end of the day, remember there was plenty of bloodshed that went into shortening the workday to just eight hours.

Padrone

It was a great bit of luck to find that newspaper article. Not only did Tony grow up surrounded by crime on the Levee, but his father also ran a saloon in the scummy part of town – and had an arsenal of a hundred guns stashed in the basement. What more could you ask for? But there was more. *A lot more.*

White wing   Library of Congress photo

I found a second newspaper article from 1886, in which the reporter had actually visited Luigi Colgioni's "grocery." Inside, the reporter found 200 Italians, "of the type usually seen at work on the streets," lounging around Luigi's big storeroom and in the back, where the saloon was located. What were all those immigrants doing there? Luigi was a man who, according to the reporter, "has probably brought more men and women to Chicago than any other man in the city. . . it is said he has gotten rich off the business." [CT, "Padrone"]

Luigi was a labor padrone, a man who had developed a parasitic relationship with those Italians the reporter observed in his store. Luigi began this relationship by offering to loan steamship tickets to desperate farmers over in Italy to come to America. Immigrants who came had to pay him back double. And that was just the tip of the iceberg. Once they got to Chicago, Luigi got them jobs as "white wings," street sweepers who cleaned animal manure off the streets of the City, for a dollar a day. The work was often sporadic. He charged the immigrants a fee for the job and then skimmed off the top of their wages every time they worked. He provided credit at his grocery store - at double the going rate. The Italians paid him inflated rents to live in his overcrowded, run down tenements in the crime infested red light district. Luigi was a one-man company town. The reporter described Luigi as a "money shark" who realized "astronomical profits."

According to Jane Addams, the padrone "fleeced them unmercifully." [Addams, 1910: 198-230] Also, garbage, manure from horse, chickens and goats, and the offal of animals slaughtered in basements piled up in the streets, breeding disease. City sanitation employees were exposed taking graft from landlords, who did not want the expense of installing

Drawing of the Levee by Norah Hamilton

running water and toilets in their buildings. The lack of proper sewage disposal contributed to the spread of water borne diseases, including the 1902 typhoid fever epidemic. [Addams, 1910: 298]

Italian immigrants were not savvy in the ways of conducting personal business in America. They put their trust in the padrone to help them write and send letters back home, and to help them with legal matters, like filling out naturalization papers. [Harney, 109, 105-6] The padrones brought immigrants over from their home area in Italy – in Luigi's case, the Cosenza area of Calabria in Southern Italy. Immigrants trusted the padrone, because of *Campanilismo* – an Italian term denoting the solidarity felt between all those who lived within range of the sound of the *campanile*, the bells of the church tower in their hometown. [Schiavo, 55]

Padrones were in the habit of making loans to their immigrants, but at usurious rates. [Harney, 110-118] Luigi himself acted as a banker, lending money, for which he charged "enormous rates of interest." At their request, he also banked his immigrants' money and sent it back to Italy. [CT, "Padrone"] In theory anyway, because I found bankruptcy records that showed Luigi went belly up, not once but twice, on savings his laborers had entrusted to his care.

Nefarious as their business practices were, padrones operated more or less within the legal system. Many were even highly influential people in the Italian community in Chicago. [Harney, 106] And in fact Luigi was described in newspaper article as being "regarded as a leader among a large section of his countrymen." [CT, "Italians"] and one of fifty "prominent Italians of Chicago." [CT, October 19, 1894, p. 3]

Big Man Around Town

Yeah, Luigi was a big man around town. In 1888 and for a number of years following, he was the elected President of the prestigious Italiano Bersaglieri di Savoia. The Daily Inter Ocean described it like this :

The society . . . has for its patrons the Presidents and officers of all the Italian societies in the city. [DIO, December 23, 1888, p. 6]

Luigi was an officer in another society, the Societa Christoforo Colombo, for whom he served as treasurer.   [Schiavo, p. 156]

Luigi was also given a place of honor in a number of parades down Michigan Avenue in Chicago, such as the Memorial Day Parade in 1894, when he was dubbed "Col. Luigi Coglioni, Commander Italian Guards."   The following year, he marched at the head of a "Platoon of Police" in the Italian Unity Parade.

APPEARANCE OF THE MOUNTED LEADERS OF THE PROCESSION.

Chicago newspaper drawing of the Italian Unity Parade

In 1890, "Capt. Luigi Colgioni" even commanded the "Italian Guards" of the Grand Army of the Republic, in a GAR parade of Union Army soldiers, who had served in the American Civil War. Luigi would only have been a five-year old boy at the start of the war. He probably wasn't even in America, because I found no records for Luigi in America before the early 1880's.   A living history re-enactor suggested to me that the rank of captain had merely been an honorary title given to Luigi, for being a big man around town who controlled lots of jobs. "He was in the center of the web – he pulled the strings. He may have done somebody in the GAR a big favor."

Paesani

You have to wonder, why Italian paesani would come to America under such a hard indenture. Many of them were destitute in the late 1800's, because farming conditions on the hillsides of Calabria had changed dramatically, due to deforestation of mountain tops. Signore Meli, secretary of the Christopher Columbus Society said that farmers tending the olive groves and vineyards on the steep slopes found that "storms have carried away the coating of the earth and hillsides are burned up." [CT, March 4, 1886] Meli knew Luigi because they were both officers in the Christopher Columbus Society and also the Bersaglieri de Savoia mutual aid societies. [Schiavo, 156]

Immigrants in steerage crossing the Atlantic – photo LOC

Another problem was that property taxes in Italy ran as high as 30%. According to Chicago Consul, Count Jacini, the paesani who owned land in Italy were "mortgaged up to the eyes," because they had borrowed from loan sharks who charged as much as 60% to 125% interest. [CT, March 4, 1886] Some Italians hired out as work hands to big farms, making as much as 34 cents a day. That was the men. Women made from 10 to 20 cents a day. [Peck, 59] When paesani saw émigrés returning to Italy with enough cash to buy a house, put meat on the table, and keep pigs, goats and chickens - that was living proof that the streets in America were paved with gold. [Iorizzo, 63] That's why a note to a farm-boss back in Italy, tacked to a shovel, read, "Signore, do your farming yourself. We are going to America" [Peck, p. 62]

The padrone offered ship passage to America, a place to live, food to eat and work at a triple the wages that they could make in Italy – all with no money up-front. All the paesani had to do was mortgage the next year or two of their lives. [Iorizzo, 85-90]

Drawing of paesano - LOC

Luigi kept a tight rein on his immigrants, by taking the deed to their little plot of land in Italy and holding it until their indenture was paid up. There were rumors that people who escaped before they were paid up were hunted down. [CT, "Padrone"]

The number of Italians in Chicago quadrupled in the decade, between 1880 and 1890, growing from 1357 to 5591 people. [www.encyclopedia, 658] Luigi was just one of a number of labor padrones bringing Italians to Chicago, but the reporter who visited Luigi's store in 1886 wrote that Luigi had brought more Italians to Chicago than any other padrones. [CT, "Padrone"]   He was still bringing his fellow countrymen over in the final decade of the 19th century, when the number of Italians had mushroomed to 16,008 by 1900.

Camorra and N'draghetta in Italy

The padrone's business had a shadow aspect to it, whose roots reach back to Italy, where they mingle with the roots of organized crime.   Not the "Mafia."   There were more organized crime syndicates back in Italy, the *Camorra* in the Basilicata region and the *N'draghetta* in Calabria.   All three groups are still alive and well today.   In fact the N'draghetta, has grown into an international crime syndicate that now reputedly controls the European cocaine market. [Scherer]

But the Mafia, the Camorra and the N'draghetta each began as rural mobs, guarding large tracts of farmland in Italy.   They protected the land from marauders and thieves, more by their reputation as tough men who would mete out retribution, than by actual policing.   In other words, if you mess with this farm estate over here, their protection syndicate is going to find out you did it and kill your whole family. [Bandiera]

Secret Societies in America

There were rumors that connected the Chicago labor padrones with organized crime. It was thought that the secret societies in Italy were acting as agents for the padrones, feeding them émigrés. The Italian Foreign Minister in 1894, complained of the "protected complicity between emigration agents who carry on the . . . slave trade in Italy and the padroni, who in American ports enroll by force our emigrants for the profit of the local *camorra* and *mafia*. [Iorizzo, p66]   One Italian in a Clark Street saloon ventured, "there are secret societies in Chicago, controlled by Neapolitan bosses, I am certain." ["Neapolitan" here refers to provinces in southern Italy that were formerly part of the Neapolitan empire, i.e. Southern Italy.]

Another guy in the same bar said, "I have heard of a secret society existing among them. . . a sort of secret terrorism among the immigrated Neapolitan peasantry. . . . de Stefano and Bartolo, a friend of his, know more than they will tell you. "[CT, "Padrone"]

More Padrones

Who were de Stefano and Bartolo? Bartolo was a padrone and a sorcerer's apprentice-type, who was always in the wrong place at the wrong time. Once he shot at and missed the president of the Nineteenth Ward Italian Republican Club and had the entire club on his heels chasing him. Another time he was president of the same club. The incident that took the cake was when a man he had sent out on a job took ill, and Bartolo brought him a doctor. The sick guy then underwent either an attempted vivisection or a hallucination that a medical student was going to dissect him. Bartolo was then arrested, but shortly afterward released and the guy who look ill was taken into custody. This happened in the 1880's, when Bartolo was located across the street from Luigi when he lived on Customs House Place, in a block that was full of brothels. [Stead, 1894, map of brothels]

Emilio de Stefano was another padrone on the Levee and he was often implicated as a Camorrista. It was even said by a priest that de Stefano was the head of the Chicago Camorra and his brother in Italy was sending him immigrants. In a letter to the editor, published in the Trib a week later, de Stefano denied belonging to any secret society, claiming that he was only a member of the Christoforo Colombo Fratellana. That's the same mutual aid society who elected Luigi as Treasurer in 1890. [CT "De Stefano"] The reporter who visited Luigi at his storefront also went over to take a look at de Stefano's, a large, four story brick building on South Clark Street and Taylor, where forty families lived crammed in the upper floors. This Levee neighborhood was called the Badlands, and was located between Taylor and Roosevelt Rd. Saloons, basement barbershops, and pawnbroker's lined the streets. There were also Chinese laundries and herbalists, and chop suey joints. Two Tongs, Chinese gangs, ran brothels, gambling joints and opium dens, the latter of which were legal until 1905. [Tim Samuelson, 2012] [www.gangresearch]

In the 1880's, the Badlands were also home to brothels like "Black Susan" Winslow's a rundown brothel. When her place was raided, the 449 pound "Black Susan" did not fit through either the front or back doors, so the police sawed a bigger opening through the back of the house to remove her. A few doors away, "The Dark Secret," was run by a madame called Big Maud, where the price of a woman - or a drink - was twenty-five cents. [www.chicagocrime]   Also peopling Clark Street were child labor padrones, described by one reporter as, "lynx-eyed, hard hearted," old men, who ran child slaves out of basement apartments. The kids were orphans, lost children and daughters and sons that had been sold for a pittance by their own father to the padrone. [CT, "Work"] In 1884, the Chicago police, along with the Humane Society, [then organized for children, not pets],

Child labor   *Photo: Library of Congress*

"unearthed three or four begging nests" on S. Clark.   [CT, "Padrone"] The padrone sent them out every day on the streets to pick rags, beg for coins, sell items like gum, shoe laces, matches, flowers or figurines of Italian art, shine shoes, pick pockets, or busk dancing or playing the harp or violin. Child padrones were notorious for their vicious treatment of children. A grocer, whose store was adjacent to one "nest," confided to a reporter that "most of them have had their ears boxed the night they were born and have been whipped every day since." [CT, "Padrone"]

The two storefront windows at de Stefanos read "Banca Italiana" on the left and "Beer" on the right. The reporter opened the door in the middle and came upon a scene of another two hundred immigrants, in a hub-hub of Italian conversation. He wrote, they "crowded about the bar drinking cheap wines or smoked and played cards." [CT, "Padrone"] [CT, "From Rome"]

In the midst of the crowd the reporter found Emilio de Stefano, playing with a solemn-eyed baby. The reporter described him as, "a suave man, given to hair-oil and jewelry."

HOTEL LUCANIA

416 S. Clark St.   **CHICAGO**

Emilio De Stefano — Proprietario

Si offrono agevolazioni agli Italiani che vengono a Chicago per visitare l'Esposizione. Camere ben fornite. Ottima cucina all'Italiana. Vini e Liquori di prima qualità importati direttamente. — **PREZZI MITI.**

Emilio de Stefano's Chicago Expo L'Italia Ad: September 16, 1893. Offering on credit to Italians who come to Chicago to visit the Exposition. Well appointed rooms. Optimal Italian cooking. Wine & spirits of the first quality, imported directly. Medium priced.

De Stefano confided to the reporter, "O, I have about 600 men now." [CT, "Padrone"] He sent them out to places like British Colombia, for work on railroads and in the mines. [CT, "From Rome"]

You don't see much of that in Hollywood Westerns, the immigrants who were brought over from Italy by padrones and sent out west to work on railroad gangs and mines. Working conditions in the wilderness were difficult and hazardous. Overseers were known to beat workers, or hold them prisoner until the job was done. Sometimes workers were bent out of their pay. Some workers even died on the job. [CT, "Hits"] The work was uneven, thus the crowd hanging around at Stefano's.

The reporter queried de Stefano, "How much do you get for securing work for them?"

De Stefano threw up his hands. "Not a cent, not a cent," Stefano ejaculated. The baby kicked up a fuss and howled at the same time. "Ah sir, they are my brothers."

The reporter asked him if those "slaves," as he called them, made de Stefano rich. "Have some wine," Emilio smiled unctuously, pouring from a wicker flask. "It's Chianti and, ah – divine.'"

Then the reporter heard a ruckus coming up from the basement and went down to investigate. There he found the source of the din: sixty "unwashed," half dressed "slaves," dancing, yelling and singing. The flop house was a long and dark room, filled with 200 bunks made of straw and boards. A guy was stretched out on a bunk, playing "a growling, monotonous tune" on a southern Italian-type bagpipe. That would be a *zampogna*, made from the entire skin of a pig. The pipes come out of the pig's snout and the blow-pipe is located on one of the front feet. And if you think I'm kidding, go to youtube.com and type in "zampogna" and you will see tarantellas played on just such a pig.

The reporter took aside one of the dancing "slaves" and asked, "Are you a free man?"

The Italian smiled blandly. "Sicuro. Gimma cigarra." [CT, "Padrone"]

Votes

Labor padrones were courted by politicians, because they delivered votes, quite literally. Hundreds of southern Italian aliens were driven from polling place to polling place "like sheep," to vote repeatedly. [CT, March 4, 1886] Money also exchanged hands between politicians and padrones during elections, as Stefano himself pointed out, in a letter to the editor of the Trib, when he said, "I am the person who returned to Mayor Harrison the $500 bill he lost on election day, and although a reward was offered, refused to accept any compensation for returning to a man his own goods." [CT February 23, 1890] [CT "De Stefano"] With skyrocketing Italian immigration, the illegal Italian vote that padrones could deliver was a real boon to those seeking office. The Italian population had grown from 1,357 in 1880 to over 45,000 by 1910. [Schiavo, 25]

June 2, 1894 L'Italia ad: Importer and Dealer of Food Items from Italy, France, Spain and America, Large Assortment of Wines, Spirits, Cigars Imports, Wholesale and Retail

The Connection

The Levee in Chicago was a small world, perhaps a mile long north and south between Van Buren and Roosevelt, and half a mile wide east and west, between Wabash and Clark. Emilio brought over paesani from his home province of Basilicata. Luigi brought immigrants from Calabria. The two padrones lived just a few blocks away from each other. They were allied in Italian social clubs, such as the Christopher Columbus Society, identified by the Trib as "the principal Italian organization," in 1886. [CT, "Chicago Italians"] They had to have known each other.

I read that when Big Jim Colosimo was a teenager, he lived in Emilio de Stefano's household. [Bilek 38] In fact, Emilio's son Rocco grew up to become the lawyer for Colosimo's crooked empire. Ties between the two families would explain what my Dad was doing at Big Jim Colosimo's funeral, since Emilio had been Colosimo's stepfather.

Maybe if I took a closer look at Luigi's activities, I could find a connection between the families of Emilio and Luigi. I wondered about that arsenal of 100 rifles that Luigi had at his store for the Italian Sharpshooters. It certainly seemed like an excess of guns. I looked up Italian Sharpshooters to see if I could find out more about what they did in newspaper archives. There were organizations in other cities, like Boston, that had large Italian communities, but I couldn't tell what they did.

Then there was the fact that Luigi was President of the Bersaglieri di Savoia. That Italian word, "Bersaglieri" was a mouthful. Since

Bersaglieri on the lookout for brigands in Italy

I knew it was a mutual aid society, [Schiavo, 55,56], which is a group that helped its members' families out in case of sickness or death, I thought the word Bersaglieri was related to bursars – people who held money. But when I looked up the name on the web, I found there was more to the Bersaglieri than mutual aid. The Chicago club had patterned themselves after a real military unit called the Bersaglieri, who were Italian sharpshooters that were part of the army which had helped bring about the unification of Italy. So that explained who the Italian Sharpshooters were and what Luigi was doing with all those guns.

The Chicago Bersaglieri wore the same dark blue uniforms striped with green, with gold epaulettes and short infantry swords as the real unit. The Bersaglieri's distinctive hat was worn pulled down over the right eye, to block the sun when firing. The hat sported a profusion of dark green plumes, thought to camouflage the presence, of the real Bersaglieri, when they were sent in ahead of the main body of infantry, to draw out the enemy. The Chicago Bersaglieri armed themselves with that arsenal of 100 rifles that Luigi kept in his store. A Trib reporter, who observed them marching in a parade, described the guns as having "wicked looking sword bayonets." [CT, "Their Fourth"]

Who was in command of this quasi military unit? I found out when I read about an Italian Unity celebration, in which the Chicago Bersaglieri were a featured entertainment, along with fireworks, dancing and carnival games. A reporter wrote:

> A man with lots of feathers and a healthy pair of lungs blew several blasts on his bugle and everybody rushed for the pavilion where Maj. Coglioni was shouting himself hoarse to the sharpshooters. They gave a pretty drill. [CT, "Their Fourth"]

That's right. Luigi – Maj. Coglioni as he was called, was their commander. Another Bersaglieri drill was given at the 1888 Bersaglieri Ball. The reporter wrote that The men looked exceedingly well in their soldier's garb and danced as only the military can, with grace and manly bearing. [DIO, December 23, 1888] And who should be on the Reception Committee, but President Luigi Coglioni and fellow labor padrone, Emilio de Stefano!

Luigi served together with Emilio as honorary vice president for a masquerade ball held during Carnivale, in 1888. Costumes included "bersaglieri, peasants, monks, nuns, bandits, Neapolitan boatmen, soldiers, brides and footmen." After the unification of Italy, the real Bersaglieri were sent to the South, to suppress bandits, also known as the people's resistance leaders. That's also what the N'draghetta and the Camorra did – chase bandits off large farming estates. The Bersaglieri had a particularly tough time of it with a resistance leader/bandit king named Crocus in Basilicata. Emilio was also from Basilicata, in the arch of the boot of Italy. Emilio wrote several letters to the editor of the Chicago Tribune, protesting the allegations by reporters that he was the leader of the Camorra in Chicago. In one letter, he says

> In your paper issued yesterday, one of your reporters attributes to me some of the information received on account of the existence of the "Mafia" in this city. What I said about the Mafia and the Camorra was only what I had read in some romances many years ago, when the southern part of Italy was under the government of the Kings Borboni. [The Bourbon kings] But now such societies are entirely gone. [CT, "In Defense"]

As ridiculous as the statement about the Mafia and Camorra being only something he had read about in novels, the statement that "now such societies are entirely gone" is completely untrue, both in Italy and Chicago.

In a second protest letter to the Trib, Emilio wrote even more fantastically, "In regard to my membership in secret societies, I deny the existence of anything of the kind among Italians." That was that same letter in which he he mentioned that he "returned to Mayor Harrison the $500 bill he lost on election day." [CT, "De Stefano"]

Luigi hailed from Calabria, the toe of the boot of Italy, where the real Bersaglieri had been sent to quash the activities of bandits, a function also of the secret society, the N'draghetta. In Chicago, Luigi was the commander of a quasi-military unit of sharpshooters, armed with swords and a hundred rifles with bayonets. Sure the rifles were for show, but the rioters were after them for more than just a splashy display of manly grace. And the Chicago Sharpshooters had been patterned after the real Sharpshooters, who had a hand in putting down bandit rebels, the same as secret societies also did in rural southern Italy. If you were a paesano from Calabria, who had signed the deed to your land over to Luigi and owed him hundreds of dollars for your room and board in America, you might be imagining the kind of retribution that could be meted out by a guy with a Bersaglieri arsenal, if you skipped your indenture.

But the most interesting committee that Emilio and Luigi turned up together on had to do with secret societies. In 1891, they were members of a "permanent committee of seven," formed in response to the killing of eleven Italians by a mob of vigilantes in New Orleans. [DIO, "Italians in Chicago"] The eleven Italians had been tried for conspiracy to murder New Orleans Police Chief Hennessey.

Apparently Hennessey had been the victim of a Mafia *vendetta*, for his zealous pursuit of evidence that would have brought about a conviction for some earlier vendetta-type murders, which were part of a feud between rival Italian wholesale fruit vendors. [Boston Daily Globe] An incriminating note was found in a police search of one of the accused men's homes, in which the Mayor of the city was fingered as the next victim of a secret Mafia, who vowed to kill any other officials who got in their way. [Cedar Rapids Evening Gazette]

Half a year later, the eleven Italians accused of conspiracy to murder the Police Chief were tried and acquitted. Vigilantes viewed this as a license for an *auto da fe*. They broke into the jail and killed all eleven men. The committee formed in Chicago by Luigi, Emilio and five others, meant to work in tandem with other committees in other cities to seek reparation for the wrongful deaths, and to clear the name of Italians in general from being associated with Mafia-type activities. In the late 1800's, discrimination in American against Italians was real. So was the Mafia and other secret societies. [CT, "Cheering"]

There was another de Stefano who was a labor racketeer. Giuseppe Saverio de Stefano, or G. S. de Stefano, was a ballsy guy who pushed the legal envelope several times. Referred to in the press as an "Italian boss," he got into trouble for selling registration cards to immigrants at $5 a piece. These cards entitled them to civil service jobs in the City's Water Pipe Extension office. These were cards they could have just gotten for free from the City. [CT, "Arrest"].

Like Luigi, G.S. de Stefano was another big man around town. Or at least he had been, until he got into hot water and apparently fell from grace. Three years earlier, in 1895, "Grand Marshal G.S. De Stefano" and staff had lead a double platoon of police, at the head of the huge Italian Unity parade. Guess who was first on the list of staff of "the Platoon of Police" - Luigi Coglioni. The parade gathered in the infamous Haymarket Square.

L'Italia ad: August 14, 1909, Seal – Member of the Italian Chamber of Commerce, Chicago, Office of Work Placement, with a license from the State of Illinois, Agency for Oceanliner and Rail tickets, Bank of Exchange, Sending of money to all the Post Offices of Italy and to principal cities in Europe, Notary Public, Branch office of United States Express Co. for Money Orders in the United States and Canada. Author Translation

Following de Stefano and Coglioni's lead were 30 Italian societies, Italian political societies, marching bands, 200 decorated carriages, the congregations of a half dozen churches, and a score of wheelmen on decorated bicycles. [CT, "Italians in Parade"]

G. S. de Stefano lived a few blocks away from Emilio, on Polk St. and worked in the same kind of business. His ad in L'Italia delineates all the padrone type services he offered. G.S. was also listed as the first pall bearer in Emilio's obituary in the Inter Ocean. [DIO, Feb 17, 1896]

Luigi Coglioni was connected through many club and committee activities to Emilio de Stefano. Both the men were labor padrones who lived and worked a few blocks away from each other. Emilio had another brother, G.S., who was also a labor padrone. Emilio raised Big Jim Colosimo along with his own son Rocco. Although Emilio had been long gone by the time Big Jim was executed, Emilio's son Rocco de Stefano, had grown up to become Colosimo's crooked lawyer. That's why my Dad and Minnie were at Colosimo's funeral. They were there along with the Coglionis, as friends of the family.

Levee Street

It all fit together like a jigsaw puzzle.

My Dad was the child of -

Minnie, who was the girlfriend of -

Tony Coglioni, who was the son of -

Luigi Colgioni, a padrone who was the associate of -

Padrones **G.S. de Stefano and Emilio de Stefano;** Emilio was the father of Rocco de Stefano and stepfather of

Big Jim Colosimo.

And that is the world my grandmother walked [in]to when she arrived in Chicago in 1916 with my Dad. She was a young mother with no place to go, who fell into a trap with an Italian American family living in the heart of Chicago's brothel district, headed up by a saloon owner and padrone. There was no way in hell anyone could have gotten mixed up with that bunch and come out okay. Minnie and Dad were at Colosimo's funeral because they belonged there.

Purveyor of Italian and Foreign Foods, Hotel and furnished rooms by the week and adjoining a Beer Saloon stocked with the best, most renowned wines and spirits , [Luigi was running his own rooming house and hotel as part of his business]

Please Note: the street numbering system was different in the 1800's. The old 500 block of State Street is now at 12th and Roosevelt.

Present day location of Alderman Kenna's Workingman's Exchange, still inhabited by pawn shops, cheap eats and a men's hotel. On So. Clark Street. Photo: Todd Kendall on www.chicagocrimescenes.com

Panel House on State and Congress from Wooldredge

Chapter Eight

಼ಀ಼ಀ಼ಀ಼ಀ಼ಀ಼ಀ಼ಀ಼ಀ಼ಀ

Crazed Levee Madams

It was midday and I was heading to the Federal Archives, again, on the far South Side of Chicago to have a look at Luigi's bankruptcy records. On the map it looked like a good way to cross over the several miles from the Lake Shore Freeway to the west end of the South Side. But instead of arriving early, I got stuck in a traffic jam several miles long. I was on South 93rd Street in one of those neighborhoods, where hundreds of people were hanging out in the street, creating traffic hazards left, right and center, that made for over an hour of white knuckled driving. It was a nice, hot summer day, and people were crossing and recrossing the street, weaving on foot around cars like mine, crawling along in the traffic jam. Other traffic hazards had their butts hanging out inches from passing autos as they bent over to talk to the driver of a parked car. Some stood on the painted yellow line in the middle of the road, like it was a traffic island. It took me five or ten minutes of intense concentration to drive a single block. So much for my short cut.

When I had finally crawled my way over to the Federal Archives, it was after 3:00 p.m., pretty late in their day. The clerk told me he couldn't fetch the files, because they were supposed to be ordered ahead of time. But when I had called two days before, *that* person told me to just come in and ask for them. Rules, rules, rules. Then on top of it, the clerk told me they didn't have anyone to pull records, because everybody was in a meeting. Well, after all that crazy driving, I wasn't going to take no for an answer.

So ten minutes later, a bland, pasty-faced bureaucrat arrived behind the counter, who had been pulled out of that meeting. He was the kind of guy who looked like he had never actually been in the sunlight. You know, like he lived there, under the anemic artificial fluorescent tubes hanging overhead and slept on a bed under the counter. With stiff formality, he dutifully took down my file request, but I could see he had smoke coming out of his ears. In the next breath, he growled through terse lips. "You know, you are *really* overstepping your bounds! You come here right before closing time, without calling ahead, and you just expect us to just drop everything and get your records!"

"'Overstepping my bounds?' What bounds?" I retorted, hotly. "I expect to place my order without having to turn the place upside down or get a lot of lip. Who do you think you're talking to, one of your employees?" I could see he was confused by that. He was one of those petty bureaucrats with a Napoleon complex.

That etiolated bureaucrat had his chance for revenge next time I came to the Archives.

Federal Archives Trip #3

A few months later, I left for Chicago in my "Artmobile," an old minivan, into which I had frantically stuffed my artwork, files and computer. Just a block away from my apartment in rural Wisconsin, the river had crested its banks. The volunteer fire department was hauling people out of their apartments in boats. Accompanying this scene was the surreal "boom, boom, boom" of a maniacal construction crew a few yards away, digging up sewer pipes as though nothing out of the ordinary was going on.

A crazy storm had loosed all that water the day before. Thunderclouds dumped down volley after volley of rain and a tornado sailed by overhead. I had been showing my jewelry at a craft show and dove for cover in the basement of a historic house museum, where the docent regaled a handful of storm refugees, myself among them, with tales of its history. Not a bad way to wait out a storm. But then the next day, between the flooding, the fire department boats and the construction crew, I had had it, and headed down to Chicago to study those files I had ordered on Luigi's bankruptcies.

L'Italia ad: May 26, 1894, Banker and Money Changer, Sending money to Italy and the cities of Europe, Transatlantic passage to and from Italy, Rail tickets for all points

This time, I got smart and took a short cut someone from Chicago told me about: 57th Street. The drive was a piece of cake. Even though I had ordered the records on my last trip, and made an appointment to look at them today, they still hadn't pulled the records yet. You have to wonder, what were all those rules for? So, I went back out to my car to eat my lunch while they retrieved the files. It was worth the wait, because I found a gold mine of information on Luigi's crappy business dealings. I took pictures, made notes and got back out to my minivan about 3 o'clock, feeling buoyant because I had a head start on rush hour traffic. I reached into my pocket for my keys, but they weren't there. When I looked in the minivan and I could see them through the window of the minivan, hanging from my ignition. Oy vey! My spare keys were also locked inside the van. Fortunately, I had left the window about half an inch ajar.

So I went back into the Archives and asked the young, well-dressed receptionist for a coat hanger. She relayed the request back to the archivists, who relayed back they had nothing. NOTHING. I went back outside and grabbed some long sticks from the ground and tried to get the door lock to pop. One by one a string of employees came out, not to help but to yak, like they had nothing better to do? I tried to be polite, but it took a lot of concentration to work that lock. Then that little Napoleon bureaucrat slithered out from his crack in the Archives and shoved a print-out of neighborhood locksmiths at me. "If you don't get your van out of there by 5 o'clock," he sneered, "we'll shut the gates to the parking lot and lock it overnight"

Old Levee scene by Norah Hamilton

"You would do that?" I asked, incredulously, picturing South Side hoodlums breaking in and stealing my computer and wrecking my artwork while my van was parked there overnight. I left the bureaucrat in the parking lot in disgust and went to call Triple A from the receptionist's phone. While I was giving Triple A my location, a different chubby, moon-faced bureaucrat, leaned over the receptionist and butted in, "We're going to lock up at 5:00. You gotta get your van out of here by then." I tried to ignore him.

Then I walked over to the military compound, next door, where I found a couple of guys hanging out outside dressed in camo, who loaned me a twisted up coat hanger. I hurried back to my car, but the coat hanger wasn't long enough to pop the switch. I went back in to the receptionist desk. She was gone, but I reached over the desk to call AAA again, waited until a human came on the line and they told me that their truck had already come and gone, because the driver couldn't find the place and I didn't answer my cell phone. "What cell phone?" I said. "I don't have a cell phone. You mean you called my house in Wisconsin when you got here?" It was now about 4:30.

Then another bureaucrat popped his head in, one I hadn't seen before, and uttered sternly, "We're going to lock that gate at 5:00." Where did they get these guys? Christ on a bike! They were like wind-up toys somebody cranked up and sent hopping after me.

I stomped back out to my car. The receptionist, bless her heart, drove up in an old, dull-black, fastback car driven by her boyfriend. He opened the trunk, pulled several hangers off a pile of shirts he had in there and helped me make a double, twisted coat hanger with a bend on the end to trip the lock. I slid it in through the crack in the window and – music to my ears – heard the lock pop. As her boyfriend climbed back in the car, I hollered to the receptionist, "Hey, give your guy a big kiss for me!" They grinned. What a nice gal! She could have just breezed on past me in her boyfriend's car and never given me a second thought.

I left with 12 minutes to spare. And that was the last time I went to the Federal Archives.

But boy, did I net the information that day. Luigi filed for bankruptcy not once, but twice. Each time, he came up short on money his immigrants had entrusted to his care. Apparently nine times out of ten, padrones bilked gullible Italian immigrants out of their savings. "Who could believe it?" the victim would wail. "He was from my home town!'" [Schiavo, 43] Immigrants had faith in *Campanilismo* – but the ringing of the bells of their church back home couldn't be heard in America. The padrone took their money and spent it .

Right before that first bankruptcy in 1894, a new law had been passed, making it illegal for padrones to bring Italian immigrants over to America. [source?]   At the same time, the entire country had sunk into a depression following the Panic of 1893, the same year those unemployed Italians rioted at Luigi's store. The first time Luigi went bankrupt, he declared $25,000 in assets. But by the time of his second bankruptcy in 1900, Luigi had no assets whatsoever *on paper*. [CT, "News"]

The levee on the Chicago River - drawing by Norah Hamilton

However, one of the Italians Luigi swindled out of his life savings was a 60 year old guy, who repaired harps for a living. The guy filed an objection to that second bankruptcy in 1900, complaining of Luigi's "intent to defraud," because Luigi had shuffled his assets by transferring them to his wife and brother-in-law. Further, the complaint read that Luigi was currently operating a "large and lucrative grocery and meat business," under his wife's name. It was a typical ploy of crooks to use their wives's names to conceal assets, launder dirty money and provide a front for financial operations. [Siebert, 168]. Luigi disappeared for a few years from city directories around the turn of the century. I checked prison records and ship passage records, but could not find a listing for him. Apparently he just disappeared on paper.

That was some role model for an Italian family of kids growing up in the scummy Levee – a father who went belly up on the savings poor immigrants had entrusted to his care. But then, in those bankruptcy records, I discovered intelligence that threw open a window onto the Levee of the 1890's, that gave me a clear view of the horrifying life that madams and prostitutes led there.

Madams

In May of 1892, Luigi took out a one-year lease on eight adjoining properties in the 200 block of Customs House Place, from the Chicago Western and Indiana Railroad Company. These properties lay right across the street from the Dearborn Train Station. Some of the row of addresses he leased may have served Luigi as convenient warehouses, since they were across the street from the train station. Or he may have rented out some as tenements for his immigrants.

But I found that three addresses had been subleased to Tilly Madison, Florence Davis and Annie Fishbeck. This fact intrigued me, because they were all women. The three properties were all in a row on Customs House place, just north of Taylor Street, an area notorious for brothels. [Stead map] The Dearborn Train Station was right across the street where tourists would arrive in the City. Given the location, I wondered if those sub-lessees might actually be madams. The more I dug, the more interesting their stories became.

Tillie Madison's name appeared on a list of twenty-eight panel house managers on the Levee, who were arrested in 1898 and convicted the following year. [Wooldredge, 46] Panel houses resembled regular bordellos, but with one important difference. When a man had his pants off and was otherwise occupied, a hand appeared out of a secret panel and removed his valuables from his clothing, sitting on the only place in the tiny room he could put them - a single chair placed right next to the secret panel. According to Detective Wooldredge, the Sherlock Holmes of the Chicago Police force, the property owners who rented out those panel houses in 1898 were also indicted in a City-wide sweep. [Ibid] Looks like Luigi missed that one by five years.

Annie Fishbeck

When I sleuthed out Annie Fishbeck's history, the trail of stories she left behind in the Chicago Tribune were some of the most interesting but pathos-filled stories I had ever read. A few years before she rented that brothel from Luigi, Fishbeck had been hauled into court by police, for packing two revolvers and a straight razor. She had been out that day hunting down Sally White, who was apprehended an hour later by the police, hopping mad, and armed with a club, a gun, and a knife. White swore to a Trib reporter, "she would have the Fishbeck woman's life." [CT, Oct 30, 1890]

Wooldredge in disguise as a bum

The incident stemmed from a love triangle, because the next day, the Trib reported that Sally White, "in a spirit of revenge for her husband showing a partiality towards Annie Fishbeck," threw all of her husband's clothes into a box and chucked it out of the window. Then she ran out into the street, which happened to be just a few blocks away from Luigi's, poured kerosene over the box and lit it on fire. Shortly after that, the police arrived and hauled away her husband, because White had sworn out a warrant charging him with vagrancy. He had to borrow some clothes to go with the officers to the station. (CT, Oct 31, 1890]

These were just two episodes in an ongoing feud between White and Fishbeck. Papers had reported the week before, that a "riot among the dusky females," had broken out, when White and five other women stormed into Fishbeck's "disreputable house" and threw Laura Johnson out of a third story window. By the papers' description, Annie Fishbeck was a madam who ran a brothel. She may have been visited by a group of women on a fact finding mission from the Indiana Women's Christian Temperance Union. Along with their police escort, the women made the rounds of the Levee brothels on a Saturday night to interview inmates, including "a colored house on Customs House Place," on the same street corner that Annie Fishbeck had been renting from Luigi. Outside they noted many fancy cabs and carriages belonging to wealthy men. [CT, "Go Through Slums"] The committee found that the women in the brothels hailed from nearly every state of the union and had originally left their homes in the country to seek legitimate work in Chicago.

Detective Wooldredge in disguise as a stockman - fat with cash after delivering his cattle to the yards

And who was Fishbeck's adversary, Sally White? I found an article reporting that she had been indicted in 1898 for keeping a brothel. [CT, Dec 31, 1898].

So she was a madam, too. But White was known on the Levee for more than running a cathouse. A reporter was privy to the following scene in a neighborhood drug store:

Gimme two bits' wuf Sally White's luck," asked a Senegambian of a drug clerk on South Clark Street the other day. The clerk proceeded to pour shellac, saltpeter, sulphur and other ingredients onto the pan of the scales until the five ounce weight swung at a balance.

That was a secret luck formula invented by Sally White. That formula was burned like incense, the fumes were inhaled, so your luck would change. Maybe that box she lit on fire in the street, contained more than just clothes. Another White formula was comprised of "verbena, pennyroyal, tansy, cedar, cloves and white rum," and went in the bath. In either case, the Trib reported, the ritual was carried out, "with the greatest care and secrecy." [CT, "Luck"]

That sounded to me like Vodun or Vodoo magic spells. Sure enough when I jumped on the web, I found lots of the same kind of formulas, available from purveyors in New Orleans who offered luck for love, jobs, money, fertility and luck for unhexing the luck someone else did on you. White's knowledge of Vodun rituals suggests Saint Domingue and ultimately West African roots, that may have come by way of New Orleans. That's where many French colonials and mixed French/Africans landed, after a revolt began in 1791, on the French colony of Saint Domingue.

It was often remarked that women born of Saint Domingue French/African liaisons had delicate features and high cheek bones, with silky hair and light cafe au lait or even white skin. [Duggal, 157-178] Perhaps Sally White was such a gal. Her last name suggests a light complexion. One thing is sure. Sally White was a Voodoo Queen. And prone to violence. Annie Fishbeck must have been one tough cookie to tussle with her.

Laura Johnson

I wondered what became of the hapless Laura Johnson. Was she a defenseless waif who Sally White and her posse flipped out of Fishbeck's brothel window? Or was she just a gal who was in the wrong place at the wrong time? Did she die in that fall, or did she live to piss someone else off another day? Turns out she lived to be involved in quite a few more brouhahas. The tale was like one of those Russian nesting dolls: you open it up and inside is another Russian doll and you open that one up and inside is another Russian doll and inside that . . .

A year and a half after sailing out of that third story window, Johnson was in good enough shape for Detective Wooldredge to chase her over the Twelfth Street viaduct between Wabash and State Streets. Wooldredge reported the chase began when he heard cries of "Police! Thief! " rising up from below from Johnson's latest victim. He was a soldier and a manager in a military hospital, who had been wandering around on furlough on the Levee with a big wad of cash. He had been fleeced by Johnson, when she led him down into an opium den, where he wanted to investigate the pharmaceuticals, or so he claimed. [Wooldredge, 349, 352]

Detective Wooldredge as himself - photo from his book

Wooldredge knew Laura Johnson well in his work as a police detective, describing her as "a notorious colored footpad." [Wooldredge, p. 349] You would not want to have met Johnson on the street, because footpads were ferocious, strong arm women who worked in pairs, prowling the Levee with revolvers, razors, brass knuckles, knives and sawed-of baseball bats. [Asbury, 127] Under cover of darkness, they trolled for their next mark. When they got him they threw him against a doorway, pressed a razor to his throat or socked him a couple of times with brass knuckles, and relieved him of valuables he was foolish enough to flash in some Levee saloon, burlesque show or opium den.

Johnson was afraid of nothing. The Trib reported that she tangled with notorious Levee footpad and panel house madam, Emma Ford. [Wooldredge 46] [CT, "Two Men"] Known as "The Levee Terror," Ford was the last person anyone in their right mind would pick a fight with. Wooldredge described her as a woman who was "as fearless as she is ferocious." He reported that "no two men on the police force were strong enough to handle her." [Wooldredge, p. 47, 48] Wooldredge nicknamed her the "Colossus." She stood six feet tall, weighed in at 200 pounds, had "muscles of steel" and arms that reached to her kneecaps. She had already been apprehended for killing a man while robbing him. But when she was tried and acquitted on a technicality, she was chased to the train station by a lynch mob, who she narrowly escaped by hopping on the back of an eastbound train, seconds ahead of the pack.

Emma Ford

Johnson's showdown with "Levee Terror" Ford took place in the heart of the brothel district, at Customs House Place and Taylor Street, where the two adversaries fired revolvers at each other. They missed hitting each other, but seriously wounded two male bystanders who were taken to the hospital. Must have been quite an adventure for the police to tackle those two seething-mad women, disarm them and drag them off to jail. Johnson finally did some time in prison, not for that shootout or for holding someone up, but for assault.   She got into an argument with another woman over a man, when Johnson reportedly "carved up" the other woman with a knife, nearly severing her arm. [Wooldredge, p. 352]

Pandora's Box

My suspicions about Luigi's sub-lessees had opened a Pandora's Box of their noxious exploits. Tillie Madison was a panel house madam. Annie Fishbeck was a brothel madam. And she was not just any madam, but a well known, desperate Levee character. Her travails, and those of other Levee women, whose names stood side by side with hers in the press, paint a vivid portrait of the pernicious life on the Levee.

The accounts demonstrate how severely women on the Levee suffered from the psychological effects of trauma. These were women who had been broken to a life of prostitution at a tender age, with terrorist techniques specifically designed to break their will. They had been coerced to service an endless stream of men, with the continued daily application of assault, humiliation and mutilation by pimp and customer alike. Now they were madams, perpetuating the same violence. The violent behavior of these women towards each other was echoic of the violence that had been done to them – not by each other, but by managers and consumers of the prostitution industry. This dynamic of human misery, proliferating unchecked on the Levee, was a truly frightening picture, because my Grandmother was headed for pretty much the same world in Chicago, a generation later.

What was equally frightening was that the father of the man my Grandmother went to Chicago with was a brothel landlord, in addition to his other nefarious businesses as a saloon owner and padrone. What culpability does a brothel landlord have? Plenty. Luigi was just one of a throng of people who grew fat of the sale of women and children. The Chicago Vice Commission wrote:

> Some of the profit sharers must be dispensed with
> through the force of public opinion or by means of

heavy penalties, before the growth of vice can be checked. These include those who profit off the place - the landlord, agent, janitor, amusement dealer, brewer, and furniture dealer; those who profit off the act - the keeper, procurer, druggist, physician, midwife, police officer, and politician. [CVC, 231]

In a 1894 expose of prostitution conditions on the Levee, William Stead publically humiliated brothel landlords by publishing their names in his book, *If Christ Came to Chicago*. He also published a map showing the location of brothels in the one hundred block of Customs House Place. [Stead, map] Luigi had his home and his business in this block several years before, in 1886. But by the time of Stead's book came out in 1894, he had relocated to 12th and State, The 200 block of Customs House Place, where Luigi was subleasing houses to madams, is tantalizingly absent from the map. But in any event, Luigi would have neatly escaped the public humiliation of having his name published on the list. He was hidden from view as an invisible sublessor, because he was subletting to madams property he was renting from the Chicago Western and Indiana Railroad. In that panel house cleanup Wooldredge performed, in which he netted Tillie Madison in 1898, indictments were also handed down to property owners who rented these houses out. [Wooldredge, 46]

I shared my research findings on Luigi's bankruptcy with Tim Samuelson, who marveled, "You just keep finding amazing information on this project. It's eerie."

"That guy was a crook who left a paper trail a mile long after him," I snorted.

Luigi profited from prostitution as a brothel landlord. He skimmed off the labor of poor immigrants, whose money he banked and spent on himself. He was a big man around town, a man given a place of respect in huge parades, the Treasurer of the Christopher Columbus Society and the president of the Italian Sharpshooters Society. He was armed with an arsenal of 100 rifles which he kept for the Sharpshooters. He was rumored to have ties to sinister secret societies. He knew both Emilio and G.S. de Stefano, fellow labor padrones who counted gangster Big Jim Colosimo among their family members. He ran a saloon in the crummiest part of town, tucked in between brothels. This is the father of the man my grandmother went to Chicago with. What kind of man raises his children in the heart of depravity? Luigi was a master parasite, who lived with his family in the same cesspool he worked in - the Levee, Chicago's red light crime district, where you could do whatever you wanted, as long as you made your pay offs to the police.

This is the man who raised a family of crooks in Satan's Mile. And one of those sons, Tony Coglioni, brought my Grandmother and my Dad to Chicago. When I took a closer look at the Coglioni family, it wasn't too hard to figure out what Tony had in mind for her.

Row of dives on the Levee

Boys shooting craps

Chapter Nine

❧ ❧ ❧ ❧ ❧ ❧ ❧

Children of Satan's Mile

In 1886, when that reporter visited Luigi Coglioni's store, that was at 151 Customs House Place. This block is now renamed Federal St., stands between Polk and Harrison and is part of Printer's Row. Detective Wooldredge, wrote:

> Here at all hours of the day and night women could be seen at the doors and windows, frequently half-clad, making an exhibition of themselves and using vulgar and obscene language [Wooldredge, 482-3]

They were in all states of undress, including "the garb which nature gave them when they were born" [Wooldredge p. 483]. Wooldredge observed prostitutes here soliciting passersby with what he called "indecent gestures and remarks." They offered services he described as involving "every low and demoralizing phase of life that the human mind could think of."

The brothels, according to William T. Stead's map, were located mainly on the even side of the street. Across the street was Luigi

Coglioni's "grocery," where upstairs he raised his family of growing boys.

The Coglioni's neighbor was brothel madam and white slaver Mary Hastings, who lived across the street at 144 Customs House Place, beginning in 1888. [Asbury, 118] There she held "Circus Nights" several times a month, featuring a floor show of sex acts. She bragged that no customer could think up something her girls couldn't perform. [Asbury, p. 118-9]

Hastings made hefty payoffs to the officer on the beat and police detectives and captains at the Harrison Street Station. When she once complained the payments were too high, a police captain was reported to have replied, "Why, damn you, what are you made for but to be plundered?" [Asbury 118] Hasting also paid Aldermen Kenna and Cougliin. Some of that money went into a defense fund for Kenna/Coughlin supporters, who kept two attorneys on retainer at $10,000 per year. [Wendt and Kogan, p. 79]

Kidnapped girls escaping from Hastings' brothel with sheets they tied together to form a rope

Satan's Mile

By 1893, Luigi had moved his padrone/grocery/saloon business *and* his family into the 1100 block of State St., between Taylor and 12th now called Roosevelt Rd. [City Directories] Now the family was straddling two even tougher areas of the Levee.

The Coglionis were just a block south of Hell's Half Acre, which ran the block of Satan's Mile, or State Street, between Taylor and Polk. Hell's Half Acre housed brothels, saloons, gambling dens, and assignation hotels used by streetwalkers. Detective Wooldredge's described this part of his beat:

> It was a continual scene of revelry, debauchery, depravity and every sin and crime in the blood stained catalog of vice. . . The most defiant and reckless characters that ever menaced society made it their home . . . It was a hotbed of crime and a cesspool of vice. . . In 1893, 1894 and 1895 there was no place in Chicago or the whole country that could compare with it in depravity. [Wooldredge, p. 313]

Nice place to raise a family. The area was so tough that the police were reluctant to enter.

A block away, between State and Plymouth Court lay "Dead Man's Alley." Here unsuspecting tourists were cornered and robbed, men who had just arrived in town at the Dearborn Train Station at Dearborn and Polk. Kitty Adams was a "strong arm woman" known as "The Terror of State Street, who worked with Jennie Clark, a pretty woman who lured men into alleys. There Adams would be waiting to jump on their latest victim from behind, grab him in a head lock and stick a razor to his throat, while Clark plucked his valuables. [Wooldredge, p. 122-3] [Asbury, 112-113]

Kids running down Dead Man's Alley would come across a hundred or more people engaged in

> pitching quoits and horseshoes, some in dog fighting, card playing, crap shooting and telling filthy and vulgar stories, while others lay on the garbage boxes or in the old hacks and slept off the effects of a night's dissipation. [Wooldredge 316]

Just imagine the Colgioni kids hanging out with that pack. One evening, Detective Wooldredge appeared with a detail of policemen, inadvertantly causing a stampede.

The part of Satan's Mile where the Coglioni's were actually living was called "Coon Hollow," which ran south of Taylor. Detective Wooldrege noted that the tough saloons there were the resort of "the most desperate burglars, thieves and sure-thing gamblers. Midnight thieving raids were planned in the back rooms; the criminal went there for protection; and in the neighborhood were 'fences' and pawnshops in which stolen property was disposed of." [Wooldredge, p. 315]. Imagine what the Coglioni children saw going on in their street as they were growing up. Brawls were a daily event. Gambling such as craps, stud poker and policy "were conducted openly and in defiance of the law." Pullman porters and dining car workers from the nearby train depots hung out on the streets during their lunch hour and after work, and told "filthy stories in the hearing of all who walked along and sang ribald songs." In the evening, well-to-do slummers "arrived at all hours of the night in their cabs and hacks" to buy "painted females, half-clad in finery . . . women of all ages, colors and degrees of depravity. . ." who went from saloon to saloon with their escorts, holding "high carnival . . . singing and making coarse jests." [Wooldredge p. 315]

In addition to being a crime-infested part of town, the area was also an Italian neighborhood of densely populated tenements. There were churches, schools, groceries, and drug stores peppered in and amongst crooked enterprises. Rapid transit on the Levee was provided by a horse drawn car that ran on Dearborn Street, and a cable car that ran on Clark Street. But with all that crime going on, kids like the Coglionis could get a leg up on illegal trades, right in their own backyard. Wooldredge wrote,

> Even the children here were taught to steal. Barefooted boys would rush out and jump on the footbars of the street cars as if to steal rides, and then snatch pocketbooks from women. [p. 122]

By the time my Grandmother arrived in 1916 with my toddler Dad, the Coglioni kids were all adults. With a father like Luigi raising children in the worst neighborhood in Chicago, I had to know: what do the children of Satan's Mile become when they grow up?

Census records told me Tony came from a family of eight kids who lived in a rented apartment above Luigi's "grocery." The U.S. Commission of Labor, studied the Levee a few years after Tony was born in 1891. They called it "one of the most openly and flagrantly vicious in the civilized world," and a "Nursery of Crime." They wrote

TYPICAL LOT BELOW STREET LEVEL

> Little idea can be given of the filthy and rotten tenements, the dingy courts and tumble-down sheds, the foul stables and dilapidated outhouses, the broken sewer-pipes, the piles of garbage fairly alive with diseased odors and of the number of children filling every nook, working and playing in every room, eating and sleeping in every window-sill, pouring in and out of every door, and seemingly literally to pave every scrap of yard. [Schiavo, 34]

Tuberculosis was rampant, along with deformity and high child mortality. There were babies who looked "starved and wan," like that "solemn-eyed baby" at Stefano's. [Schiavo, p 34]. The City Homes Association also studied conditions on the Levee, where Italian immigrants lived for the cheap rents. They wrote,

> The Italians . . . have lost to criminality many
> children. . . Thousands of . . . Italian children are
> growing up in tenements inhabited by the
> wretchedly poor, by drunkards, criminals and
> immoral women. Almost every word these
> growing children hear and every action they see
> corrupts their minds and destroys forever their
> purity of hearts. No one who becomes a part of the
> life of these tenements can escape the contaminated
> and corrupt atmospheres. [City Homes, 149]

What does it do to children to grow up in the midst of
prostitution, gambling, drinking and drug use? In 1910, the
Chicago Committee on Vice found that children witness "scenes
of depravity through the windows of their houses," at all hours,
and "become familiar with scenes of debauchery and drunkenness
until they are careless and indifferent." [CVC p. 237] The
Commission also reported

> Bad home conditions often drive the daughters of
> the family into prostitution and the sons into lives
> of crime. In such cases the parents are indifferent
> or ignorant. They allow their children to seek
> improper amusements without question or
> guidance. [CVC, 245]

Even conscientious parents on the Levee could not prevent their
children from being constantly exposed to the brothel trade, while
playing in the streets and alleys, going to stores, or even walking
to school. Kids were surrounded not only by prostituted women
and girls, but also pimps, procurers and madams, the industry
managers, who knew how to transform a neighborhood girl into a
cash cow. The Chicago Vice Commission investigators observed
such scenes as a prostitute luring "two boys in knee pants to enter
and offering as an inducement 'two for a quarter.'" [CVC, p. 238]

The Levee was also a playground for pedophiles, who sexually
assaulted young boys and girls. [CVC, p. 240] The Commission
found there were

men are afflicted with chronic venereal diseases, who have a superstition that they can be cured of their trouble by transferring it to a virgin. Many prostitutes have this same belief. As a result innocent children, both boys and girls, have been contaminated.

Photo Library of Congress

And in fact, the Commission discovered that in a twenty-seven month period of time in the Cook County Hospital, 600 children *under the age of twelve* were treated for syphilis and gonorrhea. [CVC, 241] Also contributing to the spread of venereal disease were overcrowded living conditions, often supplied by the padrone, in which entire families resided in a single room, whose daughters were sexually assaulted by fathers, uncles and boarders. [Addams, 1910: 296]

Many Levee children and teenagers were also working out on the streets and bars, selling flowers, matches, gum, newspapers and shining shoes. [Bilek, 33, 34] Many of them were sent out by child padrones, like Jim Colosimo was as a kid. Messenger boys ran errands at all hours for prostitutes, fetching carry outs from restaurants and running to drugstores to fetch toiletries, cocaine, morphine and needles, which some curious boys sampled for themselves. [CVC, p. 242, 243].

Tony Coglioni

When Dad told me Tony was a "minor Mafioso," did he mean bootlegging, or was he being cryptic about another dimension to Tony's illegal activities? Bootlegging didn't come to Illinois until 1919 and my Dad and Minnie got to Chicago in 1916. The following year, when Tony filled out his 1917 draft card, he claimed exemption from military service because he supported "a sister and her child." Tony did have one a sister, according to census records, but she was divorced, childless and living with her parents. In all likelihood Tony was referring to Minnie and my Dad, when he claimed exemption from military service. And whether he was actually supporting them, in what my Dad described as "a boom and bust existence" is debatable.

Dad told me about some choice advice Tony had given him one time, when Dad was five years old and had gotten into a fight with some other boys. He came running into the basement workshop with a bloody nose, after another kid had lobbed a brick at him.

"Get the other kid back good!" Tony hissed.

Dad picked a hammer up from the worktable, ran back outside and broke the other kid's nose. The *vendetta.* Christ! You could just see where that kind of parenting was going to lead.

So what was Tony up to all that time from 1916 to 1919? What was his racket? It was hard to imagine he didn't have one. He did have an official job as a railroad clerk. However, it was often the case that men in labor racketeering, like Luigi, would put friends and relatives into jobs that had no duties to speak of, but yielded a paycheck and perks. When I looked at the lives of Tony's brothers and sister, I found that six out of the eight had some kind of documentable nefarious activity.

Raymond

Two of the older brothers helped Luigi in the family "grocery." In addition to helping his father, one of those brothers, Raymond, also opened up his own pool room in 1923, at 12th and Wabash, just around the corner from the grocery. [Chicago Telephone Book, 1922].

What kind of a place was a Levee pool hall? It was a smoke filled joint with several billiards tables, that attracted all kinds of Levee characters: pool hustlers facing each other down in tournaments, "the sporting crowd," and "every type of con man, racketeer, grifter, pimp and just plain bum." [Waller, 56] Illegal gambling was the main event, with games like poker, craps, and roulette. You could also buy numbers tickets, place off-track bets, get in on baseball pools or play slot machines. Young boys were a frequent sight at billiards parlors in the vice district, where they were observed smoking, playing slots and getting schooled in illegal activity by thugs hanging out there. [Thrasher, 96]

Green screen photo for the movie - LOC

During Prohibition, perhaps the Coglioni family hooch may have been for sale at Raymond's pool hall, too. When saloons were shut down by the Volstead Act, U.S. Representative La Guardia observed that liquor was clandestinely served in "delicatessen stores, pool rooms, drug stores, millinery shops, private parlors, and 57 other varieties of speak-easies selling liquor and flourishing. " [LaGuardia]   And what about the Coglioni "grocery," that Luigi ran, with Raymond's help?   Luigi was still operating his business, until he died in 1925.   [CT, Obituaries, Feb 15, 1925]   What happened to that saloon during Prohibition? They wouldn't have been selling Italian specialties like Coglioni hooch under the table in the "grocery," would they?

Signora Colgioni

Tenement living ⌐photo Library of Congress

Luigi became a widower after Tony's birth in 1891, but six years later, he fathered two more sons, with his second wife, an Italian gal, who would have been brought into the family to raise Luigi's half dozen, half-grown kids. So what was Signora Coglioni up to? If she were a typical Italian wife, she'd have been expertly stoking a wood stove, simmering some spicy southern Italian food all day long back in their apartment, while tending babies and helping out downstairs in the "grocery." Luigi's second wife was referred to in his 1900 bankruptcy. That guy, who had been bilked out of his life savings, swore that Luigi had hidden his assets under that second wife's name.

How much did she know about what her husband, her kids and step kids did? Antoinette Giancana, daughter of Chicago crime boss Sam Giancana, revealed that business was a forbidden topic of discussion in her family, proclaiming it was "a real no-no." That was to protect the Giancana women from prosecution and keep them safe. That way they wouldn't have to rat on their own family in a courtroom or be sentenced for contempt if they refused to talk. [Giancana, 20]

An Italian Mafioso *pentito*, who had been a bank robber and killer before he turned informer, confessed why he kept things secret from his wife. "When we first got married, she would always ask. Then I convinced her never to ask me to explain anything. Because she was a woman and I did not want her to get involved in my life. I tell her, she tells a friend; because women mutually confide anything can happen. On occasion, when I told her, listen, I did this or that, she would burst into tears. Either way, I lose! " [La Sorte, 2007]

Luigi and Anna's two younger sons each had a brush with the law. The older brothers had no arrest records, not necessarily because they were not involved in illegal activity. Rather, they may have been more savvy because their father was still operating his well-oiled, nefarious activities at full tilt when they grew into adulthood. You can still see, even in the illegal careers of the younger brothers, that someone was at work on their behalf behind the scenes. As Al Capone explained, "Your brother or your father gets in a jam. What do you do? Do you sit back and let him go over the road without trying to help him? You'd be a yellow dog if you did."

Edward

Edward was the baby of the family, born in 1902, who was listed in the 1920 census as an eighteen year old railroad clerk, just like Tony. But he got into trouble in 1923, when he was facing charges of armed robbery, along with two other young guys, twenty-two year old Thomas Leahy and eighteen year old Gerard Nisivaco. A Grand Jury indicted the three men for an incident at the office of the Wartburg Publishing House, a Lutheran concern that published stuff like hymnals. According to the indictment, they were accused of "violently, by force and intimidation," robbing a guy working in the office, at gunpoint, to the tune of several hundred dollars. [Grand Jury Indictment]

Another Levee street

The tortured legal twists and turns that followed in Edward's case, illustrate how a court case was "fixed," so that none of the defendants actually had to serve any time. First, the case was continued four times over the next four months, at the request of the defendants. Then through a series of changes of venue, again requested by the defendants, the case moved through four courts, finally landing in Judge Lindsay's. Now seven months after the crime, the States Attorney offered a plea bargain, dropping the armed robbery count against the three. Nisivaco and Leahy pleaded guilty to Grand Larceny and were sentenced to restitution and a year probation. Not bad considering they started out charged with armed robbery. Even for Grand Larceny, they weren't even going to have to do a minute of time.

Edward Coglioni, initially accepted the plea bargain. But then a few weeks later, in a bit of legal trickery, he changed his plea to not guilty, waived his right to a jury trial, and was found not guilty by the *judge*. Clearly, Edward had really good connections. There were standard rates for various crimes with the First Ward Aldermen's fixer, who would then pay the judge a portion of the money to let the defendant off. Of course, the fixer got some of the bribe, too, and the aldermen got the rest. [Bilek, 277]

The two crooks that Edward went on that armed robbery junket with, both went on to lead lives of crime. Thomas Leahy violated his parole and did hard time in Joliet prison. Two years later, he was paroled, violated his parole again and was sent back to prison. Finally, he got out nine years later in 1933. But shortly after that, he reportedly walked into a bar with a friend, who held up the bartender at gunpoint. As luck would have it, a police detective was sitting at the bar and shot Leahy's friend, who died a week later in the hospital. Leahy himself was recaptured by the police. [CT, August 15, 1933].

The other man, Nisivaco managed to get through his period of parole, but was then convicted several times later for heroin dealing. In 1952, when he was fifty years old and just getting out of the joint for the third time, he bragged to the press that he had once been a member of the Capone gang and had lived at the Metropole Hotel. Of course, by this time, Big Al had been dead of syphilis for five years. [CT, April 11, 1952]

John

The other young son of Luigi and his second wife was John. And he was the only Coglioni brother who actually did time in prison. Six years younger than Tony, John plodded along in an uneventful career as a taxi driver, until he grew to be a portly, middle-aged man, with big, droopy eyes and jowls. Then things got interesting when he served as a First Ward poll clerk for the Democratic Party. By this time, Hinky Dink Kenna, had long retired. But Democratic Alderman John Coughlin, was still wheeling and dealing, still representing the First Ward's Levee and Loop in 1936, having pretty much put himself in office in 1893 and every election after that until he dropped dead.

Coughlin was famous for election tampering and he did it with the likes of men like John Coglioni, who was convicted of election fraud for wrongdoing during that 1936 primary.

Perhaps John Coglioni had been under the impression that he had that rap "fixed," because he hadn't served any time nine months later, when he was arrested by a couple of sheriffs at his home at 13th and S. Michigan Ave. John, along with another election clerk and two election judges, were all sentenced to a year behind bars. They appealed and received reduced sentences of 90 days in the county jail. [CT, June 24, 1938] Apparently, he did the time. Who knows exactly what those election officials did, but voting the dead in cemeteries, voting resident aliens found in flop houses, and voting non-residents of Chicago found in Levee assignation hotels, were all popular ways to tamper with local elections. A Chicago judge ordered 700 such registered voters struck from the First Ward roster in 1914. [Bilek, 169]

Chain voting was another fraudulent technique favored by Coughlin. Ballots pre-marked "Bathhouse John Coughlin" would disappear from the polling place. They would be issued to illiterate "voters" who would pull a switcheroo, in the privacy of the voting booth. Then they would turn in the pre-marked ballot. When they exited the polling place, they turned in the blank ballots they had smuggled out to First Ward precinct captains, who paid the voter for their trouble, sometimes in booze because saloons were closed on voting day. This blank ballot was then filled out for Coughlin and turned in at the polling place, by another paid voter. Or even at another polling place, by the same voter. [Behr, 175-6] Such First Ward election tactics prompted Al Capone to quip, "Vote early and vote often."

Conclusion

Here was an Italian American family, with what appeared to be legitimate jobs and businesses, whose members also ran parasitic or downright illegal activities. During Prohibition, several Coglionis including Tony were also involved in bootleg manufacture in the Illinois Perfume Company. And the family made protection payments for bootlegging operations andperhaps also for the sale of liquor in blind pigs, like the family grocery and billiards parlor, operating on the South Side in Mob territory. No Colgionis were ever arrested for anything, except those two youngest sons. There were a few more Coglionis, all involved in bootlegging one way or another. Some of them also crossed paths with Minnie and my Dad.

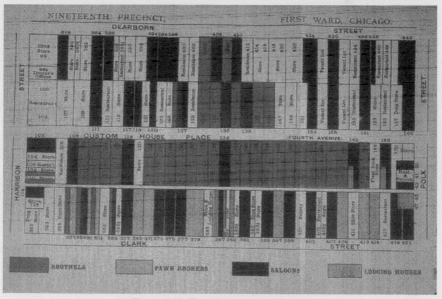

William Stead's 1894 map of the Levee

Luigi's grocery was located at 151 Customs House Place

Gettin' it while the gettin's good!   photo: *Library of Congress*

Chapter Ten

ờ ờ ờ ờ ờ ờ ờ

The Illinois Perfume Company

Yes, the Coglionis must have been a pretty interesting family with Tony making hooch on the South Side, Luigi selling it under the table along with Italian cheeses in the "grocery," Raymond presiding over his billiards parlor full of crooks, the baby of the family getting arrested for armed robbery and the other young brother fixing the election. And then when Prohibition came along, more Coglionis rolled up their sleeves and got busy, working in Torrio turf, which later became Al Capone territory.

Prohibition

The Federal Volstead Act went into law in 1920, making it illegal to manufacture, sell or transport alcoholic beverages. Booze, except for beer, had already been outlawed nation-wide, in 1918. That was so grain could go for food instead of liquor, during the last of the Great War. In 1919, Chicago itself went completely dry along with the rest of the State of Illinois , one year before Federal

Prohibition went into effect, on January 20, 1920. But no matter how many laws were passed, no one could legislate people's desire for the forbidden substance. Thus was born the wild world of speakeasies, gangsters, turf wars, bootlegging and moonshining.

Before Prohibition came along, nurses, social workers, and religious community organizations such as the Salvation Army, were dealing with the serious problems resulting from families headed by drunks. When fathers squandered the family paycheck in bars or lost their jobs for being constantly drunk, mothers and children went cold and hungry and couldn't afford medical care. Of course, plenty of married women worked, but the starvation wages women were paid for unskilled labor did little to make ends meet, for a family with children. Women and children often suffered domestic violence when breadwinners came home drunk.

The proponents of Prohibition thought, take away the liquor, and you take away the problem. But, the manufacture of alcohol is not rocket science. It's easy to cook some up at home, on the farm, and in illegal factories. To make hard liquor, you add yeast and sugar to corn mash, ferment it for a week, and then distill it. Equipment was basic. A pot or large vat for fermentation. Fire and some copper tubing for distillation. Bottles or canning jars for the finished product. Thus the manufacture of alcohol went underground with ease.

Al Capone quipped, "I am like any other man. All I do is supply a demand." A gigantic Black Market sprang up almost overnight. Illegally manufactured liquor popped up everywhere. So did speakeasies and blind pigs, which were legitimate businesses that offered their customers booze under the table. Drinking acquired a new glamour and mystique it didn't deserve.

Prohibition unleashed a host of unforeseen ills, spawning mobsters, turf wars, rum running, moonshining, bath tub gin, and sickness and death from unregulated poisons sold as hooch. People switched from beer to hard liquor, because that's what speakeasies offered. Or they drank needle beer, which was near beer - legal because it had no alcohol - that was then spiked in the speakeasy with a syringe full of "whiskey." In both cases, it got people drunker, faster.

Only 6 more days left til Prohibition kicks in

The Mob

Passing the baton

It's a relay race. A big, hulking bear of a man is running at the head of a pack of crooks, wearing an impeccable white suit with diamond studs on his shirt. A bunch of hard-faced men run behind him, in tailored suits and fedoras, their wide ties flapping in the wind. Suddenly a pistol is raised and a shot rings out. The guy in white drops to the ground. His dark eyes stare down eternity.

Improbably a nondescript man with middle age pudge, wearing a bowler hat and trench coat, leaps over the white bulk and takes over the lead.

He leaps behind the wheel of a moving Model T. The pack of crooks jump onto the running boards and hang off the car, with their Thompson submachine guns blazing. They pick off other cars following them. Bodies fly off the automobiles into the streets and drip blood into the sewers. The plain guy takes a hit, swerves down an alley, crashes and a Packard takes the lead.

A young, fat man, with a big scar on his cheek and a grin on his puss, sits in the back with thugs on either side. They screech to a halt in front of the office of the Mayor of Cicero. A police officer looks on as the fat guy rushes up the marble stairs, grabs the Mayor, and slaps him down the steps.

Prohibition was a boon to crooks. With the Mafia at the helm, the illegal market in bootleg liquor boomed. U. S. Representative La Guardia remonstrated that instead of generating taxes, the wealth generated from selling booze on the Black Market went "into the pockets of bootleggers and in the pockets of the public officials in the shape of graft." [La Guardia]

The huge profits of bootlegging made the Mob rich, fat and unstoppable. In Chicago, the power Big Jim Colosimo had accumulated before his execution, was consolidated and expanded – first under Johnny Torrio's stranglehold, then under Capone's full nelson. The Mob could afford to buy any city official they wanted, who had a price tag hanging off of him. Mobsters operated their business with impunity, outside the law. Over seven hundred men were gunned down in the Chicago Beer Wars. That included Johnny Torrio himself, who took five bullets in a hit by the Bugs Moran gang in 1925.

Johnny Torrio was ruthless. But he dressed like a banker and kept a low profile. He was soft spoken and plain. He didn't smoke, drink, or swear. He kept regular business hours. He came home to his wife every evening, to their apartment on S. Clyde Ave where he changed into slippers and they played pinochle or listened to opera records after dinner. Mrs. Torrio declared he was "the best and dearest of husbands," and that their marriage was "one long, unclouded honeymoon." [Schoenberg, 62] Yeah, right. Except for that day in 1925, when her husband was shot 5 times in front of their apartment, when they were coming home from a shopping trip and the family dog was killed in the fray.

So, if he didn't have expensive taste and went home every night for a quiet evening with his wife, what was he in it for? Power. Torrio was a killer. He murdered Colosimo's Black Hand extortionists. Torrio managed Colosimo's brothels, where he exploited women to death. He himself was arrested for heading a white slavery ring, that operated in New York, Milwaukee, St. Louis and Chicago. But prosecuting attorney Clifford Roe found insufficient evidence to convict Torrio. Maurice Van Bever and his wife Julia, however, who supplied Colosimo brothels, were both convicted. Finally, Torrio had Big Jim executed with a bullet in the back of his head, giving new meaning to the term "hostile takeover."

It's often written that Torrio knocked off Big Jim, because Colosimo didn't want to plunder the profits from illegal booze, and just wanted to play with his new wife. But hard liquor and wine had already been made illegal in 1917 and 1918, during the Great War in Chicago. And then in 1919 the entire State of Illinois went dry, one year before the rest of the country. So Prohibition had already been going on in Illinois for some years. As for wanting to play with his new wife, Colosimo and Winter had already been carrying on a love affair for six years, so there was no novelty in that.

Torrio's booze was sold to speakeasies, along with "protection" from the law. Torrio paid out an estimated $30,000 a week in graft, which led him to assert, "I own the police." [Allsop, 66]

Torrio also contributed heavily to the election campaigns of corrupt Mayor "Big Bill" Thompson, under whose leadership Chicago experienced a break down of law and order. The $30 K per week Torrio doled out went not just to police, but also to city officials, aldermen, the Mayor and Prohibition agents. Even Governor Len Small got his share for dishing out pardons, through the State Board of Pardons and Paroles, for Torrio's convicted felons - like Jack and Anna Guzik. In fact in the eight years of his incumbency, Small pardoned 950 convicted felons, in a direct purchase program operated under-the-table. [www.homicide, 18] Nearly half of Torrio's workforce were paroled and pardoned convicts. [Asbury, 325-6] Torrio retooled them into bootleggers.

By 1923 the "Beer Wars" were well under way, between Torrio and Dion O'Banion, Spike O'Donnell, the Gennas, and Bugs Moran. The conflict was characterized by the kind of mob violence Chicago became famous for: hijacked trucks, bombings, kidnappings and murders. In 1925 Johnny Torrio himself was shot five times in the neck, chest, arm, and groin, in an execution attempt by bootlegger Bugs Moran and his gang. Moran attempted to deliver the coup de grace, by aiming his pistol at Torrio's head point blank, but found he was out of bullets.

Torrio, covering up his neck wound

After a month-long stint in the hospital, Torrio was installed in prison for nine months, after his conviction for violating the Volstead Act at the Sieben Brewery. Upon his release he spent some time in Italy, but then retired back to New York. It's thought he functioned as bootlegger emeritus to the Mob there, run by an old Five Points Gang pal - Lucky Luciano.

When Torrio left Chicago, he handed the reins over to twenty-five year old Al Capone, who consolidated Colosimo's and Torrio's empires into an unstoppable syndicate. [Binder, 9, 27] Capone found small suburban governments easier to own than the City of Chicago, and moved many of his vice resorts to places like Cicero, where he rigged elections through violence and intimidation. Much of Capone's booze was manufactured in Wisconsin, or brought in from Canada to northern Wisconsin, where Capone and his brother Ralph had north woods retreats. [Hollatz, 71, 81]

Big Al was a native New Yorker, the son of Italian immigrants. In 1919 Capone came to Chicago at age twenty, and looked up Johnny Torrio. In New York, Capone actually had worked for Torrio as an errand boy, when Torrio was a member of the tough Five Points Gang and Capone was a Five Points Junior. When Capone got into hot water in New York, he started over in Colosimo's operation, with a job Torrio gave him as a bouncer in a brothel.

By 1923 Capone was running a brothel, in the South Side "Tenderloin" at Indiana and 24,[th] a shabby, brick two-story with peeling paint. "Al Brown," as he like to call himself, was coming down the stairs, just as eyewitness Irle Waller and his friends were going up. The group passed "a swarthy, heavy-set fellow with hairy arms, and with part of a hairy chest also exposed - the weather was quite warm - and a long ugly scar diagonally across his left cheek." Inside under the light of a single bulb which hung from a wire in the ceiling, was a dilapidated parlor with bare floors, a few kitchen chairs, and a half dozen young women, wearing high heels and dressed in "flimsy undergarments called 'chemises' or 'Teddy Bears.'" In the back and upstairs were tiny cubicles called "cribs," which were furnished with a narrow bed, a pitcher of water and a basin, soap and a towel. "She would ask did you want the first-class job, which was three dollars, or the two-dollar 'trick,' also about venereal protection with a twenty-five cent rubber. When you finished she would bring out a small coin container for any extra gratuity you might wish to deposit for her alone. " [Waller, 88]

When Capone took over, he bought everyone in the City government who was for sale.

I got nothing against the honest cop on the beat. You just have them transferred someplace where they can't do you any harm. But don't ever talk to me about the honor of police captains or judges. If they couldn't be bought they wouldn't have the job.

WANTED:
PUBLIC ENEMY #1
ALPHONSE GABRIEL CAPONE

DESCRIPTION:

Born: January 17, 1899 **Birthplace:** Brooklyn, NY **Height:** 5'9" **Weight:** 225 lbs.

FBI Bulletin 3 JC 31178F CN-G 61551   **Issued by:** J. Edgar Hoover   **Dated:** June 15, 1931

But once he had bought them, he was then on intimate terms with how rotten they really were. He expressed his contempt like this:

A crook is a crook, and there's something healthy about his frankness in the matter. But any guy who pretends he is enforcing the law and steals on his authority is a swell snake. The worst type of these punks is the big politician. You can only get a little of his time because he spends so much time covering up that no one will know that he is a thief. A hard-working crook will-and can-get those birds by the dozen, but right down in his heart he won't depend on them - hates the sight of them.

Coglioni Cousins

There was another Coglioni cousin, who lived in that same brownstone on So. Michigan. Tim Samuelson found a Charles Coglioni listed at the same address, in that same 1922 phone book, where he also ferreted out this gem of information: Charles worked for the Illinois Perfume Company at 3713 Wentworth Ave., a half mile from the brownstone on Michigan Ave.

"That's suspect!" Tim announced, grinning.

"What do you mean?" I asked.

"Oh, yeah! There's a nice job!" Tim proclaimed sarcastically. "Perfumers could get industrial alcohol during Prohibition. It was an easy matter to rebottle it for the streets."

Yeah. When I thought about it, the name did sound dubious. The *Illinois* Perfume Company. Ha, ha, ha. The Oriental Nights Perfume Company, yes. The Illinois Tire Company, yes. But the Illinois Perfume Company? Could a name like that inspire glamour? It was comical, you know, the kind of name thugs would dream up. I like to pronounce it with the "s" on the end of Illinois. You know, the Illinoise Perfume Company.

Turns out that Tony and Charles Coglioni weren't the only ones who had the idea of going into the perfume business. New York City Prohibition Administrator, Chester Paddock Mills, knew just how that racket worked:

> Suppose, for example, that a manufacturer of perfumes has a permit to possess large quantities of

denatured alcohol. Were he dishonest, he might sell this alcohol, labeled as "perfume," to an equally dishonest wholesaler. Then the wholesaler sells the "perfume" to a bootlegger, who re-distills the alcohol and uses it, sparingly, in the making of intoxicants." [Time]

In the haste to satisfy the thirsty market and to make a buck, this last step – redistilling - was frequently skipped. Denatured alcohol in its original form contained poisons, as required by government regulation, to prevent people from drinking it. "Bathtub Gin" was made of denatured alcohol, that had been diluted and flavored with something like juniper berries, which is what real gin is made from. In other words, the poisons were still in the hooch when it hit the streets. A barrel of industrial alcohol cost from $300 to $400 dollars, but cut with water and flavorings like prune juice, it was worth $1000 on the Black Market. [New York Times, "Warn"]

Just a year after the Volstead Act had gone into effect, the Federal Prohibition Director for New York State, Charles R. O'Connor, remonstrated to a group of bona fide perfumers, that "many unscrupulous persons, seeking to enrich themselves at the expense of the law, saw in the diversion of alcohol from non-beverage to beverage purposes, an opportunity for enormous profits." O'Connor called into question most of the permits that had been issued that year for perfumeries, proclaiming them as "not legitimate," and gotten through "fraud, perjury and deceit." Before Prohibition, only 125 manufacturers held permits in the State but in the first year of Prohibition, a thundering herd of 3,000 manufacturers garnered permits. [New York Times, "Warn"]

Charles Coglioni wasn't too hard to find in the public record - I located him in the census. He was born in 1897 in New York, but by 1920 lived with his wife on Chicago's South Side and worked as a salesman for an importer of table goods. And then in 1922, when he was 24 years old, he lived at Tony and Minnie's brownstone on 41st and So. Michigan Ave. Since Charles was born in New York and there were no kids named Charles in Luigi's household, I figured he was probably a young cousin from another branch of the Coglioni family out East.

I discovered yet another Coglioni at the brownstone, a middle-aged cousin, named Daniel, who lived there in 1922 and 1923, according to his naturalization records and city directories. Somewhere along the line, he and Minnie's family may have crossed paths, because Daniel worked in Philly as a ladies' tailor in 1910. At the same time, he also had a brother who was a ladies' tailor, and a sister engaged in dressmaking, both working in Philadelphia. [U. S. Census, 1910] When Daniel's wife died in 1916, he headed for Chicago, sometime before 1920. [U. S. Census, 1920] By 1922, when he was just over 40, he was filling out naturalization papers there, which showed him to be a wiry, Italian guy who was 5'6," weighed 125 lbs., with black hair, brown eyes and a dark olive complexion. In those naturalization papers I found that one of his witnesses also worked at the Illinois Perfume Company.

Daniel's presence in the So. Michigan Avenue brownstone intrigued me. His occupation as a ladies' tailor is the same as Minnie's mother, who owned the *Frank Ladies' Tailoring and Dresses* shop, back in Philly. [Phila. City Directory] Daniel Coglioni was living in Philadelphia and working at the same time that Mommie and Poppie were operating their shop. So not only did Tony Coglioni have a family of cousins in Minnie's home town, but three of them, all siblings, worked in the same profession as Minnie's parents did. That might be how Minnie and Tony met.

Tony could have hopped a train to Philadelphia, with the unlimited travel pass that railroad clerks usually received as perks, to visit his Coglioni cousins in Philadelphia. [www.railroadiana] Daniel or his brother or sister might have known the Frank family, or even been employed by the Franks when they still had their shop. For sure Tony and Daniel knew each other, because they were later living in the same building in Chicago, along with young Charles Coglioni, employee of the Illinois Perfume Company. Charles may even have been a nephew of Daniel. I had certainly unearthed a lot of people who worked in ladies dressmaking in Philadelphia. I had two Coglioni bootleggers at the same Chicago address, along with a Coglioni tailor, living with my Dad and Minnie. Very interesting.

Cleaners and Dyers Connection

I also found a significant connection between the occupations of the two Colgioni cousins living at the brownstone. Before he became a bootlegger, Charles had been a salesman of table goods in 1920. Daniel, of course, was a ladies' tailor. They don't seem related, but both occupations actually had ties to the Mob in Chicago, according to Art Bilek and Bill Helmer, who wrote in the *St. Valentines Day Massacre:*

> The Granddaddy of Chicago rackets was the cleaners and dyers business, which included laundries, **tailors** and suppliers of everything from hotel bed sheets to **restaurant napkins and**

tablecloths, as well as the neighborhood shop that handled household washing and dry-cleaning. [Bilek & Helmer, 74]

How did the Mob control the cleaners and dyers business? By artificially raising prices and eliminating competition. The Mob then skimmed a percentage off of the top of the profits. You can recognize the Mafia in the violence used to bring uncooperative business owners in line or shut them down – breaking plate glass windows, detonating explosives hidden in suits in a pile of commercial laundry, beating recalcitrant business owners with a revolver or a tire iron, lobbing bombs into the store front, or if all else failed, committing murder.

The Mob also controlled truck drivers - teamsters as they were called from the days when they were horse drawn - by letting them know "whose establishment to tend." [Bilek and Helmer, 74] Uncooperative drivers were "convinced" with terrorist tactics, for example a mobster throwing gasoline onto the goods in a delivery truck and lighting it - with the driver inside. [ICS, 979 – 997] The cleaners and dyers business was so corrupt by the time Al Capone was running things, that people sent their laundry out to the suburbs, because it was a lot cheaper. [Bilek and Helmer, 74]

Tony had an older brother, Joseph, who was a teamster between 1910 and 1920. [U. S. Census, 1910, 1920] Who knows who he was delivering for? During Prohibition, he became a Deputy U.S. Marshal. That's right, Joseph worked on the other side of the law. What did a U. S. Marshal do? The Department of Justice website states they "arrested bootleggers and seized all of their equipment - cars, trucks, breweries, and warehouses." [www.usdoj] In other words, they were the principal enforcement agents during the first seven years of Prohibition. [www.usmarshals]. How did a man get a job as U. S. Marshal? Politics.

Tony's brother Joseph was a tall, portly man with big, droopy eyes and bulldog jowls. In 1925, he actually ran against incumbent Alderman Coughlin. Joseph lost out to Coughlin, who had been fixing elections and milking the vice district for all it was worth since 1893. [CT, Jan 31, 1925] No wonder Joseph couldn't win. Coughlin may have recommended Joseph for that U.S. Marshal job, as a bone thrown to him to get him to back off in that 1925 election.

It seemed unusual to me for one of the Coglioni kids to be busting up barrels of confiscated beer and padlocking saloons, while other Coglionis were making hooch. But, according to crime writer Art Bilek, "Their brothers were policemen," he wrote. "They hung out in the local politician's bar; they would drink shoulder to shoulder with policemen. It was just an entirely different world." [Bilek, Email] [Bilek, Email]

Green screen scene with Tony and his cousin making deliveries of Illinois Perfume Company hooch   Background photo: Library of Congress

A bootlegger, explained it like this: "We know the officers and they know us. You know, the same as you know football players on another team" [Callano]

After the U. S. Marshals had been on the job for seven years, they didn't appear to be making any headway against bootleggers. So the U. S. Treasury Department created the Bureau of Prohibition to enforce the law in 1927. Sure the U. S. Marshals poured plenty of booze into sewers, seized account books and padlocked saloons. That's what made paying bribes to them so appealing to the Mob.

In 1928, Treasury Agent Eliot Ness and his handpicked men were sent to Chicago. They had a special, armored truck to storm Capone breweries, you know, like you see in TV and the movies. They crashed through loading docks, busted up beer barrels and stills with axes, and chased down fleeing workers. The press called them "The Untouchables," not because they couldn't be *shot*, but because they couldn't be *bought*. [Ness] Ness grumbled that the Mob had greased so many palms, that every time they pulled off a raid, the mob had already been tipped off beforehand and Ness and his men would find "the birds have flown." He beefed, even if they did make a "pinch," the case never ended up in court. [Ness, 12]

Many U.S. Marshals and Prohibition agents, in fact, proved to be bootleggers. [Binder, p. 16] For example, one former Deputy U. S. Marshal by the name of Strook, was accused of operating the West Hammond Brewery in partnership with Johnny Torrio. Both men were convicted and paid hefty fines. Incidentally, Torrio had the brewery sheltered on paper, under a lease to his own Puro Products Company. There's a nice name ha, ha, the "Puro Products Company." Kind of reminds me of the *Illinois Perfume Company*. [ICS, 912]

Graft subsidized modest federal salaries and made possible high flying lifestyles. "I have heard of $2,000 a year prohibition agents who run their own cars with liveried chauffeurs," groused U. S. Representative La Guardia. [La Guardia] The Assistant Attorney General of the U. S., Mabel Walker Willebrandt, the woman in charge of Prohibition cases for 8 years, griped that many prohibition agents had gotten their jobs solely through political connections. That's because there were no job requirements, other than a letter from a local or state politician. She also carped that many of them were "stupid," and as short on "honesty and integrity" as the bootleggers themselves. [New York Times, "The Inside"]

Beer down the sewer

The administration of City of Chicago itself was lubricated by the bootlegging industry, which contributed heavily to elections and got payback after their man made it into office. Since the government was functioning on behalf of the bootleggers, a group of businessmen formed The Secret Six, for the purpose of putting mobsters behind bars. The chair, Robert Isham Randolph, blustered, "Chicago has the most corrupt and degenerate municipal administration that ever cursed a city – a politico-criminal alliance formed between a civil administration and a gun-covered underworld for the exploitation of the citizenry." The scheming of the Secret Six was instrumental in the appointment of an honest, capable agent like Eliott Ness to Chicago, and in the conviction of Al Capone for tax evasion. In 1931, Capone bemoaned their efficacy: "The Secret Six has licked the rackets. They've licked me." [CHE, July 30, 1931]

It's hard to tell just what kind of U.S. Marshal Joseph was, but one thing was sure, he was one busy guy. On a *single day* in 1930, Joseph closed not only the Club Algiers - which had been bombed the week before, perhaps for refusing to pay for "protection" - but also padlocked twenty-five other saloons, delicatessens, drug stores, restaurants, and malt-and-hop shops, all for Prohibition violations. [CT, March 4, 1930: 9] Joseph also arrested local official Deputy Sheriff John McCleverty, for conspiring with five others to violate the Volstead Act. Apparently, Joseph wasn't just ferreting out booze and crooked deputy sheriffs either, because on another day, after raiding a storeroom and seizing 1,000 bottles of home brew, he busted a female impersonator at a club called "Entre Nous." [CT, August 9, 1931]

Joseph also found time to chase the Capone brothers. While Florida police were arresting Al Capone, and their State's Attorney was filing a petition to padlock Big Al's Palm Island state as a public nuisance due to the presence of gangsters and alcohol, Joseph was hard at work back in Cicero. He padlocked Al and Ralph's Cotton Club and Ralph's Monmartre, for dry law violations. [CT, "Capone Free"]

A year later, Joseph raided the Capones' Cotton Club, broke open a safe with an acetylene torch, and seized a treasure trove of financial goodies, "a check book, canceled checks, account books and I.O.U's." These items were later presented as evidence in Ralph Capone's tax evasion trial. [CT, "U. S. Raid"] That might have been the same club where Andrea's father played. When Al Capone was convicted on tax evasion, he did time in a cushy, well

A peek into Al Capone's cushy jail cell. Photo courtesy of Marzena

appointed cell in Atlanta.   Two years later, Capone was among
the first prisoners to be installed in the new, no-privileges,
maximum security federal prison, where his cell was like every
one else's: bare. Capone went to Alcatraz on a cross-country
train, escorted by none other than Joseph Coglioni. [Waterloo
Daily Courier] [CDT, "Al Capone"]

Hmmm.   Must have been nice to have a brother in law
enforcement, when you worked for the Illinois Perfume
Company!

After the 1933 repeal of the Volstead Act, believe it or not, Joseph
was employed in a Loop handbook on W. Washington, a joint
where off-track bets were taken. This type of gambling was
legalized in 1927 in Illinois. And one day Joseph was walking
downtown on Wells, by the Madison St. L station, when a car

pulled up and two guys jumped out and tried to shove him into the car for a one-way ride. Colgioni, six feet tall and weighing 250 pounds dropped to the sidewalk, and squawked, "I dare you to drag me in that car!" They yanked, but couldn't budge him. So they shot him in the leg and drove off. [CT, "Former Federal Deputy is Shot by Gang in Loop," November 28, 1936, p. 2]

Not very many people survive a one-way ride, but O'Donnell gang truck driver William "Shorty" Egan did in 1923, after he was forced into the back seat of a car along with another truck driver, by Frank McErlane, who was a rival bootlegger. McErlane rode shot gun in the front seat. Literally. McErlane loaded his sawed off shot gun, dispatched the other guy with a couple of blasts and reloaded. "I guess you might as well get yours, too," he sneered at Egan and shot him in the side. "Then he gimme the other barrel right on the puss," Egan fumed. Next, McErlane climbed into the back seat, opened the door, and shoved the two men out of the car, going 50 miles an hour. The other guy was dead. But Egan rolled and passed out in a ditch of icy water and came to just as the sun was coming up. [www.crime]

Joseph Colgioni recovered from his gunshot wound and left town for Kansas City, Missouri. But two years later, after a three day drinking binge, he was fatally wounded in a domestic dispute with his wife, who shot him with his own gun when he dared her to do it. [Waterloo Daily Courier]

Deputy Who Took Capone to Prison Killed by His Wife

Kansas City. Mo.—(INS)—In 1932, Joseph Coglioni, the deputy U. S. marshal who accompanied Al Capone to prison, fled Chicago fearing gangland reprisal.

Thursday, he lay dead—shot to death by his wife.

Manufacture and Quality Control

> *They call Al Capone a bootlegger. Yes, it's bootlegging*
> *while it's on the trucks, but when your host at the*
> *club, in the locker room, or on the Gold Coast hands it*
> *to you on a silver tray, it's hospitality.* --Al Capone

Prohibition era booze was produced by an entirely unregulated industry, so the quality of bootleg and how safe it was to drink varied widely. That's why, if you were well off, you bought the bonded stuff. That was booze which had been smuggled in from other countries, where alcohol consumption was still legal. You could get Canadian whiskey, Cuban rum, or even European champagne, sporting foreign government seals to prove it had been inspected.

Some bootleggers pasted fake bonding labels on their bottles, to fool their customers into believing they were buying real government inspected booze. Here's an account of a Harlem cocktail party that served up bootleg, along with weenies and olives on toothpicks:

> Our hostess had a fine array of liquor with impressive labels on the improvised bar. Once she had recommended her bootlegger to us, but we had stopped his visits when we found his labels were often not yet dry and no two like bottles had similar tastes. Since most of the people were connoisseurs no more than we were, they eagerly drank the badly cut liquor and got high. [West]

Your average drinker bought whatever was manufactured locally and available on the black market. A lot of it was made in homes right down in Chicago, because a stinking haze of fumes from cooking, fermented mash hung over entire neighborhoods. [Allsop, 34, 35] Hooch was made where ever people could hide it from view – in the basement, the bathtub, the attic, the backyard. Booze was also manufactured in unusual locations, such as a still that had operated underneath the grease rack in a mechanic's garage in Pullman, near Chicago. [Samuelson]

Booze distilled from mash or industrial alcohol might come from stills that had lead solder or lead piping could contained toxic levels of lead. Other bootleg recipes were made from equally poisonous materials, like antifreeze, creosote, sulfuric acid and embalming fluid. [Asbury, 272-273, 283]. Industrial alcohol was by its very nature poisonous. Some bootleggers just cut to the chase, diluted, colored and flavored that industrial alcohol and turned it out on the street without redistilling it, where they made quick bucks. After all, who was going to stop them? Denatured alcohol was cut with mineral oil or soap to give it smoothness. To approximate the taste of whiskey, it might have added caramel coloring and flavoring, like oil of rye from the drugstore, or burnt sugar, (Sinclair, 1962, pp. 200-201), or even iodine, which was poisonous in large quantities. Whiskey Sours and Old Fashioned cocktails are Prohibition era recipes, designed to cover up the taste of bootleg whiskey. [Allsop, 34-5]

Jake Foot

None of these flavoring agents had any effect on the poisons contained in industrial alcohol. There was even a special name for the effects this kind of liquor: Jake Foot. And a lot of blues songs were written about it.

> I can't eat, I can't talk
>
> Been drinkin' mean Jake, Lord, now can't walk

[recorded by Austin and Lee Allen in Memphis on May 5, 1930]

Industrial alcohol physically and mentally demolished many people, who drank too much of it.

> The victim of "jake paralysis" practically loses control of his fingers. . . . The feet drop forward from the ankle so that the toes point downward. . . When he tries to walk his dangling feet touch the pavement first at the toes, then his heels settle down jarringly. Toe first, heel next. That's how he moves. "Tap-click, tap-click, tap-click, tap-click," is how his footsteps sound. [Shepherd]

Dr. Ben L. Reitman, described what he called the "peculiar psychology in the effects of the poison."

> They see four tailed elephants and green giraffes and all the other different animals so long associated with delirium tremens. And then there is a peculiar half-blindness. They look at you, but they can see only half of you -- the other half, say the upper half, simply dissolves into space. [CDT, *"Green Giraffe"*

Jake Foot was a very serious condition, which also brought about paralysis, blindness and even death. In 1927, t here were 12,000 deaths by alcohol poisoning reported in the U.S. [Mendelson and Mello, 1985]

However the Illinois Perfume Company manufactured their hooch, it was an ephemeral enterprise. It didn't exist in 1920 and by 1928, the Illinois Perfume Company was no more, and Charles and Daniel disappeared from the record in Chicago. [City Telephone Books]

Speakeasies and Blind Pigs

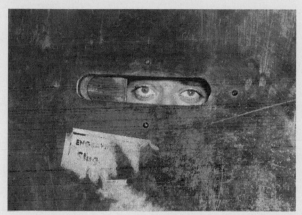
"Joe sent me"

Speakeasies were entirely unregulated, too. When taverns were legal, laws regulated the hours they could be open. But speakeasies were open day and night. All night. In saloons, women were forbidden from the barroom, as an anti-prostitution measure. A special side entrance was reserved for women to enter what was called the "family room" or "wine room," where plenty of hanky panky went on anyway. But in the deregulated world of speakeasies, women drank side by side with men. A lot more coffee was sold in the Roaring 20s, to help people sober up or to function the next day, with a hangover.

Speaks were hidden away from view in basements, attics, warehouses, and apartment houses. The entry door was locked and guarded by a lookout, who gave you "the once over" through a peephole in the door. You were supposed to *speak* the secret password, so they knew you weren't a Prohibition agent. [Yancey, 61] "Blind pigs" were places with a legitimate store front, like a vegetarian restaurant, a real estate office, a dry cleaner's, a bakery or a cigar shop, where liquor was dispensed under the table or in a secret back room. [Yancey, 62] Luigi Coglioni's grocery store could easily have been a blind pig, where you could knock back a snort of the "Italian specialties," while shopping for sheep cheese, olive oil and spaghetti noodles and do your banking. And you know who would have been making that hooch.

Restaurants also got in on the action, serving booze and charging for it in crafty ways. One diner on Coney Island was looking over his bill and noticed extra charges for a lobster and a crab, that his party hadn't ordered. That's because "lobster" and "crab" were code names for two items they did order: a Manhattan cocktail and a bottle of wine. "To cure them of the error of their ways we pinched the place," quipped the diner, who happened to be working as an undercover federal officer. [Einstein, 105]

Another New York joint, called the Wine Cellar was run by a big Italian. It was a hole-in-the wall type place that reportedly "looked like the catacombs--a series of caves leading into each other," with a sawdust floor.   Located in the Village, the cheap restaurant attracted writers, bums and the "ultra-Ritz from Pawk Avenue who went crazy about the 'atmosphere.'"

An eyewitness to the place explained how they dealt with the police. They

> kept a big bruit of a dog chained under the steps, and he had it trained to bark like hell at the sight of a blue coat and a double row of brass buttons... That pup never failed to yelp 'jiggers' when a cop snooped around, and zzst! would go the bottles into the storeroom in the back, so when they walked in, there was a nice respectable spaghetti joint. [Tramp Poet]

It was like stepping on a trapdoor to Hell, when Minnie fell into the clutches of the Coglionis. They were a family up to their eyes in questionable business practices and illegal trades. As children,

Tony Coglioni and his brothers were raised in Satan's Mile, in the midst of prostitution, gambling, saloons and organized crime. Their father Luigi was a big man around town, a Levee saloon owner and a padrone who made a parasitic living off his fellow countrymen. He profited directly from prostitution as a brothel landlord. He declared bankruptcy twice, squandered the savings of poor immigrants who had trusted him with their savings, and sheltered his property and business under his wife's name.

When his boys grew up, they helped out in their father's parasitic business on the Levee. The activities of several brothers were tied to crime. Raymond presided over crooks in a Levee billiards parlor, Edward got off scot-free when he was arrested for armed robbery, John went to jail for election racketeering, and Joseph worked on the other side of the law, at least in theory, during Prohibition. And then there was Tony and his cousin Charles, bootlegging on the South Side. The Coglionis knew how to grease the right palms to stay out of trouble with the law and use the Aldermen's fixer. The Coglioni kids grew up a the world of their father's choosing - the scummiest part of town, inhabited by poor Italian immigrants, pimps, prostituted women, madams, pickpockets, thieves, embezzlers, con-men, footpads and pedophiles.

When the Coglioni children grew to be adults, they followed in the footsteps of their father and other parasites on the Levee. Minnie and Dad didn't stand a chance.

Crashed bootlegger car, paddy wagon, plain clothes cops and spectators

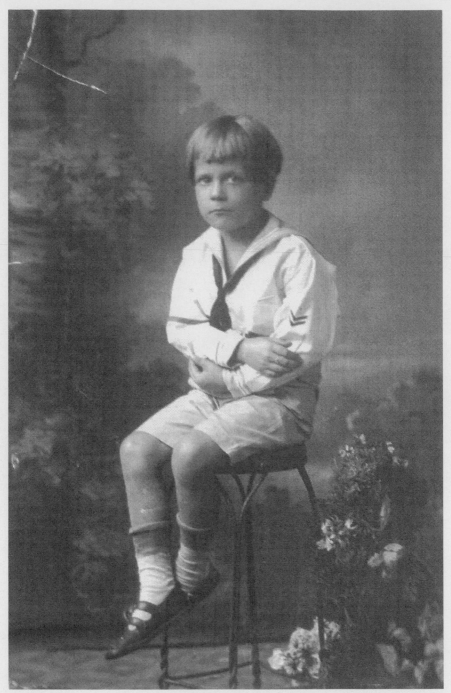

My Dad in Chicago, about four years old

Chapter Eleven

৵৵৵৵৵৵৵৵

No Life for a Child

Now that the Colgioni kids were adults, they were running the Levee they had grown up in. Dad was growing up that same world of thugs. I wondered a lot about Minnie and Dad's lives, the prostitution connection and the roller coaster of a boom and bust existence. Lily mentioned her sister Minnie's fiery disposition: "you know her temper," she wrote. That, along with their up and down finances, were just part of the reason why, according to Dad, Minnie and Tony fought a lot.

It was the emotional roller coaster of a life in prostitution that was really devastating. The relationship between prostitute and pimp is complex and sinister. It seemed unbelievable to me, but I read over and over again that pimps coerce their wives or sweethearts into prostitution. [Reitman, p. 76] [Wis Vice, p. 15-17] I read that pimps "have a high need for sadistic gratification," [Parker] In the Roaring 20's, Ben Reitman, M.D. observed that prostitutes were "not only temperamental, emotional, moody, unstable, irritable and flighty, but are often impossible." [Reitman, 22] These are precisely the characteristics of people suffering from

Post Traumatic Stress Disorder, identified many decades later as "characterized by anxiety, depression, insomnia, irritability, flashbacks, emotional numbing and hyperalertness." The same researcher found that "PTSD is normative among prostituted women." [Farley, 2004, 1104-5]

High Life, Low Life

What kind of lifestyle did they have? Reitman, himself, was in the know, as a doctor who treated pimps and prostitutes professionally in county institutions and brothels. He also enjoyed hanging out with them socially, because they liked putting on the Ritz. They dressed to the nines because they could afford it, drank giggle water, threw money around, gambled, and hung out in speaks and cabarets with the rest of the racketeers. [Reitman, 35, 92-3] They went to places like the Colosimo Café or the Black and Tan cabarets. That tallies with what my cousin Doris, my Grandmother's niece, told me once on the phone about Minnie: "She played fast and loose." Reitman related that prostitutes and pimps blew wads of cash, which also matches what Dad recalled, about living "high off the hog" one day, and "scraping the bottom of the barrel the next." Depending on how flush Minnie and Tony were at any given time, their "boom and bust existence" took them to either decent second class hotels [Reitman, 34] or shabby rooming houses or that cheap Michigan Avenue brownstone. But wherever they lived, they were surrounded by other pimps, prostitutes and racketeers.

Induction

How do pimps reel a woman in? Joe Parker, the director of an organization helping prostituted women wrote, that "a pimp is on the lookout for a certain kind of pliant person to enslave, particularly someone cut off from their families or seeking escape from an abusive family." [Parker]. In Philadelphia, Minnie was desperate and ripe for exploitation. She had been kicked out of her family home and had the responsibility of a baby to care for.

Minnie was unemployable in 1914, because she was a single mother. And she was unhappy at her older sister Olga's, because

Apache dance , a rough exhibition dance

Photo: Library of Congress

Lily wrote that she wanted to get away from them. When a pimp first meets a girl he wants to put to work, according to Reitman, he has to "put on the dog for her," and show her he is loaded and that "nothing is too good for her." [Reitman, 93] He impresses her by wining and dining her, showering her with glamorous clothes and expensive gifts. That could be how Tony convinced Minnie to go to Chicago with him, along with some choice lies, like, "Let me care a' you and the little shaver," or "I gotta line on a easy job for youse that pays a lotta dough."

Lily described it this way: "She grabbed at the first straw, which was all wrong. That was the greatest tragedy. By nature, your mother was not born for that life. . . She was not a mercenary person [i.e. a prostitute]. Only wanted love, home and family." Once Tony got Minnie and her little boy to Chicago, who was there to prevent Tony from doing whatever he wanted with her?

Drinking

With her defiant nature, Minnie had the almost superhuman strength to endure and suffer through the daily tragedies of prostitution. In addition to her personal strength, there was alcohol. She lived by the philosophy that "a dollar a day can make you a king." I found that quote in Dad's VA psychiatrist notes.

Prostitutes were expected to drink all night with customers. That's because brothels made as much or more on the sale of alcohol, as they did on selling women. The constant consumption of liquor was all in a night's work.

Jane Addams observed first-hand the death grip that alcohol had on prostitutes -

> Whoever has tried to help a girl making an effort to leave the irregular life she has been leading, must have been discouraged by the victim's attempts to overcome the habit of using alcohol and drugs. Such a girl has commonly been drawn in the life in the first place when under the influence of liquor and has continued to drink that she might be able to live through each day. Furthermore, the drinking habit grows upon her because she is constantly required to see liquor and to be 'treated' [to it]. [Addams, 1912, 188]

Pimps also use liquor to get their women to perform, because who would want to service five, ten or fifty men a day? [Reitman] Who would want to perform when they were injured or feeling sick?

Alcoholism had gotten a hold of Minnie. Dad himself told me Minnie was an alcoholic. By that time she was in her 50's, she had already been hospitalized several times for delirium tremens. My Mom described her mother-in-law as, "a drunk with a cold personality."

Money

Where's the money? Prostitutes are continually kept impoverished. It's part of the plan. Brothels keep them indebted, charging sky high prices for electricity, booze, towels, sheets, and clothing. And then on top of that, they don't get to keep the money anyway. The Philadelphia Vice Commission reported: "Their earnings are constantly taken from them by, or turned over by them to, their pimps and lovers, so that they have no money of their own." [Phila Vice, 17]

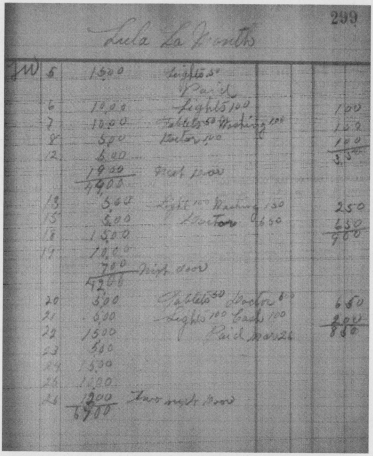

Deductions for washing, lights, medicine and doctor visits

Sex

Do a pimp and prostitute have sex together? According to Reitman it was an infrequent event, because after a woman has had 2 to 50 contacts with men a night, by morning she is exhausted and has no need for sex. Reitman also noted, no opera diva ever gave her manager more trouble, particularly at the end of the night, when she is "at the breaking point." [Reitman, 25]

Brutality

Apache dance inspired by real events on Paris streets

How does he get away with it? Reitman observed that pimping was largely a part-time undertaking - many pimps came from the ranks of bootleggers, fixers, and even policemen and police detectives. [Reitman, 41, 184] Any of these occupations would have provided an "in" with the law, which makes sense when you think about it. After all, a bootlegger would already be buying protection from those fixers, cops and detectives. Of course I knew Tony was a bootlegger from Dad's VA records. Courtroom convictions for pimps were few and far between.

What does a pimp do? He has to get his woman ready for the evening's performance, get her dolled up, get her loaded with drinks, and most importantly – lord a continuous reign of terror over her. [Reitman, p. 20] Reitman treated hundreds of women with black eyes, cut lips, skull fractures, bruises, women who had been horribly mutilated, in his words, by "their loving men." [Reitman, 44] No wonder Lily wrote, "One saw what it done to her. It completely changed her expression." Reitman noted such brutality was often followed by paroxysms of remorse, in which the pimp begged her forgiveness, shed tears, made love to her. *He beats me, he ain't no good, but I love him so.* Plenty of blues songs were inspired by that scenario.

Fifty years later, this peculiar phenomenon of human nature was identified as the "Stockholm Syndrome," named after a botched bank robbery in Stockholm, Sweden in 1973. Two robbers trapped in the

The Apache dance mimed a fight between a prostitute and pimp   Photo: Library of Congress

bank held two employees hostage, for over five days. Police were surprised to find that, as time went on, the hostages formed more and more of an alliance with the hostage takers. The hostages spoke on the robber's behalf, and even continued a relationship with them long after they were freed. [Parker]

Why don't the women just walk away? Lily wrote Minnie had "a lovely, generous nature, very sentimental. Was a beautiful girl." She added, "A girl like that is prey." She was referring to Davis, but Tony fits the bill, too.

> It is important to understand the huge psychological differences between a pimp and a person being forced into prostitution. People who become pimps typically are psychopathic and sadistic. The feelings and needs of others have no controlling effect on them. The victims, on the other hand, usually are normal, ordinary people, who feel empathy, concern, and loyalty to those around them." [Parker]

Thus, when ordinary people with good mental health are trapped in a prolonged relationship with a a pimp, they suffer "serious psychological harm." [Herman, 116]

Herein lies the ugly, hidden underbelly of prostitution. [Farley, 2007, 83] The pimp is a strange bird, a man with a Jekyll and Hyde personality. He terrorizes, brainwashes, and assaults his wife or lover, so that she will keep performing with customers and keep raking in cash – to his pockets. His deliberate actions, executed behind the scenes, are designed to inflict maximum psychological damage and yield him total control over his woman. [Phila Vice, 16] The pimp deprives her of food, sleep and medical care, threatens to harm her child, commits verbal, sexual and physical assault on her, confiscates all monies paid to her, and forces her to engage in sexual violence with johns. [Parker,]

But the pimp is not done, yet. He follows his punishing behavior with affection, gifts and treats, applying the balm of remorse, apologies, and expressions of love to the wounds his brutality has caused. This powerful combination of love and hate demolishes her will, producing "trauma bonding." [Farley, 49-50] Trauma bonding is, in fact, "one of the most potent methods of behavioral conditioning known to social scientists." It is employed in military torture, hostage situations, concentration camps, and cult initiations. Trauma bonding causes "psychological degradation and disorganization" - damage which paralyzes an individual's sense of self-preservation. [Farley, 2007, 51]

Popular thought throughout the 19th and early 20th centuries blamed the prostitute for being in prostitution, labeling her a "fallen woman," "a soiled dove," a "social outcast," with a "ruined character." [Phila Vice, 15]. But is it really any different now, when many people think that an underlying masochism leads the prostitute to live a perpetually tormented existence? The victim of sadism does indeed suffer from psychopathology that is real. That's why Lily wrote that what happened to Minnie "was the greatest tragedy." But that psychological damage is not a *preexisting* condition. Rather, it is *caused* by sadistic abuse. [Herman, 116] Lily believed, "By nature, your mother was not born for that life." And she knew Minnie better than anyone. Sadistic behavior cannot be explained or understood by examining the personality of the victim.

Women in prostitution can't just walk away from it. The pimp threatens to kill her or harm her child if she leaves, backing up his threats with assault and battery and even torture. A woman interviewed in the late 30's, explained:

> Then, when I tried to leave him, he beat me up and gave me a couple of black eyes. After that when I came in at night, he took all my money and told me he'd cut my throat if I tried to hold out on him. [Big Bess, 5]

Even if the pimp eventually disappears, the damage remains, the will is demolished. There is no self-preservation mechanism to prevent another pimp stepping in and taking over.

Children

Why didn't Minnie and Tony have other children? In order to make it possible for the woman to continue performing without the lengthy interruption of pregnancy, abortion was used as a birth control method in early 20th century prostitution. And prostitutes who had abortions usually were back performing, before they had had adequate time to rest. Since most had been exposed to gonorrhea by the time they had that abortion, the organism then traveled deeper into the body. In the days before antibiotics, this resulted in Pelvic Inflammatory Disease, a very painful condition, which caused sterility and even death. Both gonorrhea and syphilis caused miscarriages. [Reitman, 114-119]

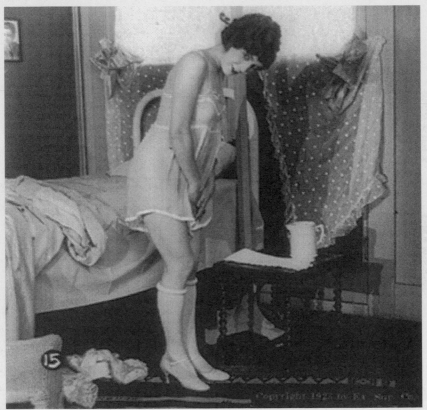

French postcard from Library of Congress

Thus, children were usually born to mothers *before* they became prostituted, as in Minnie's case. [Reitman, 115] And those children they brought with them to a life of prostitution, suffered from lack of supervision and bad role modeling. As a result, it was common for children of prostitutes to become juvenile delinquents and "third-class gangsters." And many children entered "the racket" when they grew to be adults. [Reitman, 119] Dad was left to his own devices for at night. He was in danger of growing up to be a thug, just like the racketeers in the hotels and rooming houses they lived in. Their brownstone apartment housed several bootleggers, including Tony himself. Plus, the brownstone neighborhood was, in and of itself, teeming with vice nests in cabarets, brothels, assignation flats and buffet flats.

Finally, in 1922 after six years of living together, Minnie and Tony had a knock down, drag out fight. That's when the guy my seven year old Dad thought was his father stormed out, and never came back. Exit Tony.

Freddy

Enter Freddy. You can see from this picture of Freddie, he has the good looks, fancy suit, expensive car and panache that Tony Coglioni lacked. He looks like a nice guy, but who knows what he really did or what happened to him? Bootlegging was an illegal occupation, as fraught with ingenuity as it was with violence.

A Prohibition agent discovered this strange piece of bootlegger ingenuity in Florida –

> a strip of metal to which is tacked a wooden block carved to resemble the hoof of a cow, which may be strapped to the human foot. A man shod with a pair of them would leave a trail resembling that of a cow . . . Officers believe the inventor got his idea from a Sherlock Holmes story, in which the villain shod his horse with shoes, the imprint of which resembled those of a cow's hoof. [Evening]

Violence and Bootlegging

Competition among Chicago bootlegger gangs resulted in a series of 700 murders, known as The Beer Wars. Targets ran the gamut from small time bootleggers [like Tony and Freddy] to Mob leaders, like Johnny Torrio. After his attempted assassination by the Bugs Morgan gang, Torrio took his exit cue and turned the reins over to young Al Capone. Several years later, Capone ordered the most famous hit in history - the St. Valentine's Day Massacre in 1929, killing key members of the same Moran Gang.

The Cow Shoe

Bugs Moran was not present in the garage that day, but he and Capone continued to strike at each other regularly, until Capone had to leave his bodyguards and bullet proof car behind, and go to prison in 1931 for tax evasion.

Capone died a few years after getting out of prison – of syphilis. Moran finally died of lung cancer in prison, while serving his second sentence for armed robbery in 1957.

Rum Running

In addition to manufacturing hooch, the Chicago Mob picked up booze on the shores of Lake Superior and carted it down to Chicago. This was premium booze manufactured with government seals in Canada and Europe, a boon not just to the Mob, but also to foreign wineries, breweries and distillers. For example, imports of champagne from the French Moet et Chandon winery to Canada increased ten-fold during Prohibition, because entire shiploads of it were smuggled over the U.S./Canadian border in the Great Lakes. [Behr, 130]

Large sailing vessels carrying this kind of premium hooch anchored off the shores of America on the East Coast, the Gulf of Mexico, and the Great Lakes. Their cargo was loaded onto small boats under cover of darkness. The clandestine process of ferrying it in to shore was called "rum running."

In 1923, the U.S. government seized 134 foreign ships carrying large quantities of liquor destined for American shores. The following year 236 foreign ships were seized. Feds at Sturgeon Bay, in Lake Michigan, busted the ship Geronimo, when she was carrying 4,000 cases of Canadian ale. In spite of such efforts, the Department of Commerce estimated that in 1924, $40 million dollars in liquor made it into the country anyway.

In 1930, the Feds were hunting for the Ansterborg #18 in Lake Michigan. The ship had been confiscated rum running the summer before and had recently disappeared from it's anchorage. It was found by the Coast Guard at the tip of Door County, loaded with 5,000 cases of Canadian liquor, worth $120 on the street, bringing the total value of the confiscated booze to $600,000. It was thought the ship was rum running for Capone. [CT, "Sieze"]

Capone also had it flown over the border. He had an air strip built on his country estate in northern Wisconsin near Couderay, for landing planes carrying Canadian whiskey, with those nice government seals that brought a high price when it hit the streets of Chicago. [Kyvig, 153]

Many bootleggers were enlisted to haul Canadian liquor down to Chicago over the roads. They headed up to Lake Superior, by way of Milwaukee and Green Bay, and north to Spread Eagle. Then bootleggers picked up Highway 2 going west, the only paved road up there at the time. They loaded up somewhere along the Lake Superior shore, between Hurley and west to Superior. [Richard] Bootleggers favored sturdy automobiles, like the Buick and the Ford Model A, so that the glass bottles wouldn't break on the long trip down to Chicago. They took out the back seat and stacked cases of booze on the floor. To keep the car from riding too low when it was loaded down and arousing suspicion, they installed overload springs. [Monte]

Rum Run to Superior Wis.

Bootleggers liked to soup up their engines to run at high speeds, so they could out maneuver police cars in chases. They invented high speed driving secrets, like the "bootleg turn," a trick they used to change directions instantaneously. First the bootlegger throws the car into 2nd gear, turns the steering wheel sharply into the oncoming traffic lane. The car skids, turning itself around 180 degrees and voila! The bootlegger flies off in the opposite direction. The sheriff's car in pursuit meanwhile, is still traveling in the same old direction, perhaps with the sheriff's mouth hanging open, at the bootlegger who just whizzed past them. [Monte]

I read about one flamboyant bootlegger, who drove the pilot car of a caravan of sturdy Packards and Cadillacs. Those cars were expensive, but they were the kind bootleggers could afford, because as he remarked, "only suckers work."

> I'd hang behind the loaded cars. When the patrol started chasing us I'd hold 'em up, block the road on 'em, to let the boys with the loads get away. We had a smoke-screen on the pilot car. We'd come hell-roaring down over that line and hit back roads all the way home. We had hideouts in barns and garages along the way. Some of the people we had to pay, some we just had to leave a case of beer. [Callano]

Women in prostitution were recruited to drive for bootleggers. One such woman reported,

> The gang liked me and they gave me a job driving a booze car down from Canada. I got a hundred bucks a week for three trips. When they lost some of their cars they took mine away from me [Big Bess, 3, 4]

Here's a snapshot from Dad's photo album, of Freddy the bootlegger, smirking as he raises his glass to the camera, like Franz Hals' painting, *The Merry Toper*. He looks pretty smashed, perched in front of the wooden spokes on the wheels of a 1926 Willis Knight. [Anderson] Minnie is leaning back on the running board, grinning in an expensive looking 20's flapper dress made of "scales." Imagine a seamstress cutting out and sewing all those little pieces of fabric! Dad penciled underneath it in his photo album, *Superior, Wis., 1925.*

I showed this picture to my family friend Jeanette Suchanek, and her partner, Richard, one night when the three of us had just finished a fried pork chop dinner in her kitchen in Milwaukee.

"What do you think they were doing in Superior in 1925?" I wondered.

"Rum running," Richard beamed, without hesitation.

Richard is a big, lumbering Finn in his 70's, from Superior, Wisconsin. His dad had been a policeman way up in there in Superior in the twenties, so Richard heard a lot about bootlegging growing up. With a goofy smile on his face, Richard explained, "It was difficult country up there. They would illegally import liquor from Canada. There was probably more money going up Lake Superior than down. Ha ha."

"Why is the liquor so dark in the picture?" I asked.

"Sorghum," Jeanette replied matter-of-factly. "They used it for flavor." She was in her 80's and knowledgeable on country ways, because her parents had raised her on the edge of town in Janesville, right next to farm country. There wasn't any sorghum to be had at the grocery store, but the next time I went to my local county fair, I picked up a pint jar of it. It was tasty, kind of like a cross between molasses and maple syrup. Not icky sweet, but I could see how it could improve the taste of liquor.

"So, what was going on up in Superior in 1925?" I asked Richard.

"Coal, iron ore, bootlegging," Richard ticked off the industries on his meaty fingers, like breakfast links. "And prostitution."

That last one was no surprise. I had already read that in Superior a "fixer fine" was paid by houses of prostitution directly into city coffers in the town in 1913. That fact was uncovered by the Teasdale Commission, investigating vice conditions all over the state of Wisconsin. In the transcripts of testimony, no city officials would admit under questioning that those houses of prostitution had been fined. However, the owners of the brothels told a different story. Each and every one who testified complained of having to pay $53 to the city every month to stay in business. [WLI, 177, 178, 259]

Quid Pro Quo

Richard revealed a story about hidden corruption up in Superior way back when - one that the Commission hadn't discovered. "Yeah, the Chief of Police and one of the brothel owners were good friends. In fact, the Chief was collecting a little monthly stipend. Once in a while the cop gets a little token of appreciation, you know, on Thanksgiving and Christmas." Richard rose up out of his chair, his bulk filling the small kitchen. In a sing-song voice, he mimicked the police chief, "We're looking

Captured still at Crandon Lake Courthouse - Photo Courtesy of Mike Monte

for them, the brothels. They're under investigation, but we need more money." Richard smiled and put his hand behind his back palm up, and wiggled his sausage fingers. Then he shoved his hand in his pants pocket, like he was stashing some cash. Big grin. "We're looking for brothels. They're under investigation, but we need more money." Wiggle, wiggle.

In addition to Lake Superior rum running, there were also plenty of stills cranking out moonshine up there and Richard explained how they got their supplies. "People would order 100 lbs of sugar to make booze with. It wasn't an unusual quantity for berry canning, except there aren't many berries up there." He paused for effect. "a lot of people including my family, who raised diary cattle, bought large quantities of corn because of the short growing season way up north. It would be nothing unusual to get an extra 100 pound bag or two of corn, to go with that 100 pound bag of sugar. Nobody would raise an eyebrow."

Richard's dad the cop was downtown one day in a basement storefront called the FW Club. "He wasn't there to drink soda pop," Richard quipped, his face lighting up with a smirk. "It was a speakeasy. Someone came in to get him, because apparently there was a guy driving around in circles on the main street in the middle of the intersection. My dad came up out of the speakeasy and flagged down the car.

"'What do you think you're doing?' he demanded."

"The guy replied, 'I needed a cop and I couldn't find one, so I thought if I drove around in circles, someone would go get one.'" Now that he was wound up and running, Richard told another bootlegging story, in that same, silly, sing-song voice. "My uncle was visiting someone's still up in Douglas County, in the middle of the woods. Douglas County was full of woods, more woods and if you turned around you found another tree. There were very few roads in all those woods, so the road that led to this still was one a lot of people knew about. They were all having a little party down there, including my uncle, at the bottom of a hill. All of a sudden, there were headlights and the sound of a heavy motor.

Nobody they knew had a car that big, that heavy duty. Bootleggers liked a souped up engine. Some of them would just raid a still, not bother to buy the hooch, but steal it at night when they thought no one was there. The feds liked heavy engines too, and they liked to show up unannounced. Somebody in the party had rifle, a big one, bigger than you would want to shoot a bear or a deer with, and they fired between the headlights. All of a sudden the motor stopped, the car backed up the hill and they never saw it again. Ha, ha." Richard shook as he chuckled, all 270 pounds of him. [Richard]

Boys' Gangs in Chicago

Back down in Chicago, Minnie and Dad had another urban problem to deal with, besides all those thugs on the South Side. The City had 1313 neighborhood gangs of boys, ranging in age from six to nineteen or twenty years of age. [Thrasher, 1927: 74 chart] Benny Goodman, five years older than Dad, recalled street fights when he was a boy in Chicago's Douglas Park "and how you were afraid to cross the bridge 'cause the Irish kid on the other side would beat your head in." Packs of young boys hung out on the streets and alleyways, along the canals, in vacant lots, abandoned buildings, old barns, garages, under L tracks, in poolrooms, carnivals, arcades, amusement parks, vaudeville shows and burlesque theaters. [Thrasher, 1927: 96] What were they doing? Gang boys played games and pranks, got into fights. Sometimes their activities involved vandalism and other kinds of juvenile delinquent crime.

Was Dad hanging out with gang kids when he lived in Chicago? Could be. There was that street fight he had with another kid when he was six. And he also told me he played craps as a kid, a favorite activity of street boys. Dad told me another childhood tale: he and his buddies used to go to vaudeville shows, where they would sit down in front, next to the orchestra and taunt the woodwind musicians, by sucking loudly on slices of lemons during the performance. The object of the prank was to make the musicians salivate so hard they couldn't play their instruments.

Some gang boys played destructive pranks like dumping glue into car engines, tearing down street signs, and breaking windows. They wrought havoc on neighborhood merchants, by robbing them when their backs were turned. [Thrasher, 1927: 94] Boys got into fistfights with kids from rival gangs. Among Italians, the

Street fight   Photo: Library of Congress

vendetta was brought into juvenile quarrels - like when Tony told my Dad to "get the other kid back good." [Thrasher, 1927: 8] The lure of the gang made boys play hooky from school to spend the day with their buddies, playing baseball, fishing, shooting dice, pilfering, drinking, smoking, roughhousing, ogling French postcards, wrecking stuff, running betting pools on prize fights and ballgames, dreaming up secret rituals, and taunting females going about their business on the street.

Some boys struck out on their own for days and nights at a time, going on thieving sprees for food or money, sleeping in a shed or an abandoned building or even a cave. Dad had the freedom to do any of that, because he was unsupervised. He mentioned playing hooky, but didn't go into details. He probably didn't want to give me and my brother Rob ideas when we were kids.

The gang was also a school for crime. Boys learned to steal bikes and even cars for the thrill of joy riding. They learned how to snatch purses, pick pockets, shoplift, roll drunks, pick locks, sell

Boys playing craps on the sidewalk

This Library of Congress pic made an ideal green screen backdrop in the movie

stolen goods to fences, get guns, hold up stores or break in at night and burglarize them. [Thrasher, 1963: 270] They also learned to taunt the police and to outrun them. [Thrasher: 1927, 83-84] What did they do with their cash? Buy candy, ice cream, luxury items like canned shrimp, play pool, go to movies, vaudeville shows, burlesque theater, peep shows, buy smut, shoot craps and lose it all.

As boys grew to be teenagers, their predilection for disorder, violence, and warfare with other gangs could escalate until they became uncontrollable to their families, social service agencies and the police. In the 1919 Chicago Race Riots neighborhood gangs of teenage boys, under names like "The Dirty Dozen" and "The Murderers," were out on the streets riling things up, beating and killing black people who were just going to their jobs. [Thrasher, 1927: 6, 47, 65]

Kids were even drawn into the bootlegging industry. Teenage boys made bootleg runs in cars and trucks, laden with hooch. But even young boys were brought into the business, recruited to stoke stills and make deliveries on foot. [Thrasher, 1927: 46] Many gang kids grew up to be bootleggers themselves, becoming young men like Freddy – someone who could command respect and admiration in the neighborhood, with expensive clothes, fancy cars and their pockets stuffed with cash. Hundreds of young bootleggers were killed in the Beer Wars in Chicago before they had even turned 30, casualties of the *vendetta*. Mob warfare was waged with hand guns, rifles, bombs and the newly invented Thompson machine gun.

Boy Gangs and Hoodlums

Bootleggers, gangsters and even Mob bosses got their start in crime as hooligans in gangs of boys. Al Capone was only 26 years old when he became head of the Chicago Outfit in 1925. But his years as a kid in the tough New York Five Points Juniors and later the adult Five Points Gang itself, gave him hands-on experience in crime and intimidation, before he even arrived in Chicago at age twenty. The vicious Five Points Gang had also spawned Capone's predecessor, Johnny Torrio, who executed *his* predecessor, Big Jim Colosimo, in a *vendetta* for divorcing Torrio's aunt. Infamous New York crime boss Lucky Luciano was another Five Points Gang member.

Chicago mobster Sam Giancana had been raised in Chicago around the same time as my Dad. Giancana climbed to the top of the pile to become mob boss in 1957, twenty six years after

Capone went to jail. Dad was six years younger than Giancana, who grew up in a Chicago boy's gang. According to his daughter, Antoinette Giancana, her father learned "the arts of murder and terror" as a kid in the 42's Gang. Many of the 42's grew up to form the core of Giancana's Mob. [Giancana, 16, 32]

Crashed bootlegger car   Photo: Library of Congress

Minnie Sends Dad Away

I can see how my Dad was going to grow up to be a thug, living in that world. Minnie couldn't walk away from that life. But she could save my Dad. Sometime after that rum run to Lake Superior with Freddy, she put Dad on a train back East when he was eleven years old. "It was no life for a child." That's what Dad said. He might have been quoting her when he told me that. Was there some incident that made her put him on the train? Was Minnie in some kind of trouble? Did she have to do time in prison? Or did a child welfare agency intervene, and say that "it was no life for a child?" I checked the Children's Court records in the City Archives, a special court established during the Progressive era in the 20's, but they did not have any records on Dad. And I checked admissions to the Bridewell House of Corrections during that time, but her name didn't turn up. However in 1925, there was a significant change in prostitution. An intensive campaign of vice raids, in which prostitutes were arrested and brothels were shut down, were carried out under orders from Police Chief Morgan Collins. Brothels left the City and relocated operations in Chicago's south suburbs. [Bilek and Helmer, 275]

One thing I know for sure - my Dad didn't come of age running loose in a world of crooks. Minnie made sure he was going to have a different kind of upbringing, than what she could provide. He didn't grow up to be a Chicago crime lord, like Al Capone and Sam Giancana, or a thug like the men that worked for them.

But there was a price. Lily wrote that Minnie only wanted "love, home and family." I read that "one of the most painful events in the life of prostitution is losing custody of children, regardless of how good the reasons for that loss may be." [Parker] It must have been the hardest thing she ever did - to send away the one person who loved her.

And what happened to the little boy she sent away? Dad was raised by the one man who was never going to forgive Minnie for giving birth to him: Poppie.

Dad was supposed to go to Lily, but something went wrong. Lily would have been a great mom for Dad. She was willing and she had a lot of love to give, a stable home, and a steady income. But Minnie and Lily had an older sister, Heddy, who convinced their parents to intervene, because she said, "Lily's household isn't moral enough to raise a child." That's because by the mid 1920's, Lily was living together with Jack, an older man she ran a roadhouse with in Oceanside, New Jersey. Jack was a Catholic and separated from his wife, who he couldn't divorce. So he and Lily didn't marry until 20 years later, when his wife died.

Dad's father, Davis, of course was out of the picture. But I found out in my research that when Davis married someone else, a couple of years after Dad was born, that he and his wife never had any children together. So Dad was a boy without a father and Davis was a man without a son. If Davis or Poppie had played their cards differently, they could have had Dad's affection -- but neither Poppie nor Davis were the kind of men to let feelings dictate their actions.

Lily and Jack

I found the cold, clinical notes on Dad's life with Poppie, left behind by a string of VA psychiatrists in box #2, of the six boxes of papers I received, when I sent to Kansas City for Dad's records from the VA.

Psychiatric Interview, March 10, 1959, Victor Hunkel, M.D.

[Dad was 45 years old at the time]

I have seen Army veteran Mr. Davis twice a week, for the last 6 months. The past record of this patient discloses many of his points of difficulty.

265

After he left his mother, he had no one to talk to and no one to confide in and trust. Loss of affection from her made him restless and nervous. He mentions there were many times he didn't receive a present on his birthday, or during Christmas.

The patient's Grandfather really trimmed him down. He remembers being in hot water all the time because from then on, he had a rather mercurial temper. The patient didn't see his mother again for 10 years. She married and kept this a secret.

For many years, and perhaps even at the present time in 1959, a well ingrained philosophy that he has is, "A dollar a day can make you a king." This he picked up from his mother. For his mother felt that you could buy a dollar's worth of liquor a day, and that that would make you a king.

He is looking for pleasant things in life and shunning the unpleasant, except that he is wary of others. And his sarcastic manner and his paranoid approach soon lead him into unpleasant situations.

Interview, 1960, F. L. Mooney, M.D.

[Dad was 46 years old] *At the age of 14, Mr. Davis first began to exhibit his neurotic nervous traits: panicky feelings, mostly dislike of crowds, fear of closed places, fear of darkness, fear of heights, fear of going to the dentist, sometimes fear of dying. Presently to alleviate these conditions, frequently he drinks.*

His grandfather was very austere because he never forgave the patient's mother for the circumstances of the patient's birth. The patient says he was really "hammered down" by his Grandfather. The veteran's Grandfather had retired at age 50, leaving his children to support him, and yet he remained the dominant one in the home, and was catered to.

The patient's Grandmother died in 1936 at the age of seventy-five after nine months of illness during which time her mind became deranged. His grandfather committed suicide six months later.He was seventy eight and had been despondent since his wife's death. Mr. Davis found his grandfather.

Special Psychiatric Examination, 1973, J. D. Hart, Ph.D.

[Dad was 59 years old] *Mr. Davis has been receiving treatment for anxiety since 1958. There seems to have been little change in his condition over the years.*

Dad in Philly

Minnie and Johnny in the North Country, early 1930's

Chapter Twelve

ର୍ଚ ର୍ଚ ର୍ଚ ର୍ଚ ର୍ଚ ର୍ଚ ର୍ଚ

No Man's Land

Minnie saw what the North Country was like when she went up there with Dad and Freddy in 1925. Sometime later she headed up North on her own. A lot of Minnie's story up there I pieced together from snapshots in her photo album, which my Mom was thoughtful enough to save from two basement floods, after my Dad died. Given the way she felt about her mother-in-law, I'm lucky she didn't pitch the album when it was covered in sewage.

Mom characterized Minnie as a "drunk with a cold personality." That was pretty much the state Minnie was in at the end of her life by the time Mom knew her, going in and out of the hospital for delirium tremens, and turning up drunk at family events. Like my parents' wedding in 1945 which Minnie came down from Spread Eagle to attend. My mother told me about her wedding night.

At our wedding my mother-in-law was so drunk, that she fell and broke her ankle. So she couldn't come to the reception. So on our wedding night, 'Dad,' my husband, left me and went over to be with her in the hotel with her broken ankle. And I was left all by myself in this hotel room for hours. And he came home and he had a buzz-on too. So I figured they must have been drinking those whole several hours, on my wedding night

I found a lot of weird pictures of Minnie in that photo album of hers, like the one where she's standing behind a barbed wire fence in a desolate field of snow, dressed in an expensive lamb coat. In another, she's standing with a tough looking guy in front of a rough hewn building, dressed in the same fancy coat.

Minnie changed locations frequently, because the stamps on the back of the pictures had the names of North Country places on them, like Iron River, Michigan There were pictures of friends too The one thing that struck me about all those pictures is that the women look so out of place. It was a tough life for women in that desolate country, with no place to really call home.

Very few women were up in the North Country. Rather it was a world of lumberjacks and miners who lived together in dormitories until payday, when their paychecks went up in smoke buying drink and women and gambling it away. A handwritten letter to the Governor of Wisconsin, tells how girls got up there in the first place from Milwaukee or Chicago.

"They are generally in debt here and if a man comes down during the winter and offers to pay their fare up north they are willing to go, thinking that the north is lined with gold every spring when the woodsmen are paid off. . . there are plenty of them who have been up in the woods two or three times. . .

"When they get to the land of promise they find it hard enough, god knows, and are generally kept in debt, and forced to remain where they are, or lose their clothes, being sometimes beaten . . . The life of a prostitute is one full of horror under the best of circumstances, and they are as apt to feel the weight of a "gentleman's" fist in Chicago or Milwaukee as to get a kick from a woodsman in Peshtigo." [WLI, Petherick]

A woman explains the system of debt she was subjected to by brothels.

> They charge you four times over for everything. You got to pay for the towels, for the music, for the lifebuoy, for the guys who stay overtime, . . . you got to pay off the doc who finds out you're sick, a sawbuck just to let you off, a fin to the bondsman when the house is pinched ["When You Live"]

Here is a page from a brothel ledger in Milwaukee, uncovered in the Teasdale Commission investigation of vice in Wisconsin in

Brothel ledger

1913. They show how inmates were charged for each and every thing, no matter how small - lights, laundry, dresses, hosiery, furs, perfume, shoes, soap, toothpaste, sponges, towels, Listerine, syringes, beer, gas, medical treatment, drugs, George the Newsboy's services, and fines for drunkenness.

Minnie was adrift in that wild landscape of endless pine forests and pristine lakes, until she met Johnny up there in 1929. That was the year the stock market crashed. Banks folded taking people's savings down with them. Unemployment was rampant.

Businesses closed. The hungry waited in bread lines. Folks lived in makeshift shacks and old cars. Prohibition was still in full swing.

Compared to the dire straits the rest of the country was in, Minnie and Johnny were living the Good Life up there, in No Man's Land during the Great Depression. They were newlyweds in their mid 30's, working in Houghton/Hancock, Michigan - a pair of mining towns on a peninsula sticking up into Lake Superior in the UP.

They were listed in the census as a cashier and a cook in a restaurant. Having a job was an accomplishment in and of itself, during the Depression – if those were legit. But given the fact that it was a mining town, during the Depression and Prohibition, the restaurant could easily have been a blind pig – a speakeasy, with cribs in the back. Considering that they did well enough at the Hollywood a few years later, that savvy had to come from somewhere.

Johnny was a Greek Mafioso. That's what Dad called him. But Johnny was not without his fun side, as

Minnie at Lake Superior

a snapshot of him smashed, dressed in a girl's dress, cuddling up to his "beau" reveals. Minnie herself has a look of contentment, at least in the beginning of their relationship. Johnny had come to America a decade earlier, and immediately became a creature of the lawless North Country in the Roaring 20's. Here was a place he could operate an illegal business with impunity, by entertaining the men who enforced the law - the local judge, sheriff and the DA - as he did later at the Hollywood. Often local officials were in office as an excuse to collect bribes, because those jobs didn't come with salaries.

Prohibition and the North Country

Johnny on the left

During Prohibition, stills popped up everywhere in the State of Wisconsin. And the Law was always close at hand.

Pat Printz, the "walking encyclopedia" I met up in Spread Eagle, told me that when he was a kid he saw moonshine in the making.

Pat: My grandfather was a Deputy Sheriff out in the Rhinelander area . . . He handled a lot of the bootlegging and moonshining for them, like that. He did take me to some of the stills

Genevieve: And what did you see when you saw the stills?

Pat: Just big stills, a bunch of guys working and packaging and seeing the truck loading up. I mean, these weren't little stills down in the Rhinelander area. These were big stills.

Genevieve: And where did it go then?

Pat: Mobsters. Chicago. Detroit.

Genevieve: Oh, that's interesting. Well I've read that Wisconsin was an "alky farm" for Chicago.

Pat: Right. We made it and they drank it!

[Pat Printz, Personal Interview, 2011]

That wasn't a bust Pat was talking about. It was just a visit. That's right, the sheriffs and their deputies played a role in the production of moonshine.

Rhinelander Still

I learned about another big still back home, when I stopped one day at a farm near my house to buy some beef. The farmer and I got talking, and it turns out his brother was married to a gal whose grandpa had run a big still up in the same area. Known as "The Phantom Still" had been dismantled 4 or 5 times, and each time moved to another secret location near Rhinelander, where it continued cranking out gajillions of gallons of moonshine. It had never been busted, because it seems they got "the word" from a guy who worked for her grandpa, *after* he became sheriff.

Moonshining in Rhinelander

As you can see from these pictures, the vats are huge - 12 feet in diameter and 12 feet tall.

"Grandpa had at least 10 of them cooking at one time," the granddaughter told me. "It only took a week to ferment the mash, distill it and make whiskey out of it."

"Who was he cooking all the whiskey for?" I wondered.

"They owned two supper clubs up there," she confided.

So that was one point of delivery. But they were cooking a lot more than could be consumed weekly in a couple of restaurants.

Cooking mash in huge vats

"What were they doing with the rest of it?" I asked.

"Al Capone used to visit their supper club once in a while, on his way to his estate over in Couderay," she related. That was west of Rhinelander. "But, he wasn't buddy-buddy with Grandpa." So maybe Big Al was checking out the competition.

"There were definitely regular shipments hauled down to Chicago," his granddaughter explained. "Cause I heard about one time when "Grandma" went along on a trip to the Windy City with a hired hand. They were hauling a full load of moonshine all the way down there, about 20 or 30 gallons in one gallon glass jugs, you know, what you could get in a car. They were supposed to park the car on a certain street when they got to town, leave it, and come back in an hour.

"But as soon as they got into they city, they noticed they were being followed. The hired hand put his foot to the floor and Grandma wound up hanging on for dear life in a high speed chase. They never did find out who was on their bumper, but they lost the tail. Then they parked the car as they had been instructed and went shopping for an hour." When they came back from shopping, which is probably why "Grandma" wanted to go in the first place, "the booze had been unloaded and an envelope full of bills was sitting on the seat. And that was the last time "Grandma" ever went down to Chicago on a delivery run." [Personal interview, 2011]

Still in Bevant, Wis.

It was an easy matter, with all the woods and streams in Wisconsin, to hide a moonshining operation. Much of the state was sparsely populated, and there were plenty of trees for fuel, water for cooling, and remote places to set up a still, where no one would notice the smoke, the fire, or the smell of cooking mash.

My friend Sharon sent me this picture of her Grandmother's still. How the picture got printed is a good question because someone at the local drugstore, where pictures were usually taken to be printed, would have known about it and could have squealed.

"My grandmother was born in 1906," Sharon told me. "She had been a flapper in down in Chicago and worked in a chicken processing factory." When she settled down with Grandpa it was up on a farm, near Bevant, Wisconsin way up by Wausau, with bedrock formations on the Plover River, which ran through their backwoods "They raised cows and pigs," Sharon related. "Grandma grumbled that 'the Indians tried to steal them.'" Yeah, it was the Depression. People were hungry, people were paranoid, people were racist. Like a lot of folks in Wisconsin, Sharon's grandparents made part of their income with this still in the woods, fermenting corn mash and sugar. According to Sharon, "they hid jugs of moonshine in the wall in the barn and also buried them by the river banks." Who was buying it? "I was selling to Capone," her grandmother confided. "I met him," she bragged. "I met Capone."

Picture Sharon sent me of her Grandmother's still.

On the sly, her grandmother showed Sharon the Brownie snapshots she kept stashed away in a cigar box, of her and her boyfriends in her flapper days in Chicago. "Don't tell Grandpa," she whispered. [Sharon F., Personal interview, 2007]

Crandon Lake, Wis. Stills

Pretty much everybody in Wisconsin has a family story about bootlegging, because basically, moonshining was a way of making ends meet back then. It wasn't rocket science, either. You just got some vegetable matter, like potatoes or corn, and you cooked that and distilled it and voila: moonshine. Crandon Lake newspaper editor Mike Monte explains how things worked up there, by Green Bay:

Captured still in Crandon Lake, from Mike Monte

"Conditions were pretty primitive. There was no police force to speak of. There were stills all over here. And aging houses, where they would keep a wood stove going even in summer. They'd char the inside of oak barrels, and then pour the booze in to age it, you know, so it would have a mellow taste. It was so hot in there those guys worked in their skivvies all summer, turning the barrels all the time so it would age rapidly. You had a viable product in just three weeks, instead of years."

And where was this hooch headed? "I heard of some guys who drove a load of whiskey down to Chicago to deliver it one time. They were driving on Lake Shore Drive just as the sun was coming up, and a big car pulled up along side of them full of guys with guns," Monte disclosed. "There were so many guns, they didn't know there were that many guns in Chicago. Ha ha. That car pulled them over. One of the guys got out and looked in their car and said, "You just delivered your last load of booze to Chicago, ever, right?"

"The Wisconsin guys nodded their heads, 'uh, yup, that's right.'" [Mike Monte, Personal Interview, 2012]

Yes, Wisconsin was hopping during Prohibition. And it still is. That's because, for some reason, we have three times more taverns per capita than the rest of the country. [Romell, Rick. "Alcohol Runs in Our Blood," Wisconsin State Journal, October 19, 2008] Even today, you'll find that the tiniest towns, ones without so much as a gas station or a little grocery store, have a couple of taverns.

Brewing Beer in Portage, Wis

During Prohibition, the Eulberg Brewery, in Portage, WI, managed to perk along brewing beer continuously for 12 years, first under the ruse that they were manufacturing "near beer" and malting grains for other "near beer" manufacturers. That explained the stink of brewing that spewed over the town every day. Then finally in 1931 their luck ran out, when the Feds came and seizing 4,000 pints of beer in bottles and hundreds of barrels of brew. Apparently the raid caused a temporary "drought" in the speakeasies in the State capital of Madison, nearby. [Capital Times]

Was there a quid pro quo relationship with local government, that allowed the Eulberg Brewery to crank out mass quantities of beer during Prohibition? Well, the owners, two Eulberg brothers, were both sentenced to six months in prison. However, one brother's sentence was suspended, and the other brother only served a week, before he received a pardon from the *President of the United States*. Hmmmm.

The Euhlberg Brewery   Photo courtesy of Dave Euhlberg

The Capones

Wisconsin was also the playground of Chicago Mobsters. They came to escape the heat in Chicago - i.e. the Feds, the weather and the shootouts of the Beer Wars. They liked the scenery and the peace and quiet, where they could go hunting, fishing, and swimming with friends.   [Hollatz, Tom. *Gangster Holidays*, St. Cloud, MN : North Star Press of St. Cloud, Inc., 1989, p.xiv] And they liked the way they were entertained - with prostitutes, gambling and liquor. Al Capone had his own northern Wisconsin getaway, a 40 acre wooded estate on Cranberry Lake at Couderay. He called it "The Hideout." It had a field stone lodge, a stone jail and a stone lookout tower, complete with gun slots.

Big Al's largesse up north was legendary. One guy called him "a saint," because Capone gave his family food for nine months when they had nothing to eat during the Depression. [Hollatz, 1989, p. 71]   What did the local sheriff and his men think when they saw Al Capone's Packard?   They figured, it was best to act like they didn't know who those guys were. They knew they were "out of their league." [Hollatz, 1989, p. 94]

All Capone's Hideaway in northern Wisconsin

Al's brother Ralph Capone had a bar up north in Mercer, the Rex Hotel, which had a namesake down on Chicago's Levee. A former bartender in the hotel lounge up there recalled spotting many of Ralph's "boys" in the joint, wearing shoulder holsters, under their expensive suit coats. How did the bartender deal with that? "I learned never to ask questions." At the same time, Ralph bailed out plenty of folks who were losing their homes to foreclosure, during the Depression. [Hollatz, 1989, p. 84] If somebody's house burned down, Ralph would be the first to start up a fund for them. [Hollatz, p. 83]

When Ralph Capone got out of prison, after being behind bars from 1932 to 1935, he liked the North Country so much, he lived up there, until his death in 1974 in Hurley, ten miles from Lake Superior. That's a place my mother called "the playground of the Chicago Mafia." She would know, because when my Mom and Dad were newlyweds, Minnie and Johnny took them on a tour of the bars across northern Wisconsin in 1947. They stopped in Hurley when it had 89 taverns and 150 houses of prostitution. [Reimann]

John Dillinger

The Capones weren't the only gunmen running around up north. Dillinger was up there too. And by that time he was a household name, because his face was plastered all over the newspapers. "A man to be feared and reviled," was my mother's description of him. He and his gang were spotted from time to time by the locals. One time a farmer and his wife out by Crandon Lake found the gang coming up the driveway of their farm looking for breakfast - out of the limelight, so to speak. "So my grandmother cooked up a big breakfast for 'em," Laura H. told me, you know, something like ham and eggs and potatoes and biscuits with gravy. "And the gang paid them a bunch of money for it." [Laura H] Another time, Dillinger appeared in a barbershop at the Hotel Crandon, for

Postcard of the Hotel Crandon, from Mike Monte where his grandfather barbered Dillinger

a shave and a haircut. One of his gang members sat in the shop with him, while the rest of the gang waited outside in the car with the engine running. The barber boasted to his grandson, "I could have cut his throat real easy." [Mike Monte Interview, 2012]

That 1947 bar hopping joy ride, with Minnie and Johnny and my Mom and Dad, included a stop for dinner and drinks at Little Bohemia, up by Manitowish Waters, "where they still had all the bullet holes, wherever John Dillinger had shot people," Mom told me. "They wanted to see that especially." Incidentally, you can still find a lot of people in Wisconsin today, who will tell you that bar hopping is their idea of a good vacation.

The owner of Little Bohemia, Earl Wanatka, made a cottage industry out of showing off those bullet holes in the windows, and Dillinger momentos - things the gang left behind while making a hasty exit through the woods – shirts, tooth powder, toiletries, guns, and a couple of pairs of high heels, which had been worn by the girls they left behind, too. You can still see them today in a display case. Not the girls, the stuff. I stopped in for a burger in the bullet hole-riddled dining room, when I was screening my film nearby last summer. They took me upstairs to check out the glassed-in 1930's sets, preserved from the movie *Public Enemy*, complete with a bathroom that had fake bullet holes and a partially blown-off sink.

Before opening Little Bohemia, Wanatka was down in Chicago, operating a popular mobster hangout. But after several of his best customers were murdered in the 1929 St. Valentine's Day

John Dillinger, a very glamorous guy

Massacre, he decided to get out of town and start a business up north. His piece and quiet lasted until April 23, 1934, when Dillinger holed up there, with Baby Face Nelson and the rest of the gang. Someone, perhaps Wanatka himself, leaked the gang's whereabouts to the Feds, who came storming in the next night. Dillinger and his gang fought like wildcats, spraying machine gun fire through the glass windows, before splitting up and escaping into the woods in the darkness.

A guy named Jim, from Chicago, tells of the aftermath of the battle. "My Grandpa was a doctor up in Ironwood and he was summoned for help. So my Dad, who was a teenager at the time, drove my Grandpa to the Little Bohemia lodge in the Buick. They saw the aftermath of the shootout and brought back two 'stiffs' to the morgue in the back seat of the Buick." The two "stiffs" they retrieved were Federal Agent Baum, killed by Baby Face Nelson, and Eugene Boisoneau, a foreman at the CCC camp, killed by mistake by the FBI. [Jim Crosby, e-message].

Baby Face Nelson, another object of glamour

Dillinger eluded the Feds that night, but was executed three months later by FBI men, as he was coming out of the Biograph Theater in Chicago after a movie. Two FBI agents later caught up with Baby Face Nelson, in a shootout in Barrington, Illinois, northwest of the City the same year. Both of the FBI agents, as well as Nelson, were killed in the shoot out. Nelson was another thug whose career got jump started when he was a kid and roamed the streets of Chicago with a gang of delinquent boys. "By the age of 14, he was an accomplished car thief and had been dubbed 'Baby Face' by members of his gang due to his juvenile appearance." [FBI]

The Hollywood

A few years after the 1933 repeal of Prohibition, Minnie and Johnny came down from Houghton/Hancock in the UP and bought the Hollywood Bar and Hotel in Spread Eagle. They paid cash during the height of the Depression. It was a deal that put money into the pockets of the man of the Register of Deeds who was only acting as a private citizen. An hour earlier, again acting as a private citizen, the Register of Deeds had purchased the property from Florence County, which had recently acquired it for back taxes.

My Mom visited the Hollywood Hotel three times, in the mid 1940's.

Mom: "Upstairs, they had rooms for rent, because it was called the Hollywood Hotel. We got one of the rooms they usually rent out. His mother cooked us breakfast, scrambled eggs and bacon and that. Soon afterwards, I was wandering around, peeking in some of the other rooms, and I noticed there were two toilets. And I thought that was very odd, so I asked 'Dad' about it.

"And he said, 'Well that's a bidet.'

"And I said, 'I'd never heard of that.' I heard the word, but I didn't know what a bidet was. And then he explained to me what it was and what it did. And how people used it that were up there having a good time, the man and the girl. That was a big shock. I never got over that as long as she lived – that that was the kind of place it was.

Genevieve: Oh, so that's when you learned that it was –

Mom: That it was . . . a brothel. Yeah. And I was *in* a brothel. And I then was pretty much aware of it, because I would hear doors open and shut, and people coming and going at all hours of the night, you know, I could hear "fun" going on. So this was a whole new experience for me, to know that there was a world like that out there. And that I was married to the son of one of the people.

Yeah, that's right. Only my mother could stay in a brothel and not realize it. In fact, she had already stayed up there once before, briefly, and just thought it was a regular hotel, because that's what they told her it was.

However, my Mom didn't tell *me* the Hollywood was a brothel, until after I drove up there in 2004. That's when everyone I talked to in Spread Eagle and Florence told me the Hollywood was, in their words, "a whorehouse." No sugar coating up there.

Minnie up north around age 53

Pat Printz told me that he thought that running the Hollywood was a good deal, "clean, fresh air, nice countryside, steady money, no trouble." For a gal roaming the North Country in the Depression, it was a dream come true.

But no one I interviewed remembered Minnie. They remembered Johnny, but not her. The cost of owning the Hollywood, Minnie paid in ever advancing stages of alcoholism. That's why Mom saw her as "a drunk with a cold personality." Near the end of her life, Minnie was withdrawn and emotionally shut down. Because she died before I was born, I only knew her through snapshots of her when I was a kid. Her stony face seemed scary. But now the way she looks seems more comprehensible to me.

Denial was a major factor in surviving in that business as long as she did. Here is an incredible stream of consciousness account, taken down in the same time period, from a woman in the same kind of business.

> When you live like I done, people give you a line all the time, all day long wherever you're at. All day long, everybody's givin everybody else a line, and after a while without thinkin much about it one way or another, just trying to get along you know, there you are givin somebody a line just like everyone else is doin . . . You got to lie to *everybody*, you can't believe *nobody* . . .

> but most of all you got to lie to yourself. . . when you live like I done you can't *ever* stop kidding yourself a *second* or you're through. It'd just take all the heart out of you, you'd get blind drunk and blow your top. ["When You Live"]

Dad's VA psychiatrist's notes read, "His mother was very nervous, was in the tavern business and was hospitalized many times for delirium tremors." Delirium tremens is a symptom that appears when the body is so soaked with alcohol that the person falls into an uncontrollable state of high anxiety, gets the shakes and experiences stark hallucinations. Treatment in the 1940's was primitive: hospitalization with restraints, like a straight jacket or tying the patient to the bed.

Pat Printz

In the 1930's when Pat Printz tagged along with his grandfather, they also stopped in at the Hollywood.

Pat: I was about six, seven years old when I went there with my grandfather.

Genevieve: Can you tell me what you saw when you were in the Hollywood?

Pat: All kinds of well dressed women, a lot of liquor and a lot of guys around, like that, looked like gangsters, which I knew they were. With the hats and the ties. They always wore ties, like that, and suspenders, like that and they always had guns. Everybody had a gun. Sometimes, many more.

Genevieve: Yeah, like what kind of guns did they have?

Pat: Pistols, shot guns. Tommy guns.

Genevieve: What about hunting season up here?

Pat: In November a lot of them came up to hunt in the cold weather. We always made sure they had plenty of dead deer to take back on their cars with them.

Genevieve: And how did you do that?

Pat: Go out and kill as many as they want. And have them ready for 'em.

Genevieve: And then what did they do with the deer that you killed for them?

Pat: Put 'em on their cars and took 'em home to show how they killed the deer. Well, they never really killed the deer. They were busy playing cards - which was a big thing - gambling, drinking and playing with their women.

Genevieve: Were there some famous gangsters that you know of that were up in Spread Eagle?

Pat: Baby Face Nelson and all of them came into the area.

Genevieve: Oh, so Baby Face Nelson came up here?

Pat: Oh yeah. He was going to the Hollywood, too. And all he was, was another person with guns having a good time. [Baby Face Nelson died in that shootout in Illinois, a couple years before Minnie and Johnny bought the Hollywood]

Pat: I know Al Capone had his place over by Eagle River, like that.

[Capone was sent to prison three years before Minnie and Johnny ran the Hollywood].

Nightlife in the North Country - Ironwood, Michigan   Library of Congress photo

Pat: It wasn't that there was any crime or anything. It was just the mobsters, they were coming up here doing their thing, and they were making sure that everybody in the area was happy. And it was good for us. It was good for the local economy. You could never look at 'em and think these were bad guys, 'cause they treated everybody in the area so good. And a lot of his guys were over here all the time.

The mobsters from Chicago, this is where they came regular. Not a weekend, like we think of, because it took them a couple of days to get here back then, because they didn't have the roads that you have now. And they would come up here and this is where they relaxed and enjoyed themselves. They also brought all kinds of good stuff here. Tires, food stamps, everything. They provided for the people in the area well.

Genevieve: Why did they bring tires?

Pat: That was during the time when you couldn't buy tires. You had to have stamps from the government, and you were allotted so many, because it was during the time of the War.

[Pat is now talking about World War II, which took place from 1941 to 1945.]

Genevieve: Are you talking about rationing? And tire coupons?

Pat: Yes, tire coupons and gas stamps. They would provide plenty of gas stamps for the people in the area. And the gas stamps were all black market that they would get. And they gave 'em out very lavishly to everybody. So everybody was on their side. The mobsters were the hard people that came in. They weren't afraid to kill. These are the people that worked for 'em, like your Grandmother and everything like that. And they were well taken care of, and well compensated. And they made sure that when the mobsters came up, that they were happy.

Letter

I only found one letter from my Grandmother to my Dad. When I showed it to Pat, he looked at their motto, *A Fine Place – Just Like Home*. "Geez," he pondered, "that really shows you what a nice place it really was!" The letter was in with a handful of greeting cards she had sent to Dad and just signed, "Love Mother and Dad." This is the same letter excerpted in Chapter 1. If you could pick one letter to have this would be it. Minnie really gives the flavor of their lives at the Hollywood. A couple of phrases were souped up by the voice-over actress, Triko Bronjo, who read the letter in the film. Those are in bold.

> Received your letter today so I thought I'd better answer it at once as I am the worlds worst letter riter. Well today is really one hot schorer [scorcher], and you know how I hate that, never could take the hot weather. Otherwise I'm feeling pretty good again. **No more heebee jeebees.** [In other words, she was hospitalized for delirium tremens].

I bet you sure were surprised to see Johnny down there. He likes Milwaukee very much. He's been there before of course, but it has been quite a while **so he kind of forgot about how much he likes the chassies down there.** [Johnny was probably down in Milwaukee getting more girls to work at the Hollywood, because they had recently lost an important source of income – the slots.]

The Hollywood Hotel stationary - "A Fine Place, Just Like Home"

As far as the slot machines, **those one-armed bandits,** they are positively out. No doubt you read how the governor signed the Anti-Gambling Bill. They claim even Bingo is out. If that is so, I think the Riverside will close up. They put on about three times as many enforcement **dicks**, so that will keep us closed up pretty tight as far as the one o'clock closing for a while. The operator of the slot machines was in tonight and took out all the machines, and said people shouldn't expect anything for at least two years, so I guess that's that.

As far as the Riverside down the road, right now they have an all girl band and a woman organ player, but things here at the Hollywood are kind of quiet [because they are in a financial slump]. People seem to go more to resort towns, where there is swimming boating, etcetera. Our business always seems better here when its colder, **because we know how to take the chill out of the bones here, in the winter.**

Boy it's hot. I think when we close up we will take a ride. Maybe I can get a little air.

Well Francis I guess this is all the news at present, so will bring this to a close. Rite soon.

Your loving

Mother & Dad

The bone weariness of this letter is telling of the stifling conditions under which Minnie lived. By 1945 she was in her fifties. She had traveled way down the road she had started on so long ago, as a young woman. She was a woman whose hopes and dreams of "love, home and family" were lost and never regained. She had been deserted by her fiancé, abandoned by her father and forced to send the only one who really loved her away - to save him. She had resided in a living hell her entire adult life, desperately locked inside herself, her lonely existence ground into dollars. Alcohol was a demon that consumed her.

Stockades

I hadn't really thought much about the history of prostitution right in Spread Eagle. I knew that the town already had a reputation for selling women when my grandmother bought the Hollywood in 1936, because other brothels were already established in the area. I got that from reading the Florence Mining News. But I didn't realize that long before Minnie arrived, there had been a grim tradition of unrestrained lawlessness in Spread Eagle, dating back to the late 1800's. That is, until one of my actors, Robert Golden who played the sheriff at the Hollywood, sent me this email:

> I mentioned your film project to some of my uncles
> and aunts. They remembered reading newspaper
> articles my aunt had about some guy named
> "Mudge." They said they were at a 4th of July
> parade up near Florence and Mudge and his "girls"
> even had their own float in the parade and every-
> one in the crowd knew all about them. Not exactly
> flying under radar screen.

The origins of prostitution in the North Country are about as dark as human nature gets. I already knew about it from looking through the Wisconsin Legislature *Investigations* files, where I found newspaper headlines from 1887, referring to "Stockades" and "Pineries" as "Wisconsin Hells," where "Atrocious Crimes [are] Committed in the Forests of Wisconsin." The stockades were described as "Devil's dens in Wisconsin, where American women are inveigled, enslaved, chained, guarded by bull dogs, debauched, abused, robbed and murdered." [WLI, Safeguard, No. 281]

Once I investigated my actor's lead, I learned that a stockade had existed right outside of Spread Eagle. A series of newspaper editors in nearby Florence had been terrorized and run out of town for trying to shut it down. Florence, itself, was described as "a metropolis of vice" by the man who replaced them: twenty three year old Chase Osborne. Before Osborne's arrival in 1882, the superintendent of the local mine had also tried to clean up the town, but lost his seven year old son to kidnappers, who were never brought to justice. [Bolduc and Dickenson]

Osborne's first night in town with his wife and baby was a harrowing one, because in the middle of the night, the rough building that housed both the paper and Osborne's family, was shot up. But Osborne was not to be gotten rid of so easily. [Osborne]

The Stockade, which stood a mile outside of town, belonged to "Old Man Mudge," a "white livered" poltroon, with a "sepulchral" appearance, who dressed in a frock coat and top hat, even when feeding his wolves, who stood chained at the entrance of The Stockade. Osborne and his wife, at the newspaper headquarters a mile away, could hear their "long low, blood-freezing howl" which "sifted to our ears with the pine-needle, wind rhythms." Stockades siphoned off a month's wages out of iron ore

Chase Osborne, a man to have on your side

miners and lumberjacks, by offering gambling, dancing, drink and the bodies of women and girls. But the toll that stockades took on human life was staggering.

Posing as a minister, Mudge traveled by train, trolling for prostitution recruits in a five state area. He gained the confidence of young women, particularly those with no family to protect them, to travel north with him, by telling them that he had a high paying legitimate job waiting for them. Others were lured to Mudge's after responding to ads for school teachers, sewing girls, chambermaids and waitresses in northern Wisconsin hotels.

When the trusting young women arrived at Old Man Mudge's, they were imprisoned, beaten and raped, until their will was broken. Mudge's stockade was a fort-like palisade of tall, sharpened logs, surrounding a large, rough hewn log building, that contained a dance hall and bar on the first floor, cribs on the second and dungeons in the basement. The women thus obtained were then either retained at Mudge's or sold to other stockades or brothels up north.

The young women were continually subjected to sexual violence, beatings and venereal disease until they died. Mamie Rearson, a seventeen year old inmate of a stockade, stuffed the keyhole of her door and whispered to an investigating reporter, "I have seen girls beaten and pounded until they lay insensible on the floor. I remember on one occasion a logger pounded a girl with his boots until there was not a tooth in her head. The girl screamed loud enough to have been heard three blocks away, but no one in the house attempted to interfere." ["Great"]

One girl who managed to escape was recaptured and dragged unconscious behind a wagon back to the stockade. Another shivering, wild-eyed refugee came to Osborne's house, where she reported that she had been starved, beaten, bound hand and foot with leather thongs, and left tied up in the cold, next to the wolves, whose jaws snapped at her only a few inches away. While Osborne was out making arrangements to move her secretly to safety, she disappeared. The case held no interest for the local sheriff, who was himself the owner of a saloon in town. Osborne did not find out until several years later, that the young woman had been sold to a brothel keeper in the UP, [the "Upper Pennisula" of Michigan] who murdered her one night in a dive on the shores of Lake Superior.

"Murders often occurred, but those guilty were seldom punished," because witnesses were intimidated, "run off" or even murdered. [WLI, The Safeguard, No. 281]. If a girl was murdered up there, who would know? Old Man Mudge, who had broken his own daughter to the business, thought he was unstoppable. But Osborne got himself a pair of bulldogs and several Wincester rifles for his office. He took on the prostitution gang in print and formed an armed posse, called "The Regulators." The posse was comprised of an unlikely group of men – "a fighting preacher," "that north woods oddity"– an honest deputy sheriff, his brother a "crack shot and peerless tracker," and lastly a hardware man, a bantam rooster with "intestinal courage."

Meanwhile the rest of the town lived in a "twilight zone of morals," including the Sheriff, the DA and half the merchants, who were in league with Mudge. Osborne reported that "shootings occurred by day and night, and the fight was a real battle." In spite of repeated assassination attempts on his person, Osborne galvanized the town and managed to turn things around, along with his posse, which grew in number to include most of the town. "What became of Mudge will never be told. Only a half dozen Regulators ever knew." Osborne, his wife, and children subsequently enjoyed four peaceful years there in a vice-free town.

AN INMATE OF A WISCONSIN DEN MAKING AN EFFORT TO ESCAPE.

In 1887, the State of Wisconsin's Legislature passed Chapter 214, outlawing white slavery. This bill was written specifically to put an end to the stockades and "the abduction of females for the purpose of prostitution." ["Northwestern"]

By 1893, when Osborne had long packed up and left, Mudge's daughter Mina was back in Florence operating a brothel. Osborne had described her as "a stunning woman" with a "fine animal figure" and "the cruelty of a she-hyena." Mina had also been observed down in Milwaukee in the same year, rounding up girls from River Street brothels and syphilis patients from the County Hospital, and loading them on a sleeper train bound for Florence. [WLI, Pettineck] Her method of obtaining girls differed from her late father's, in response to the new law. However, that does not mean that was the only way girls were gotten for north country brothels. Mina's ex-husband, Frank Bolduc, was arrested a number of times - after the law went into effect - for trying to trick young girls into getting on the train with him, so he could take them to his den at Iron King, near Hurley. [Daily Northwestern, "Willie" and "Mina"]

In 1911 Chase S. Osborne, the man who took on vice in Florence, Wisconsin was elected Governor of the State of Michigan on the Progressive Ticket.

Wisconsin Vice Commission

By 1913 a Wisconsin legislative committee had convened to investigate the extent and conditions of prostitution in the State. Called the Teasdale Commission, it was one of many vice commissions formed around the same time across the country.

The Commission received this letter, from the Archdeacon of Fond du Lac, concerning young women held against their will in prostitution, showing that the white slavery law enacted in 1887 was de facto nullified in the town of Fond du Lac. The letter also warned the Commission to beware of public officials.

". . . young girls were being held as inmates, [of brothels], but neither the chief of Police nor Mayor would render the slightest assistance. . . the Mayor . . . and the Chief of Police will do all that they can to prevent

your investigation and to trip it up at any stage that they may have an opportunity to do so." [WLI, Rogers]

The Commission found that prostitution was still an integral part of the fabric of Wisconsin towns back in 1913. Corruption of local officials was a recurring theme in many investigators' reports. When the Committee sent Investigator Ben Morgan out to the town of LaCrosse, Chairman Teasdale, who himself hailed from nearby Sparta, warned the investigator: "In this city please be very guarded in regard to the police and also be on the lookout for the post office officials, as they are watching what we are doing very closely."

Here is the investigator's handwritten report, that shows how deeply the town was riddled with it.

> - [Police] Detective McGraw is the man who collected 'hush money' from all the gambling and sporting houses, has full privileges [at the houses]–
>
> - The Manager of the Park Store is a hoarmaster and his clerks all have the reputation of being fast but go out only with friends of the proprietor
>
> - small house, no [house] number, a woman is practicing prostitution and claims to be protected by the Chief of Police
>
> - German Village Saloon is a bad hole
>
> – Auto Livery carries sports to the roadhouses
>
> - rooms over the Bijou Theater were being used for immoral purposes late last night
>
> - 'Hub' Saloon & Restaurant . . resort where prostitutes congregate

- Buffett Saloon . . . you can go there and hook up with a girl for purposes of prostitution

- Knitting Mills, 212 Main St. has many girls who are immoral, one said . . . she could not make money enough to dress herself at the Mills, ½ of the girls go out with men in order to make money on the side. [WLI, Morgan]

Spread Eagle

Things were essentially the same up in Spread Eagle, when my grandmother got there a generation later, in 1936. "The Sheriff didn't make a living getting a paycheck," local resident Pat Printz observed. "He never got it like that. Everything went to the Sheriff's pocket. Uh, money didn't go to the county in them days. There was no bookkeeping."

Pat was an astute observer of conditions when he was growing up,

Johnny in his 50's at Little Bohemia

like the quid pro quo relationship between brothel owners and the law. As a kid, he was friends with the sheriff's son and paid close attention to conversations he heard in the sheriff's kitchen. And talk he heard at home, too, because his father was a deputy sheriff in Florence. During our interview, he explained exactly how the kind of corruption, that the Teasdale Commission ran into 20 years earlier, was still in taking place in Spread Eagle in the 30's and 40's.

Me: Did you ever see the Sheriff or the Judge over at the Hollywood?

Pat: They all hung together and stuck together and enjoyed themselves and had their fun together, like that. Knowing that everybody had their backside covered. They were actually part of it, like that. They were an integral part of what was happening up here. The Sheriff got his – he protected the brothels. He made sure everything was okay, like that. And he got taken care of financially from the brothels, and I'm sure that the money that the brothels were giving him were coming from the mobsters also, from in their pockets, like that. So the Sheriff was taken care of from all angles. And not only him, but the Judge and the Prosecutor, like that, which were all elected officials at the time.

The Sheriff – he'd deputize who he needed at the time. And he had a select few, and they all kept their badges and their guns and everything in their house. And if he needed them, there was up to

20 people on the same phone line, and everybody had a different ring. Your ring might be one, it might be two it might be three. And there was a code on it, if the Sheriff needed his Deputies, like that, so many rings represent that you get your badge and your gun and you go and meet him. It was actually a false raid. It wasn't a real raid, even.

Genevieve: What do you mean by that?

Pat: Well, they'd be tipped off that there was going to be a raid by the State Police.

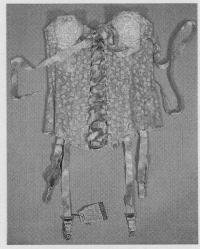

1940's Vintage bustier

I'm thinking of the Green Garage in particular, one raid. First thing they did, the Sheriff sent my dad and another guy down to warn the Green Garage that it was going to happen. They had so much stuff they got. They took it to the Sheriff's house, which was my neighbor. They had all kinds of guns, all kinds of ladies' underwear, and everything there at the house. And cases and cases of cigarettes. Cigarettes were something you couldn't get in them days. There were stamps on them, [i.e. you had to have ration coupons to buy them]. You were only allowed to buy so many at a time. And they had all the cigarettes you wanted.

And they were all ready for them. When they went there to raid it, they went through a raid, they had an actual raid with the State Police right, like that. But they didn't find anything that was that incriminating, so the State Police couldn't do anything. It was already all taken care of.

Genevieve: Oh, so this was with the *State Police*.

Pat: Right. When the State Police would come in, they'd get the local sheriff to go on the raid with them. And, after the State Police left, they came and picked up everything, like that. And took it right back to the Green Garage. It was all a game.

The final thing Pat had to say on the subject, was: "Nothing ever reached a point where it went to a major trial or anything like that. It was done right there. It was a way of doing business. That's the best way to put it, like that. Everybody was happy. Everybody was making a living. Everybody was having their fun. As bad as it might sound, it wasn't bad. It was good for the area."

Funeral in No Man's Land

After running the Hollywood from 1936 to 1948, Minnie died under mysterious circumstances. Aunt Lily, came out from New Jersey for the wake. My mother remembers, "When we were at the funeral parlor, we went to look at the open casket. Aunt Lily says "you've got to kiss her on the forehead." I said, "Oh, I can't do that." I never kissed any *body*, uh, anywhere. And she says, "You have to. That's what's expected of you. You're in the family." So I had to bend over and kiss this dead body. And it was ice cold and hard. It was such a traumatic experience for me. I'd never heard of that before. And I never want to do it again. So, I just did what I was told. But it was ugly."

There was a lot of crooked business concerning Minnie's death. "At the time that it was official," Mom confided, "it was a heart attack that she died of. That's what the death certificate apparently said. But, that was not true. It was all covered up then, afterwards. It was all very strange, bizarre and scary."

When I went up to Florence, I looked up the death certificate and it said "heart failure due to alcohol overindulgent." I asked the clerk in the Register of Deeds office about it and she said, "Oh, yeah, they put 'heart attack' on a lot of death certificates, where there's something weird that went on."

My parents out on the town

"Dad had gotten a secret long distance call, right before they left for the funeral, from someone up there - a friend of Minnie's. "Well, a neighbor lady called and talked to Dad. And she told him that there was a will and also she had been dead three days before somebody found her and realized she was gone. And she was found on the couch in their apartment. She had died of alcoholism and had died on her own vomit. That's what we were told, anyway.

"That's pretty surprising, that somebody could not be missed or not be checked on for that length of time. It was just a very unpleasant, difficult way to say goodbye to Dad's mother. Actually for him it was the worst."

By the time Mom and Dad and Lily got up there to Spread Eagle for the funeral, there was no will to be found and that neighbor lady was no longer talking. Lily urged Dad, "You might as well go ahead and take her diamond

Neighbor Lady – Movie still

ring, because it doesn't look like you're going to get anything else." But when they got back to Milwaukee, the Milwaukee Police were waiting for them as they got off the train and took the ring back for Johnny. That's how long Johnny's arm was from all the way up in Spread Eagle.

But that wasn't the end of it, Mom explained.

> So then, sometime later we contacted an attorney I was working for at the time, and had him go up there to see what he could do about finding the will, that her friend had said that Dad's mother had made. And so he went up there and he had been threatened. He came back and said "Those are Mafia people, you can't mess with them. They're not going to give up the fact that there was a will and probably tore it up already. He said, 'You'll never find out what happened up there.' And he said we should be afraid for our lives if we tried to pursue it. So that was the end of that.

As my friend Terese pointed out, Minnie may have died from drinking alcohol used to block the pain of broken bones and other injuries resulting from an assault. It was a habit of women in prostitution had, who often experienced broken bones that went unset, resulting from violence by a pimp or customer. [Baldwin,]

There were more weird things. On her death certificate, the doctor notes he saw her on the same day she died. So if she had been dead for several days, like the neighbor lady said, just imagine what a fly on the wall would have heard that day between the doctor and Johnny.

Another weird thing, Johnny had her cremated in 1948, when only 5% of funerals included cremation. Makes you wonder. But if you lived in no man's land and you showed the judge, the sheriff and the DA a good time, day in and day out, isn't the law pretty much in your own hands, anyway?

One last chilling variation, I was told by a 17 year old psychic. She saw Minnie locked up dead in a trunk for two days, after being beaten in the stomach with a baseball bat by her husband.

So what is the truth? Minnie, Johnny, the sheriff, the judge, the DA, the doctor and the neighbor lady – they're all dead now. It's too late for truth. Or justice.

All I can do is tell her story

Minnie in Chicago, 1920

Note the two men in fedoras whose silhouettes fall over her skirt in the lower right. The finger of the man taking the picture covers part of the lens, nearly obliterating her face.

She wears a lamb coat with a fox fur collar and a cloche hat pulled down low, shading her eyes from view.

Hollywood Hotel Chili - from "Frank's Mother"

My Grandmother actually made this at the Hollywood. In fact, in Minnie's probate papers, there were bills for groceries that included cans of tomatoes and bags of kidney beans. In spite of the fact that all but one of the grocery bills were dated *after* her death, the judge allowed that 50% of the total could be charged against her estate.

Thanks to my mother for preserving this recipe. If you like, add garlic and chili peppers to your heart's content.

1lb. lean chopped beef

1 large onion, chopped

2T shortening

1tsp. chili powder

½ tsp. paprika

2 bay leaves

dash cloves

1 tsp. salt

1 large can peeled tomatoes

1 small can kidney or red beans

chopped green pepper, optional

Brown meat and onion in shortening. Add remaining ingredients, except beans, and simmer 2 hours. Add beans and heat through.

"Everyone loves this chili." [Yeah, Mom actually wrote that!]

My Mom as Miss Celeste Orchid, for a publicity stunt at Fox Theaters in Milwaukee, where she was a secretary to the execs

Who's Who

Minnie's Family

Minnie - My Grandmother who died before I was born

Mommie and Poppie - Minnie's parents, from Denmark

Lily - Minnie's sister, one year younger, writer of letters about Minnie

Olga - Minnie and Lily's older sister, where Minnie lived briefly

Arthur - Minnie and Lily's older brother, painter in Paris

Auggie - Minnie and Lily's younger brother called August

Doris and Karl - Children of August, my Dad's cousins

My Family

Dad - Also called Francis and Frank Davis - my father

Mom - My mother, Helen Davis, eyewitness of events up north

Rob and Brian - My brothers

Minnie's Lovers

Davis - My Dad's father, a traveling salesman, engaged to Minnie

Tony Coglioni - Minnie's live-in lover in Chicago, a "minor Mafioso," lived with Minnie and Dad

Freddy - Bootlegger who went on a rum run with Minnie and Dad up north

Johnny Vill - Owned and operated the Hollywood with Minnie as her husband

The Colgioni's

Luigi Coglioni - Tony Colgioni's father, Italian labor padrone

Anna – Luigi's second wife, Tony's mother, sheltered Luigi's property under her name

Joseph – Tony's older half-brother, U.S. Marshal

Raymond – Tony's older half-brother, helped in the family business and ran a pool hall

John – Tony's younger-brother, election official who went to jail for election tampering

Edward – Tony's younger brother, indicted for theft

Daniel - Middle aged cousin of Tony, tailor from Philadelphia

Charles – Young cousin of Tony, Illinois Perfume Company employee

Colosimo's Circle

Big Jim Colosimo – Italian vice lord, owner of Colosimo's Cafe, bagman for Aldermen Kenna and Coughlin

Vittoria Moresco – Spouse of Big Jim Colosimo and brothel owner

Johnny Torrio – Nephew of Vittoria, Chicago crime boss 1920 - 1925, member New York Five Points Gang

Dale Winter – Singer at the Colosimo Cafe and sweetheart, then second wife of Big Jim Colosimo

Emilio de Stefano – Italian labor padrone on the Levee, step-father of Big Jim Colosimo, associate of Luigi Colgioni

Rocco de Stefano - Emilio's son, Colosimo's step-brother & lawyer

G. S. de Stefano – Emilio's younger brother, also an Italian labor padrone and associate of Luigi Coglioni

Hinky Dink Kenna – First Ward Alderman and Levee dive owner

John "Bathhouse" Coughlin – First Ward Alderman and Levee dive owner

Other Crime Bosses

Al Capone – Chicago crime boss, 1925-1932, member of Five Points Gang as a kid and young man in New York

Sam Giancana – Mobster, Chicago crime boss in the 50's and 60's

Lucky Luciano – New York crime boss 1931 to 1946, member of New York Five Points Gang

Progressives

Jane Addams – Progressive social work leader, Founder of Hull House in Chicago, Nobel Prize winner

William Stead – Progressive English Journalist who wrote about Chicago

Walking Encyclopedias

Tim Samuelson – City of Chicago Cultural Center Historian who contributed research

Pat Printz – Lives in Florence County, Wis.

References

Abbreviations: **CCRR**=Chicago Commission on Race Relations, **CDN**=Chicago Daily News, **CHE**=Chicago Herald and Examiner, **CT**=Chicago Tribune, **CVC**=Chicago Vice Commission, **DIO**=Daily Inter Ocean, **ICS**=Illinois Crime Survey, **JUV**=Juvenile Protection Association, **Phila Vice**=Vice Commission of Philadelphia, **Wis Vice**=Wisconsin Vice Commission, see Wisconsin. Legislature. Committee on White Slave Traffic, **WLI**=Wisconsin Legislature Investigations,

A

Addams, Jane. *A New Conscience and an Ancient Evil*, Macmillan Company, New York 1912

Addams, Jane. *Twenty Years at Hull-House with Autobiographical Notes*, The MacMillan Company, New York, 1910

Andrea. Personal Interview on 3/8/2088

Allsop, Kenneth. *The Bootleggers*, Arlington House, 1961

Anderson, Ken. Personal Interview

Asbury, Herbert. *Gem of the Prairie.* Knopf, New York, 1940

Austin and Lee Allen. Jake Foot song recorded in Memphis on May 5, 1930

B

Baldwin, Margaret A. "Living in Longing, Prostitution, Trauma Recover and Public Assistance," in *Prostitution, Trafficking, and Traumatic Stress*, Melissa Farley, PhD Editor, The Haworth Maltreatment and Trauma Press, 2003, p 297

Ball, Edward. *Slaves in the Family,* Ballentine Publishing Group, 1998

Bandiera, Oriana. "Private States and the Enforcement of Property Rights," Center for Policy Research, London, 2002, http://www.international.ucla.edu/cms/files/OrianaBandiera.pdf

Becky. Personal Interviews, 2009-2012

Behr, Edward. *Prohibition, Thirteen Years that Changed America*, Arcade Publishing, New York, 1996

Bell, Earnest A. *Fighting the Traffic in Young Women*, 1910

Big Bess. "The Private Life of Big Bess," American Life Histories: Manuscripts from the Federal Writers' Project, 1936-1940

Bilek, Arthur J. Email to Author on 4/17/2008

Bilek, Arthur J. Personal Interview, 2008

Bilek, Arthur J. *The First Vice Lord*, Nashville: Cumberland House, 2008

Bilek, Arthur J. & William J. Helmer. *St. Valentines Day Massacre*, Cumberland House, 2006

Binder, John. *The Chicago Outfit*, Arcadia Publishing, 2003

Boston Daily Globe. Thursday, October 23, 1890

Bowen, Louise de Koven. *Public Dance Halls of Chicago*, Juvenile Protection Association, 1917

C

Callano. "Only Suckers Work," American Life Histories: Manuscripts from the Federal Writers' Project, 1936-1940

Capital Times. July 1, 1931, Afternoon Edition, p. 10

Cedar Rapids Evening Gazette. Saturday, October 18,1890, Cedar Rapids, Iowa

The Chicago American. June 13, 1835, from
http://www.earlychicago.com/chron.php

Chicago City Directories. 1920-29, The Illinois Perfume
Company, Daniel Coglioni, Tony Coglioni

Chicago Commission on Race Relations. *The Negro in Chicago*,
Chicago: University of Chicago Press, 1922

chicagocrimescenes.blogspot.com/2008/08/bad-lands.html

Chicago Daily News. "$10,000 Graft paid Politicians Weekly by
Second Ward Vice Dens," August 15, 1921

Chicago Daily News. "Big Jim Was Her All Sobs Widow-Bride,"
May 11, 1920

Chicago Daily News. "Find Dale's Ex-Sweetheart" May 15, 1920

Chicago Daily News. "Murder Bares Ward War," May 12, 1920

Chicago Daily News. "Nab New Colosimo Suspects," May 13,
1920

Chicago Daily News. "Rehearse Colosimo Deed'" May 12, 1920

Chicago Tribune. "Al Capone Is on Way to New 'Devil's Island'"
August 20, 1934. p. 1

Chicago Tribune. April 11, 1952, p. B8 [Nisivaco braggs about
Capone]

Chicago Tribune. "Arrest of Two Bosses," Jan 7, 1896, p. 7

Chicago Tribune. August 9, 1931

Chicago Tribune. August 15, 1933, p. 2 [Edward Coglioni arrest]

Chicago Tribune. "Beach Peaches One-Piece Suits Get Suburb
O.K., August 6, 1919, p. 1

Chicago Tribune. "Black Belt the Blackest Belt in Chicago," John Kelly, December 17, 1921, p. 16

Chicago Tribune. "Capone Free After a Day," May 15, 1930: 1

Chicago Tribune. "Cheering the Stars and Stripes," 16 Mar 1891

Chicago Tribune. "Chicago Italians," March 4, 1886, "p.9

Chicago Tribune. "Cheering the Stars and Stripes," 16 Mar 1891

Chicago Tribune. "Chicago Italians," March 4, 1886, "p.9

Chicago Tribune. "Chicago's Vice is Worst in U.S., Survey Asserts," January 30, 1923, p.3

Chicago Tribune. "The City, A Sad Tragedy," 25 Nov 1863, 4

Chicago Tribune. "The Conspiracy Case," March 24, 1860

Chicago Tribune. "Conspiracy," June 16, 1864, p. 4

Chicago Tribune. Dec 31, 1898, p. 2

Chicago Tribune. "Council Orders City Inquiry on Beach Costumes," July 15, 1919, p. 19

Chicago Tribune. "Courts, Opera, Underworld to Bury Colosimo," May 14, 1920: 2

Chicago Tribune. "De Stefano Explains," 7 Mar 1886: 7

Chicago Tribune. "De Stefano Put Out" 31 Jan 1898: 1

Chicago Tribune. "Divorced Wife's Brother Tells of Family Rows," May 12, 1920, p. 3

Chicago Tribune. "Double Suicide", August 27, 1872, p. 6

Chicago Tribune. "Educational and Church News," April 12, 1912, p. 8

Chicago Tribune. "Factional Fights in a Ward Club," Jan 1, 1897, p. 8

Chicago Tribune. February 7, 1897, p. 25

Chicago Tribune. February 8, 1898, p. 5

Chicago Tribune. "From Rome to Chicago," February 23, 1890:25

Chicago Tribune. "Go Through Slums," Oct 23, 1893, p. 1

Chicago Tribune. *Green Giraffe Haunts Jag on Wood Alcohol,* Dec 29, 1919

Chicago Tribune. "Here's Sad News for Baldheaded Row of Beaches," Jul 14 1919, p.5

Chicago Tribune. "Hits at the Padroni, " Nov 8 1897, p. 7,

Chicago Tribune. "A Horrible Affair," Dec 12, 1859, p. 3

Chicago Tribune. "Houses of Prostitution," Trib Jan 28, 1864

Chicago Tribune. "In Defense of the Italians," De Stefano, Emilio, 26 Oct 1888: 9

Chicago Tribune. "The Inquiring Reporter," June 25, 1921, p. 13

Chicago Tribune. "Italians Fighting for Flags," August 31, 1893, p. 2

Chicago Tribune. "Italians in Parade," September 23, 1895, p. 8

Chicago Tribune. January 14, 1869, p. 4

Chicago Tribune. January 31, 1925, [Joseph Coglioni election]

Chicago Tribune. July 21, 1859

Chicago Tribune. June 24, 1938 [John Coglioni]

Chicago Tribune. "Lady Cops Say Scant Suits are Proper – In Lake", Lucy Calhoun, July 18, 1919, p.7

Chicago Tribune. "Lizzie Engles Conspiracy Case," April 17, 1860,

Chicago Tribune. "Luck Sold by Drugstores," Apr 10, 1898, p. 54

Chicago Tribune. February 15, 1925, [Luigi obit]

Chicago Tribune. March 4, 1886, [politicians and sheep]

Chicago Tribune. March 4, 1930, p.9, [Joseph Coglioni closing saloons]

Chicago Tribune. Trib May 4,1893 [Haymarket Riots]

Chicago Tribune. May 12, 1920 [Colosimo death]

Chicago Tribune. May 14, 1920 [Colosimo funeral]

Chicago Tribune. May 16, 1920 [Colosimo]

Chicago Tribune. May 21, 1920 [Colosimo]

Chicago Tribune. "Morals Court of Open War on Vice" March 16, 1913, p. 1

Chicago Tribune. "News of the Courts," September 11, 1894, p. 9

Chicago Tribune. "Obituaries," Feb 15, 1925

Chicago Tribune. "Obituary," May 15, 1920: 8

*Chicago Tribune. October 13, 1892: 3

Chicago Tribune. October 19, 1894, p. 3

Chicago Tribune. October 4, 1915

Chicago Tribune. "Officer 666, Vice Trust Tactics Bared By Insider, Jul 20, 1914, p. 1,2

Chicago Tribune. "Outrageous Abduction of a Young Girl," Oct 31, 1857

Chicago Tribune. "The Padrone System," Feb 28, 1886, p. 9

Chicago Tribune. "Powers Wins All Italy," Jan 8, 1896

Chicago Tribune. "Sad Death of a Prostitute," Aug 4, 1864, p. 4

Chicago Tribune. "Seize Boat; $600,000 Booze," 15 May 1930, p.1

Chicago Tribune. "Sought 9 Months in Poll Frauds; Find Him at Home," June 24, 1938

Chicago Tribune. "The Suicide Case," 21 July 1859: 0_1

Chicago Tribune. "Suicides: Prostitution and Despair – Strychnine, Laudanum and Death," August 7, 1864, p. 4

Chicago Tribune. "Their Fourth of July," September 21 1889, p. 2

Chicago Tribune. "Two Men Accidentally Shot," November 11, 1894, p. 6

Chicago Tribune. "U. S. Raid Piles Up Trouble for Ralph Capone," Mar 13, 1931

Chicago Tribune. "Vice Trust Men to be Revealed," October 9, 1912 , p. 2

Chicago Tribune. "White Slave," Oct 31, 1857

Chicago Tribune. "Work on Sympathy," August 20, 1893, p. 25

Chicago Herald Examiner. July 30, 1931

Chicago Herald and Examiner. "Big Jim Laid to Rest," May 15, 1920

Chicago Herald and Examiner. "Bride Says Former Wife Periled Both,"May 13, 1920

Chicago Herald and Examiner. "Colosimo Cortege Passing 'Big Jim's' Café," May 15, 1920

Chicago Herald and Examiner. "Hold 4 New Suspects in Colosimo Murder," May 14, 1920

Encyclopaedia of Chicago. "The Devel of Private and Public Beaches for Recreational Use," Chicago History Museum, p. 4

Chicago History Museum. www.chicagohs.org/history/stock.html

Chicago Telephone Book, 1922

Chicago Telephone Books, 1920-29, The Illinois Perfume Company

Chicago Vice Commission. *The Social Evil in Chicago,* Chicago: Gunthorp-Warren Printing Company, 1911

City Homes Association. *Tenement Conditions in Chicago,* Chicago, 1901

Clabaugh, Hinton G. quoted in Chicago Tribune, "U.S. Officials Want Police Aid to Trap Slavers," Dec 2, 1914

Cleaver, Charles, Esq. "Reminiscences of Early Chicago (1833)." *Fergus Historical Series* 19, 1882

Dorothy West. Interviewer in New York City, Cocktail Party: Personal Experience Harlem Hostess, January 10, 1939, American Life Histories: Manuscripts from the Federal Writers' Project, 1936-1940

Commissioner of Labor. *The Slums of Baltimore, Chicago, New York and Philadelphia,* 1894, p. 4, in *Schiavo,* p. 34

Cook County Circuit Court Archives. *Juvenile Cases, 1899 –1926 (with gaps)*

crimemagazine.com/frank-mcerlane-and-chicago-beer-wars

Crosby, Jim. E-message, 2012.

D

Daily Inter Ocean. Chicago, December 23, 1888, p. 6

Daily Inter Ocean. "Social Pleasures," Chicago, February 15, 1888, Part 1, p. 3

Daily Inter Ocean. "Tribute to the Dead," Chicago, May 31, 1894, p. 1

Daily Northwestern. "Mina Mudge in Court," May 22, 1888, p. 6

Daily Northwestern. "Willie in Canada," Oshkosh. August 10, 1888

D'Archangelis, James. Pasta Arrabiata recipe

darrow.law.umn.edu/trialpdfs/ILLINOIS_CASES.pdf

David, George. "Diary of George David [Extracts] – A Trip From London to Chicago in 1833" Unedited manuscript, transcribed from the original by R.P. Mason, Escanaba, Mich., *Michigan History Magazine* 18, Winter 1934, pp. 53-66

Davis, Helen. Interviews, 2004-2010

Draft Cards from World War I. Tony Coglioni, Daniel Coglioni

Duggal, Barbara Rosendale. "Marie Laveau: The Voodoo Queen Repossessed," in *Creole, The History and Legacy of Louisiana's Free People of Color,* Sybil Kein, Ed., 2000, Louisiana State University Press, p. 157-178

E

Einstein, Isidor. *Prohibition Agent No. 1,* Frederick A. Stokes Co, New York, 1932

www.**encyclopedia**.chicagohistory.org/pages/2841.html

Evening Independent. May 27, 1922, ,St. Petersburg, FL, p. 5, http://boingboing.net/2012/05/15/moonshiners-cow-shoes.html

"Evolution of Legalized Gambling In Wisconsin, www.legis.state.wi.us

F

Farley, Melissa. "Bad for the Body, Bad for the Heart," *Violence against Women, Vol 10, No. 10, October 2004, 1087-1125*

Farley, Melissa. "Prostitution: Factsheet on Human Rights Violations," Prostitution Research and Education, 2000, www.prostitutionresearch.com/faq/000008.html

Farley, Melissa. "Prostitution and Trafficking in Nevada: Making the Connections," Prostitution Research and Education, SF CA, 2007

fbi.gov/about-us/history/famous-cases/baby-face-nelson

G

Gallagher, William. Letter to his sister http://greatchicagofire.org/anthology-of-fire-narratives/william-gallagher

gambino.com

gangresearch.net/ChicagoGangs/tongs/sek8.html

Giancana, Antoinette. *Mafia Princess*, Harper Collins, 1985.

Golden, Robert. Emails.

Gomes, Mario. myalcaponemuseum.com

Grand Jury Indictment for Edward Coglioni, City of Chicago Archives

Great Wisconsin Pineries Scandal: Infamy, Horrors and Vices of Wisconsin's Vile Dens, 1889, p. 7, http://murphylibrary.uwlax.edu/digital/wisc/WiscPineries/001 00007.htm

Greenwald, Robert. *The High Cost of Low Price,* Documentary Film, 2005

H

Harney, Robert. The Padrone and the Immigrant," *Canadian Review of American Studies 5,* 1974, as quoted in Peck, Gunther, *Reinventing Free Labor*, Cambridge University Press, 2000

H, Laura. Personal interview, 2012

Hemingway, Earnest. "American Bohemians in Paris," The Toronto Star Weekly, March 25, 1922

Herman, Judith Lewis. *Trauma and Recovery*, Basic Books, 1992.

Hoffmann, Charles Fenno. *A Winter in the West. By a New Yorker.* New York: Harper & Brothers, 1835

Hollatz, Tom. *Gangster Holidays,* St. Cloud, MN : North Star Press of St. Cloud, Inc., 1989

homicide.northwestern.edu/docs_fk/homicide/ICS/ICS.18.pdf

Hotalin, G.T. and Sugarman, D.G. "An Analysis of Rick Markers in Husband-to-Wife Violence: The Current State of Knowledge," *Violence and Victims 1 (1986): 101-24*

Hughes, Langston. *The Big Sea ,* New York: Oxford University Press, 1993, p. 13

I

Illinois Crime Survey. 1929, http://homicide.northwestern.edu/docs_fk/homicide/ICS/ICS.1

Iorizzo, Luciano J. *Italian Immigration and the Impact of the Padrone System,* Doctoral Dissertation, Syracuse University, January 1966, p. 85-90

J

Johnson, Curt with Craig R. Sautter. *Wicked City, Chicago from Kenna to Capone,* Da Capo Press, Cambridge, Mass, 1998

Juvenile Protection Association Bulletin. 1919

Juvenile Protection Association of Chicago. *21st Annual Report,* 1921-22

K

Kendall, Todd D.
http://chicagocrimescenes.blogspot.com/2009/02/alderman-john-coughlins-basement.html

Kipling, Rudyard, 1891

Kyvig, David E. *Daily Life in the United States, 1920-1939,* Greenwood Press, Westport CT, 2002.

L

LaGuardia, Fiorella H. La Guardia, N.Y. rep to U.S. House of Representatives, testimony, *The National Prohibition Law,* Hearings before the Committee on the Judiciary, U.S. Senate, 69th Congress, 1st Session (1926): 649-52 , found on this web site: http://prohibition.osu.edu/content/laguardi.cfm]

Lancek, Lena and Gideon Bosker. *Making Waves: Swimsuits and the Undressing of America,* Chronicle, San Francisco, 1989.

La Sorte, Mike.
http://www.americanmafia.com/Feature_Articles_404.html

La Sorte, Mike. "Donne di Mafia [Women of the Mafia]," 2007, http://www.americanmafia.com/Feature_Articles_404.html

Osborne, Chase S. *The Iron Hunter,* Great Lakes Books. 1918.

P

Parker, Joseph. "How Prostitution Works,"
http://www.prostitutionresearch.com/how_prostitution_works/
000012.html]

Peck, Gunther. *Reinventing Free Labor,* Cambridge University
Press, 2000

Percy, George. "True Relation," p. 3
http://nationalhumanitiescenter.org/pds/amerbegin/settlement
/text2/JamestownPercyRelation.pdf

Philadelphia City Directory, 1906 City Directory, Frank Ladies
Tailoring and Dresses
PRELIMINARY SUMMARY OF INFORMATION
SUBMITTED TO THE COMMISSION ON CHICAGO LAND-
MARKS IN DECEMBER 2012 SHERIDAN ROAD MANSIONs,
http://www.cityofchicago.org/content/dam/city/depts/zlup/
Historic_Preservation/Publications/Sheridan_Road_Mansions_Pr
elim_Sum.pdf

Printz, Patrick. Personal Interviews, 2004 & 2011

R

railroadiana.org/paper/pgPasses.php Railroad Passes

Raymond, Janice G. "Health Effects of Prostitution," 1/31/6,
http://www.uri.edu/artsci/wms/hughes/mhvhealt.htm

Raymond, Janice G. and Donna M. Hughes. "Sex Trafficking of
Women in the United States," Coalition Against Trafficking in
Women, 2001.

Reiman, Lewis C. *Hurley Still No Angel* Northwoods Publishers,
1954.

Reitman, Ben L., M.D. *The Second Oldest Profession,* Vanguard, 1931

Report of the Comptroller to the City of Chicago, 1896-1898 at http://www.archive.org/stream/reportcomptroll00finagoog/reportcomptroll00finagoog_djvu.txt

Richard. Personal Interview, 2007

Romell, Rick. "Alcohol Runs in Our Blood," Wisconsin State Journal, October 19, 2008

Ross, Edward A. *Social Control, a Survey of the Foundations of Order,* New York: The Macmillan Company, 1901

S

Sanger, Margaret. *Autobiography,* Orig 1928, Dover Edition, 1971

Sanger, William M. *The History of Prostitution - Its Extent,Causes and Effects Throughout the World - Being an Official Report to the Board of Almshouse Governors of the City of New York,* 1859

Scherer, Steve. "Italy's 'Ndranghetta Mafia One of World's Strongest," Feb. 20

http://www.bloomberg.com/apps/news?pid=20601085&sid=a6OtnVJc2hGo&refer=europe

Schoenberg, Robert. *Mr. Capone,* Harper Collins, 1992

Schiavo, Giovanni E. *The Italians in Chicago.* Italian American Publishing Co., Chicago, Il, 1928

Sharon. Personal interview, 2007

Shepherd, William G. "Description of Jake Victim." *Collier's Weekly,* July 26, 1930
http://onlinebooks.library.upenn.edu/webbin/serial?id=colliers)

Siebert, Renate. *Secrets of Life and Death, Women and the Mafia,* 1996

Sinclair, Andrew. *Prohibition: The Era of Excess.* Boston, MA: Little, Brown & Co., 1962

Smith, Gipsy. In Lindberg, *Chicago by Gaslight,* 2005, 135

Speciale, Phillip J. www.great-chicago-italian-recipes.com, *Mia Cucina Pazza* [My Crazy Kitchen] and "Shut Up and Manja."

Stead, William T. *If Christ Came to Chicago.* Laird and Lee, 1894

Stead, William T. The Pall Mall Gazette, July 6, 1885, at www.attackingthedevil.co.uk/pmg/tribute/mt1.php#sthash.oN6 TKEmL.dpbs

http://**stomp-off**.blogspot.com/2011/06/visit-to-buffet-flat.html

T

Thrasher, Frederick M. *The Gang, A study of 1313 Gangs in Chicago.* University of Chicago Press, 1927

Thrasher, Frederick M. *The Gang, A study of 1313 Gangs in Chicago.* University of Chicago Press, Abridged Edition, 1963

Time Magazine. January 7, 1929, http://www.time.com/time/magazine/article/0,9171,929359,00.html

Tramp Poet. Recorded by May Swenson, American Life Histories: Manuscripts from the Federal Writers' Project, 1936-1940]

Turner, George Kibbe. "The City of Chicago, A Study of the Great Immoralities" *McClure's Magazine,* April 1907, vol. 28:575-92

Twain, Mark. *Life on the Mississippi,* 1883.

Twain, Mark. *Pudd'nhead Wilson's New Calendar,* Chapter 60, "Following the Equator," 1897.

U

United States Census. 1880 – 1950

usdoj.gov/marshals/history/prohibition/ "U.S. Marshals Role During Prohibition"

usmarshals.gov/history/timeline.html

uwgb.edu/wisfrench/library/articles/metis.htm

V

Vice Commission of Philadelphia. Published by the Commission, 1913

W

Waterloo Daily Courier. February 10, 1938, p. 2

Waller, Irle. *Chicago Uncensored*, Exposition Press, New York 1965

Watson, Sonny. Streetswing.com

Wendt, Lloyd, and Herman Kogan. *Lords of the Levee*. Bobbs-Merrill, 1943.

"**When** You Live Like I Done," American Life Histories: Manuscripts from the Federal Writers' Project, 1936-1940

Wicker, Cassius Milton. http://greatchicagofire.org/anthology-of-fire-narratives/cassius-milton-wicker

Wilde, Oscar. *Picture of Dorian Gray*, Chapter 3, 1891

Willrich, Michael. *City of Courts*, Cambridge: Cambridge University Press, 2003

Wilson, Samuel Paynter. *Chicago by Gaslight*, Privately printed, 1910 [p. 57-61]

Wisconsin. Legislature. Committee on White Slave Traffic and Kindred Subjects, *Report and Recommendations of the Wisconsin Legislative Committee to Investigate the White Slave Traffic and Kindred Subjects*, 1914

Wisconsin. Legislature. *Investigations* 1837-1945, Series 173, Box

1-44 MAD 3/10/H1-7

    Superior Transcripts in box 16, pp. 177, 178, 259

Wisconsin. Legislature. *Investigations.* **Mr. Hart** of the Civic League. "Report of the City Club on Public amusements and Morals," 1914, in DANCE HALLS AND PUBLIC MORALS, 1837-1945, Series 173, Box 1-44 MAD 3/10/H1-7

Wisconsin. Legislature. *Investigations.* **Superior** Transcripts in box 16, pp. 177, 178, 259

Wisconsin. Legislature. *Investigations.* **Ben Morgan** Letter: November 24, 1913 Memo to Sen. Howard Teasdale, Chairman of Legislative Committee on White Slavery, 1837-1945, Series 173, Box 1-44 MAD 3/10/H1-7

Wisconsin Legislature, *Investigations.* **Petherick, E. R.** Letter, Series 173, Box 1-44 MAD 3/10/H1-7, 1893

Wisconsin. Legislature. *Investigations.* **Rogers, B. T.** Archdeacon of Fond du Lac: Letter, November 15th, 1913

Senator Teasdale, Letter November 23, 1913, 1837-1945, Series 173, Box 1-44 MAD 3/10/H1-7

Wisconsin. Legislature. *Investigations.* **No. 281,** 1837-1945, Series 173, Box 1-44 MAD 3/10/H1-7

Wisconsin History.
http://www.wisconsinhistory.org/turningpoints/search.asp?id=1567]

Wooldredge, Clifton R. *Hands Up in the World of Crime,* Chicago: Charles C. Thompson & Co, 1906.

Y

Yancey, Diane. *Life in the Roaring Twenties, Diane Yancey,* p. 61

ABOUT THE AUTHOR

This is Genevieve Davis's first book. It is based on a 10 year research project, ferreting out her family's roots in organized crime. She is a filmmaker and professional artist in Wisconsin. Davis is also a living history re-enactor.

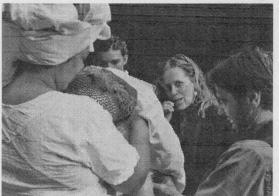

Photo by Colin Cameron

On the set of the SECRET LIFE, SECRET DEATH, making "Laura Johnson" with [left to right] actors, Sadie Beacham, Debra Lopez and Michael Denk

Gallery of Stills from the Movie
Secret Life, Secret Death
www.secretlifesecretdeath.com

Minnie and Davis – Kjersti Beth and Skip Blake

Rum Run to Lake Superior, Wis.

Actors: Kjersti Beth, Brian Miracle, Henry Shotwell

Tony, my Dad, Minnie and Freddy at Big Jim Colosimo's Funeral.
Actors: Andy Osen, Jimmy Shotwell, Kjersti Beth, Brian Miracle

"Get the other kid back good!" Actors Andy Osen, Jimmy Shotwell and
Mike Hart

My Dad in the Caboose with the conductor, on his way to Philly
Actors: Mid-Continent Conductor and Henry Shotwell

Minnie and Johnny cooling off with a fan blowing on a bowl of ice cubes.
Actors Kjersti Beth and David Flores